Rethinking Public Sector Compensation

Rethinking Public Sector Compensation

What Ever Happened to the Public Interest?

Thom Reilly

M.E.Sharpe
Armonk, New York
London, England

In memory of my father
John J. Reilly
(1933–2005)

To my mother, Marie, and my partner, Jim

Copyright © 2012 by M.E. Sharpe, Inc.

All rights reserved. No part of this book may be reproduced in any form
without written permission from the publisher, M.E. Sharpe, Inc.,
80 Business Park Drive, Armonk, New York 10504.

Library of Congress Cataloging-in-Publication Data

Reilly, Thom, 1960–
Rethinking public sector compensation : what ever happened to the public interest? /
by Thom Reilly.
   p. cm.
Includes bibliographical references and index.
ISBN 978-0-7656-3054-4 (hardcover : alk. paper); ISBN 978-0-7656-3055-1 (pbk: alk. paper)
  1. United States—Officials and employees—Salaries, etc. 2. United States—Officials and
employees—Pensions. 3. State governments—Officials and employees—Salaries, etc.—
United States. 4. State governments—Officials and employees—Pensions—United States.
5. Local officials and employees—Salaries, etc.—United States. 6. Local officials and
employees—Pensions—United States. I. Title.

JK776.R45 2012
331.2′835173—dc23   2011045384

Printed in the United States of America

The paper used in this publication meets the minimum requirements of
American National Standard for Information Sciences
Permanence of Paper for Printed Library Materials,
ANSI Z 39.48-1984.

∞

IBT (c)   10   9   8   7   6   5   4   3   2   1
IBT (p)   10   9   8   7   6   5   4   3   2   1

Contents

Foreword	vii
Preface and Acknowledgments	xi
Introduction	xv

1. Phantom Prosperity: The Great Recession — 3
  The Effect of the Great Recession on Public Sector Employment — 4
  State Approaches to Public Employee Unions and Budget Cuts — 12
  Filling the Budget Shortfall into the Future — 17

2. Seniority Rules: The Civil Service System — 18
  The Merit Principle — 19
  Barriers to Reform — 28
  New Public Wage Management Systems — 31
  New Governance-Shared Delivery — 36
  Summary — 39

3. (Public) Workers of the United States Unite! Collective Bargaining in the Public Sector — 42
  Resistance to Public Sector Bargaining — 47
  The Essence of Collective Bargaining Appears in the Public Sector — 48
  Unions Begin to Grow Through the Legislative Process — 49
  Public Unions Experience Government Backlash — 52
  The Contemporary Status — 53
  Anti-Union Push? — 58
  Public Sector Union Influence in California — 60
  Current Views of Unions — 64
  The Difference between Public Sector and Private Sector Unions — 65
  Unions as a Political Machine — 68
  Counter to Big Business — 70
  Summary — 71

4. **Public Versus Private: Who Really Makes More?** 73
   Principles for Determining Pay in the Public Sector 73
   Pay Differentials 74
   Determining the Cost of Deferred Benefits 77
   The Impact of Unions 79
   The Iron Triangle 81
   Summary 87

5. **Comparison of Lifetime Earnings** 88
   A Compensation Model 88
   The Blue-Collar Model 89
   The White-Collar Model 95
   Summary 100

6. **Pensions Gone Wild!** 101
   Public Pension Plans in the United States 103
   The Pension Benefit Guaranty Corporation 106
   Public Sector Unions 108
   The Price of Public Pensions and How We Got Here 110
   Where Do We Go from Here? 121

7. **Rethinking Public Sector Employment** 125
   Increased Transparency 129
   Conflicts in Awarding Compensation Should Be Avoided 130
   Pensions and Other Postemployment Benefits 131
   Civil Service Reform 133
   Collective Bargaining 134

Appendices
Appendix 1. Comparative Analysis of Compensation Levels.
   Hypothetical Public and Private Sector Employees:
   Janitors and Cleaners 135
Appendix 2. Comparative Analysis of Compensation Levels.
   Hypothetical Public and Private Sector Employees: Civil Engineer 143

References 151
Index 163
About the Author 171

Foreword

I was flattered when Thom Reilly asked me to write the foreword for his book, *Rethinking Public Sector Employment: What Ever Happened to the Public Interest?* although my initial reaction was one of hesitation. I have always had a high regard for Thom's professional competence as a manager in the public sector. Forty years ago as a young lawyer, I represented several public employee unions in their negotiations with their public employer. Moreover, as a former attorney general, governor, and U.S. senator, I am a recipient of retirement benefits in both the state of Nevada and the federal retirement systems. I anguished: Would there be an element of hypocrisy in my commenting on public employee benefits? After wrestling with this concern I decided to leave it to the reader to reach his or her own conclusion.

I do not subscribe to the view shared by others that all wisdom resides with those who labor in the private sector. In my 36 years of public service I have been privileged to work with extraordinarily talented and dedicated public servants. By way of contrast on more than one occasion, I was underwhelmed by those in the private sector who sought employment with state agencies. Public employees should not be required to take a vow of poverty. They are entitled to be fairly compensated. The question is one of balance: Has the pendulum gone too far in favor of employee benefits? Has the public interest been compromised by the new public employee compensation structure?

The right for workers to unionize and to collectively bargain for benefits is a comparatively recent development. The seminal event in the private sector was the enactment of the National Labor Relations Act in 1935—part of Franklin D. Roosevelt's New Deal. Public employee recognition of such rights came much later. Unlike the current debate, its genesis was often bipartisan. In Nevada, for example, a conservative Republican state senator from rural Nevada was the sponsor of the legislation that gave local government employees the right to collectively bargain with an enforcement mechanism if an impasse was reached.

In recent decades labor union membership in the private sector has declined markedly, but in the public sector it has seen explosive growth. The growth of local governments in the post–World War II era fueled an expansion in its workforce and added to the political influence of public employees. Among the first to recognize the opportunities presented were the public safety groups—fire, police, and teachers unions; they were soon followed by other public employee groups. While exercising their newfound clout they were successful in negotiating salary increases and generous retirement benefits for their members.

The collective bargaining process by its very nature lacks transparency. Local government boards and councils delegate to staff the responsibility of negotiations with public employee groups. The negotiated collective bargaining agreement is submitted to the public employee groups for ratification and to local government board members for approval. Seldom do the negotiated agreements generate front-page coverage in the press or lead the evening news. Typically, the press coverage would indicate a new agreement had been reached, covering a specific number of years with cost of living increases for each year of the new contract.

The collapse of the U.S. economy in 2007–2008 and the onset of a recession more devastating than anything since the Great Depression changed that dynamic. The decade of "irrational exuberance" as Alan Greenspan observed with reference to the stock market was over.[1]

Reeling from the impact of plunging revenues, state and local governments faced serious financial crises. Benefits negotiated with public employee groups were no longer affordable. At the same time, the private sector was shedding 700,000 jobs per month by the fall of 2008, and the financial markets were facing a potential meltdown.

Public sector managers were left with these choices, both grim: massive layoffs or reducing benefits, or a combination of the two. The dialogue between public employee unions and their local government employers became testy and often acrimonious. The provisions in the collective bargaining agreements that were previously obscure became front-page news.

Stripped of their inconspicuous presence in the bowels of the bureaucracy, many provisions that had never received public scrutiny generated enormous controversy. Comparisons were made between private and public sector compensation for essentially the same level of responsibility. The higher level of compensation for public employees was difficult to justify. Politics reared its ugly head and some sought to demonize public employee unions and blame them for the financial crises faced by state and local governments. Public employee unions mobilized to protect their benefits and joined the fray.

That debate continues to play out in state legislatures and with local governments. In hindsight, it is increasingly clear that some of the benefits negotiated, particularly public employee pension benefits as currently structured, are not sustainable. That is the setting that makes Thom Reilly's book both timely and illuminating.

Thom Reilly brings a wealth of experience and perspective to the discussion of public employee benefits. As the county manager of Nevada's most populous county (Clark County, Las Vegas), with a population approaching two million people, he has been on the firing line in negotiating contracts with public employee groups ranging from public safety unions, fire and police, hospital employees, to the staff of the district attorney's office.

Reilly's book provides the context for a thoughtful analysis of how public employees, who provide the essential services all of us depend on, should be compensated and managed. Many of the policies that evolved in recent years are no longer affordable in an era of reduced revenues. Retirement systems that have provided generous benefits for those in their fifties and sixties are no longer sustainable as life expectancy reaches into the eighties.

As the new paradigm for compensation for those who work in the public sector is debated, Thom Reilly has made an important contribution in outlining the policy choices available. The student of government as well as the informed citizen will find this book impressively researched, readable, and informative as the debate on compensating public employees unfolds.

> Richard H. Bryan
> former governor and U.S. senator from Nevada

Note

1. This phrase has its origin in a speech made by then-Chairman Alan Greenspan at the Annual Dinner and Francis Boyer Lecture of The American Enterprise Institute for Public Policy Research, Washington, DC, on December 5, 1996.

Preface and Acknowledgments

Many state and local governments across the United States are in bad financial shape, their budgets having been significantly reduced by five years of unyielding economic hardship. Their ability to perform their core functions and deliver essential services to their citizens has been seriously compromised. Large, unfunded liability costs for public sector workers' pensions and other postretirement expenses, such as health insurance, have exacerbated the problem. Increasingly, governments are asking public employees to pay for a greater share of those pensions and related costs; however, additional payments are not enough and governments are tapping their general funds to make up the difference at the expense of education, libraries, safety-net programs, road repairs, police and fire protection, and other services the public rightfully expects these state and local governments to provide. Thus, the public interest is getting left behind.

The decisions governments face, and the reforms that need to be implemented, will not be easy and do not lend themselves to simple solutions. The topics of public employment and how public workers are compensated are now more than ever under the microscope of the media and the subject of intense policy discussions. It is time to rethink public sector employment and how we compensate and manage public workers—without losing sight of their ultimate role of *serving the public*.

This book was written to focus on public sector employment, how it has evolved over time in the United States, and what reforms should be considered so as to create a system that better serves the public interest. I felt that a book like this one was needed to be able to fully address the complexity of the issues. The media have often vilified public employees, sensationalized the topic of public sector compensation, and offered simplistic solutions to the budget problems facing communities. Politicians and special interest groups on the Right and Left have predictably staked out their populist partisan rhetoric, further polarizing the conversation and leaving most citizens frustrated and angry. Furthermore, academic journal articles are usually only able to cover one or two aspects of this topic at a time and have not been able to fully integrate and address the multiple and often overlapping components. In other cases, the values and political ideology of some researchers have led to methodological shortcomings and questionable conclusions in some of the research.

Numerous factors have converged with regard to public sector employment, and the wages and benefits afforded public employees. All of the following have contributed, in part, to the current problematic situation: the length and depth of the recent Great Recession; the media coverage that has often fostered private sector envy over public employee benefits and pay; the lack of transparency and preponderance of shortsighted thinking in decisions made about the compensation of public workers; the various ways in which public unions operate and influence elected officials responsible for approving wage and benefits; and the rigidity of the civil service system.

This book focuses primarily on state and local government, and deals less with federal employees and teachers. This focus reflects the fact that my work experience has been at the local level, as a former county manager for a large metropolitan area (the Las Vegas Valley) and at the state level, as an executive who ran both child welfare and income maintenance systems.

Audience

This book is aimed at a wide variety of individuals and groups: policymakers, activists, public managers, elected officials, university students, civic and business groups, and concerned citizens from all sectors of American life. It was planned and developed as a resource for anyone concerned about the ability of state and local governments to operate in the public interest by ensuring that essential services are delivered efficiently and effectively. It was not written to criticize public employees or the public sector workforce. Quite to the contrary, I have great respect for public employees and for public service. Having worked in the public, private, and nonprofit arenas, it has been my experience that public workers are just as hard working, bright, and dedicated to their jobs as workers in any other sector. However, the ways in which we reward and manage public workers result in many of the best and brightest leaving public service early, while the less creative, less entrepreneurial, and more entrenched workers are retained until retirement.

Overview of the Contents

In Chapter 1, I examine the effect of the Great Recession on public sector employment and provide an overview of how state and local governments have responded to the financial crisis. Chapter 2 analyzes how the civil ser-

PREFACE AND ACKNOWLEDGMENTS   xiii

vice employment system evolved, and how it often rewards employees in the wrong ways by emphasizing job security and longevity over performance, entrepreneurial thinking, and connecting through a networked environment so as to attract and retain young employees. In Chapter 3, I look at how public unions have developed over time, the difference between collective bargaining in the private and public sectors, and how public sector unions have become a major political force as a result of their external political activity.

Chapter 4 outlines the principles for determining pay in the public sector and examines the empirical research on the level of pay differential between public and private workers. I also offer the theoretical model of the Iron Triangle to illustrate how elected politicians, management, and labor representatives often engage in nontransparent discussions involving public pay and benefits. In Chapter 5, a comparative analysis of the public-versus-private-sector compensation model is constructed to gauge the cost of lifetime compensation. Two public-private comparisons are assessed: one comparing a typical blue-collar employee, a janitor in the public sector to one in the private sector; and the second, a public sector white-collar employee, a civil engineer, is compared to one in the private sector. Chapter 6 examines how public and private pension plans differ. Most public plans are defined benefit plans that guarantee retirees a set income for the rest of their lives, indexed for inflation. In many cases, however, the promises made to employees were unaffordable even before the recent recession, suggesting that the unfunded and underfunded state and local pensions and retiree health care arose due to poor management and political expediency by elected officials, and not as a result of the economic crisis.

Finally, Chapter 7 considers available solutions for the current crisis, many of which have already been enacted in certain jurisdictions. These reforms address the need for elected officials to avoid conflicts of interest and to be transparent in decision making when awarding worker benefits, unfunded liabilities in employee pensions, and other postemployment benefit (OPEB) plans. At the same time, many of these measures aim to moderate the undue influence of public sector unions and the inflexibility of civil service systems.

Acknowledgments

This book had a long gestation period and was made possible by the tremendous contributions of many individuals. During this period, the ideas in this book were often presented to others, challenged, debated, and refined. In this sense, it was a true collaboration. I owe a great deal to several people who labored through drafts and offered insightful critiques and suggestions. My sincere thanks go to Rex Enoch, Guy Hobbs, Eric Schellhorn, Steve Smith, and Jason Thompson.

I appreciate the editing and proofreading provided by Christine Springer, Brooke Graves, and my mother, Marie Reilly. Jake Joyce and Jeremy Aguero provided enormous assistance with the financial overview and developing the public-versus-private-sector compensation modeling. Many thanks go to Chris Clark for his work in developing and formatting the various figures and charts, and to Debi Puccinelli for her research on public-private wage differences.

The research assistance provided by my graduate assistants—Johnny Floersheimer, Laura Cohen, Katherine Gemmell, and Ricardo Martinez—was invaluable. In particular, I offer Johnny my sincere thanks for all his dedicated hard work and research on public sector unions and pensions.

Finally, I give a very special thanks to my partner Jim Moore, and to Jon Wiercinski and Rory Reid. They have a gift for encouragement, for knowing when to react and when to listen, and for providing intellectual and much-needed moral support.

Introduction

State, regional, and municipal governments across the United States are facing dire financial distress as a result of what has been the worst economic downturn since the Great Depression. Even if the nation is slowly coming out of this recession and tax revenues start to rebound, state and local governments historically lag behind. According to many financial experts, it could take five years or longer for state and local finances to return to prerecession levels.

The drop in revenues experienced by state and local governments has been accompanied by an increase in service demands, which is typical in recessions, and the strategies put in place to deal with these record budget shortfalls have been quite harsh. The large shortfalls jeopardize the ability of states, counties, and cities to perform essential services. And unlike the federal government, state and local governments must balance their budgets—by either cutting services or raising taxes. Yet both of these choices are politically unpopular, and those jurisdictions that attempt to do either face tremendous obstacles.

While the poor economy has blown gaping holes in state, county, and city budgets, much attention has recently been focused on how public workers are compensated, particularly with regard to personnel benefits and the ability of state and local governments to fund them. The housing bubble and subsequent Wall Street collapse wreaked havoc on the nation's retirement savings, as many pension funds and 401(k) plans suffered losses of 30 percent or more. State and local governments now face huge unfunded pension and other postretirement benefit liabilities, prompting policymakers to scramble for ways to close the gap without slashing payrolls and services. Some estimates place the unfunded liability for major pensions in the fifty states at about $3 trillion with an unfunded liability of over $1 trillion, while other estimates suggest the collective liability totals $4.43 trillion with unfunded liabilities approaching $3 trillion.

Public sector unions have borne a great deal of the blame for this fiscal imbalance, but there is plenty of blame to go around. Singling out and blaming only public sector unions fails to fully address the complexity of the problem. After all, these pension deficits exist in nonunion states as well.

The real cause of the pension crisis involves multiple players whose self-dealing and questionable decisions are detailed in this book. However, the crisis has more to do with an inherent conflict of interest that elected officials encounter when they have the option of awarding pensions to special interest constituencies, including themselves, without citizens understanding what is going on and with the bills coming due only after they have left office. In order to balance their budgets and/or increase services, many politicians have refused to make the necessary contributions to pension funds or have borrowed from these funds at the same time, creating deeper and deeper future shortfalls (Schieber and Longman 2011).

The focus of this book extends beyond the troubled pension debacle we are facing in the United States and addresses how public workers are compensated as well as how they are rewarded and managed. Government workers are paid in many of the wrong ways—in ways that make life easier on public managers, union leaders, employee groups, and elected officials in the short run but create significant challenges for service delivery, government efficiency, and responsiveness in the longer run. Government pay is skewed too heavily toward pensions and retiree health care. All in all, the deferral of employee compensation costs to future generations results in a much more expensive and ethically troublesome personnel system. The public employment system emphasizes job security and time served rather than performance; seldom rewards high achievers, innovation, and entrepreneurial thinking; and is often characterized by rigid job classifications that rarely hold individuals accountable for problem solving beyond their own departmental duties.

Several different factors have recently converged to bring the issue of public sector employment to the front page of national newspapers and to the forefront of national policy debates. Each of these will be addressed in this book in more detail.

First, clearly, the current recession has exacerbated problems with the compensation and reward system for public employees. Significant shortfalls in both state and local budgets have led to painful and widespread reductions to social safety-net programs, health care, education, and overall municipal services. In some jurisdictions, pension costs now displace spending for parks, libraries, public schools, and state universities. Service reductions, program elimination, and calls for new taxes test the resolve of citizens and lawmakers alike. Since payroll makes up a large portion of local government funding, reductions are unavoidable. And the resulting layoffs, furloughs, and inability to fill vacant positions directly impact government's responsiveness.

Second, the media has fostered what might be called "public sector envy," primarily around the issue of deferred benefits. Yet the media's rhetoric often is unrealistic. However, because the political stakes are high and public administrators and other governmental officials have been slow to address this ticking time bomb in an open and transparent manner, the issue has become ripe for increased media attention. Most public employees are guaranteed a pension via a defined benefits package and also have access to subsidized retiree health care that requires little or no copayment. These types of benefits have been disappearing rapidly in the private sector. As the media highlights the more lucrative benefit packages that public workers receive, and as the recession continues to take a toll on citizens, taxpayer resentment has increased.

Third, the lack of transparency in adopting public worker wages and benefits has been truly startling. The adoption of many unsustainable benefits has occurred within a tight circle of insiders (elected officials, public managers, and union and/or employee groups) without the press or the public taking much notice or being fully informed. Shortsighted politicians, union officials, and public managers have chosen to provide compensation via deferred benefits because it is less transparent and because the cost can be spread out over time.

Fourth, the extraordinary rise of public sector unions also has played a significant role in shaping public sector employment. While union membership has been declining in the private sector for the past several decades to a record low of 6.9 percent, public sector union membership has risen steadily, in 2011 to a current level of 36 percent. In 2009, the number of union workers employed by government outnumbered union workers in the private sector for the first time. This may be due to the political power of unions having a larger impact on wages, benefits, and spending than the actual formal collective bargaining process. Public sector unions are some of the most powerful interest groups in the United States. As providers of a virtual monopoly of services, they are influential political machines that often are able to determine which elected officials will be seated across from them at the bargaining table.

Finally, rules adopted to combat corruption and patronage have become so onerous and rigid that they are now more of a problem than a solution. Outdated civil service systems impose excessive protections for employees, which in turn compresses wages, making government employment less attractive to those whose skills and talents are in high demand. Often, public sector employment attracts individuals who seek job security versus entrepreneurial thinking. As a result, government has become less creative, less flexible, and less responsive.

What often gets lost in the heated debates about wages and benefits for public workers is where and how the public interest is served. The provision of effective and efficient government services is in the public interest. The role of government is to provide and/or facilitate the delivery of these services to the public in a responsive manner.

How did we get to the point in this country where large portions of general fund budgets are being siphoned off to meet retirement promises to public employees? Such obligations crowd out essential services and safety-net programs for citizens. How did we get to the point where standard public sector personnel rules require public agencies to grant preferences based simply on how long an employee has been with the organization? Such worker protections force public agencies to keep the most senior workers even if those workers are not the most qualified or best suited to perform the job at hand. How do these practices serve the public interest? In the pages that follow, I argue that the responsibility of government is to ensure that citizens receive essential services and that this principle should drive the debate and inform the development of effective solutions.

Rethinking Public Sector Compensation

1
Phantom Prosperity
The Great Recession

Preceded by an eerie sense of calm, tornadoes can suddenly strike and wreak havoc on a landscape. Residents of tornado-prone areas know this peculiar serenity and seek shelter when they sense it. If only financial markets worked the same way. In finance, feeding frenzies can last for years. As investors and others who envy and emulate the perceived winners jump in the mix, the frenzy widens. We call this a bubble, and it when it pops, just as when a tornado touches down, the after-effects can be life altering. Unfortunately, among financial wizards and laymen alike, memory is fleeting, and many investors soon find themselves participating in the next financial frenzy, willingly adding their own air to the bubble.

By the mid-2000s, prosperity was in full swing across the United States. While a bubble from speculative technology investments—the dotcom bubble—had burst, and the terrorist attacks of September 11, 2001, had shaken America to its core, times were good for many. Interest rates had been falling for a decade and credit was relatively easy to acquire. Between 1995 and 2006, the median price of a new home rose 76.1 percent (U.S. Census Bureau 2011a). The rising prices caused homes sales to surge, with nearly 1.7 million new homes built in 2006 (U.S. Census Bureau 2011b). Fueled by rising prices, consumer confidence, and low unemployment, an unprecedented number of households took the first step toward the achieving the American dream—homeownership. Homeownership rates rose 4.8 percent over ten years, with 69.0 percent of families across the United States becoming homeowners by the end of 2005 (U.S. Census Bureau 2011c). It is worth noting that a 1 percent increase in homeownership in 2000 equated to nearly 1.2 million new homes, while a 1 percent increase in home valuation during the same year provided $139 billion in additional equity or household net worth. In turn, as home values rose, more families considered themselves, and acted, wealthier than true salaries and wages suggested they were. Consider that the average annual amount of home equity withdrawal was estimated to be $299.6 billion between 1991 and 2000. From 2001 to 2005, the annual equity withdrawal averaged $997.5 billion, peaking at more than $1.4 trillion in 2005 (Greenspan and Kennedy 2007). As often happens during periods of what former Federal Reserve chairman Alan Greenspan famously called "irrational exuberance," the bubble created an illusion that the growth could go on forever.

The Effect of the Great Recession on Public Sector Employment

As large segments of the population witnessed unprecedented levels of phantom prosperity, a "trickle up" effect occurred in the budget offices of state and local governments. From fiscal years 1996 through 2007, total state spending increased 86.5 percent, to nearly $1.4 trillion (NASBO 2010). Over the same period, state spending increased from $2,857 per capita to $4,689, a 64.1 percent increase. Adjusted for inflation, state spending per capita rose 24.2 percent. As the 2008 fiscal year budgets were being drafted by state legislatures, the boom era was reaching its zenith. Forty-two states were reporting budget surpluses for the 2007 fiscal year, leading twenty-three governors to propose tax cuts at the time. Although even more states chose to cushion their rainy day funds, the $28.9 billion in excess tax revenue was used as a bargaining chip for major tax reform. For example, Nebraska taxpayers witnessed a $420 million tax cut package; Arkansas reduced its groceries tax from 6 percent to 3 percent; and Texas reduced its property taxes by $14.2 billion for the biennium, the largest such reduction in history, after reporting an annual budget surplus of nearly $7.0 billion.

Excess surpluses also caused states to go on a spending spree. South Dakota approved a pay increase of 3 percent for all state employees. Utah lawmakers approved a $1 billion bond for roads with the debt service to be paid down from the general fund. One state actually gave surplus money back to the taxpayers. In 2005, the Nevada state legislature approved Assembly Bill 572 authorizing a rebate from a $300 million surplus to every Nevada resident who owned a vehicle. It is worth noting that subnational governments did not just go on a spending spree using the additional cash flow of tax revenue. Municipalities across the country aggressively bonded against the current influx of revenue, building much of it into increases in public employee wages. From 1997 to 2007, the average annual public employee wage grew in real dollars from $31,733 to $48,328, or by 17.9 percent after adjusting for inflation. As is typically the case during bubbles, it seemed like the growth would continue into perpetuity.

The downturn experienced by both taxpayers and tax spenders would be characterized by shock and awe. The subprime mortgage mess and the decline of home prices were like a bad headache and the recession might have been limited to, and cured within, the U.S. housing and financial markets if there had not been a larger financial cancer metastasizing. Progressing slowly, a web of debt was cast around the world by means of creative financial instruments and loosened regulation that began in the 1990s. Factors such as allowing over-the-counter derivatives, which Warren Buffet described as "financial weapons of mass destruction," to be self-regulated, the passage of the Gramm-Leach-Bliley Act, and changes to investment banks' net capital rule led to much financial risk being leveraged and spread around the globe through mortgage-backed securities and collateralized debt obligations. The subprime housing crisis turned into a global financial crisis almost overnight.

An electronic run on the banks began in the fall of 2007. In August of that year, the Federal Reserve injected $100 billion into the money supply for banks to borrow at a low interest rate; it provided two more rounds of injection, totaling another $81 billion before the end of the year. These actions did not stop American Home Mortgage and Ameriquest from going out of business. In March 2008, the government turned to JPMorgan Chase, enabling it to act like a modern-day Richard Whitney and buy out Bear Stearns, which was nearing collapse, for a sale price of $10 per share. JPMorgan had actually valued the firm at a share price of $2, even though it had traded at $133 per share within the last year. The investment bank Lehman Brothers would not be as lucky. Filing for Chapter 11 bankruptcy in September 2008, it became the largest bankruptcy in U.S. history. The Dow Jones Industrial Average had reached a peak of 14,164.53 less than a year earlier, but within a few weeks of Lehman Brothers closing its doors the Dow would fall to 8,451.19. Uncertainty with regard to stocks and assets created a major selloff on Wall Street. The first week of March 2009 would witness the Dow settle at 6,626.94, its lowest point in almost 12 years. Not since the period between September 1929 and November 1930, when the index fell more than 50 percent, had the Dow experienced a comparable decline. For a sense of perspective, consider that from peak to trough, the Dow fell nearly 89.1 percent during the Great Depression, and took over 25 years to climb back to its previous peak.

The ripple effect from Wall Street would spread to every corner of the economy in 2009. Although Congress may have helped mitigate some of the most catastrophic impacts by passing the $787 billion American Recovery and Reinvestment Act of 2009 (ARRA), the damage had largely been done, and the outcomes were terrible to behold. Household net worth fell from its peak of $66 trillion to $49 trillion, more than 3.5 million homes would be returned to the banks, and unemployment would rise to 10.1 percent as more than 14 million people who wanted to work could not find jobs.

The severity of the Great Recession is reflected in nearly every economic indicator, and although the recession officially lasted from December 2007 through June 2009, state legislatures have continued to struggle to balance budgets at a time when revenues are at historic lows, while their constituents'

6 CHAPTER 1

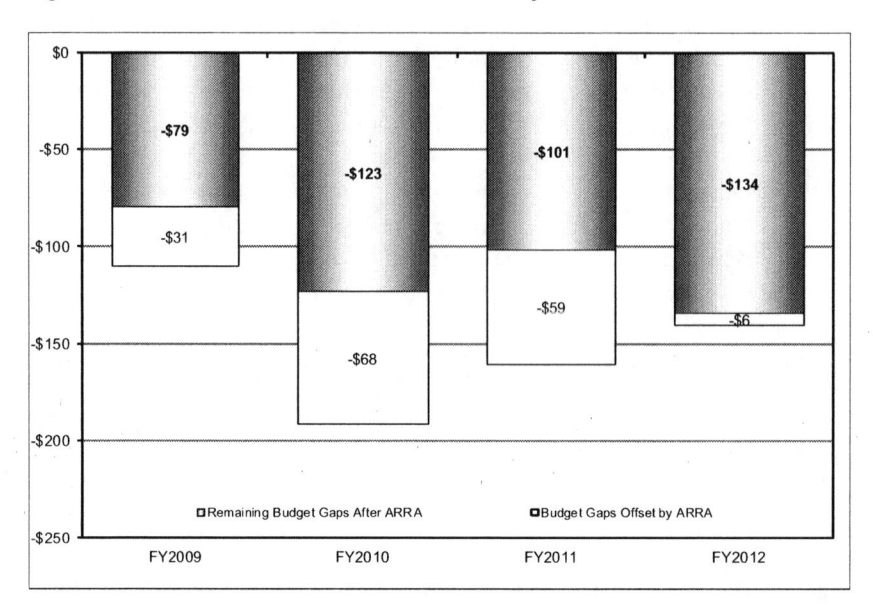

Figure 1.1 **State Shortfalls after Use of Recovery Act Funds**

[Bar chart showing budget gaps for FY2009-FY2012. FY2009: -$79 total with -$31 offset by ARRA. FY2010: -$123 total with -$68 offset by ARRA. FY2011: -$101 total with -$59 offset by ARRA. FY2012: -$134 total with -$6 offset by ARRA. Legend: Remaining Budget Gaps After ARRA; Budget Gaps Offset by ARRA.]

Source: McNichol, Oliff, and Johnson, 2011.

needs are growing with each passing year. Figure 1.1 illustrates the estimated long-term budget gaps state governments faced and what ARRA helped offset, $68 billion and $59 billion in fiscal years 2010 and 2011, respectively.

On a state-by-state basis, the severity of the fiscal year 2011 budget gaps are identified in Figures 1.2 and 1.3 in real dollars and percentage of the overall budget. As these budget gaps totaled $190 billion and $160 billion, extreme measures were taken to balance budgets. A larger problem emerges in fiscal year 2012 when 39 states project a $140 billion budget shortfall, and less than $6 billion from ARRA funds remain to help offset the revenue gaps.

Figures 1.4 and 1.5 specify the projected budget shortfall by state in real dollars and as a percentage of the prior fiscal year (2011) budget. Many states, especially those that have no rainy-day funds, are faced with going back to the drawing board to make up for budget shortfalls (McNichol, Oliff, and Johnson 2011). Budgets had been trimmed as much as possible, but many states are now using unique tactics to reel in spending and raise revenues wherever politically feasible.

States approached their fiscal 2011 budget gap issues in a variety of ways, including user fees (14); higher education fees (7); court-related fees (9); motor vehicle fees (8); business fees (6); layoffs (20); furloughs (19); early retirement (6); salary reductions (9); cuts to state employee benefits (13); across-the-board cuts (20); targeted cuts (34); reductions in local aid (16);

Figure 1.2 **FY2011 State Budget Gaps in Real Dollars**

Source: McNichol, Oliff, and Johnson, 2011.

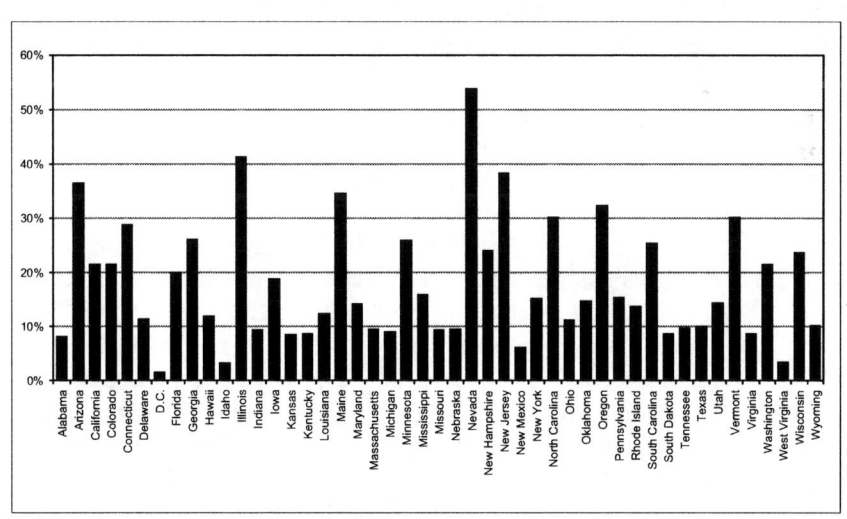

Figure 1.3 **FY2011 State Budget Gaps: Percent of FY 2011 Budget**

Source: McNichol, Oliff, and Johnson, 2011.

consolidation in agencies (12); privatization of government services (5); the use of rainy-day funds (9); and expansions in lottery (4) and gambling (4). In spite of this, 26 states were forced to make an additional $7.8 billion in cuts after their fiscal year 2011 budget was passed by the legislature.

8   CHAPTER 1

Figure 1.4   **FY2012 Projected State Budget Gaps in Real Dollars**

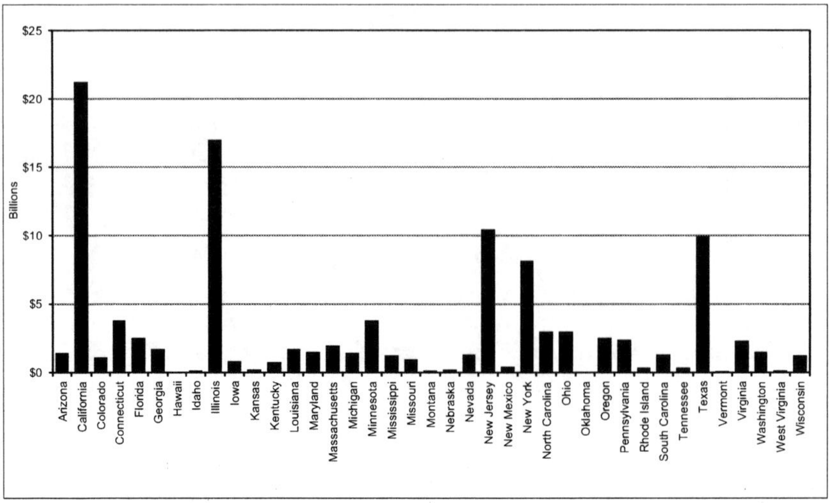

Source: McNichol, Oliff, and Johnson, 2011.

The State of New Jersey as an Example

One of the most outspoken governors, New Jersey Republican Chris Christie catapulted himself onto the national stage with his tough talk on cutting spending and used an executive order to declare a fiscal emergency so as to close a $2.2 billion budget gap during the 2010 fiscal year. Christie took on a bigger challenge in fiscal year 2011, closing a $10.7 billion budget shortfall largely with tax cuts and no major concessions to the Democratic-controlled legislature. The $29.4 billion budget that was signed into law for fiscal year 2011 was the smallest budget that the state had approved in five years. Quite amazingly, through aggressive spending cuts, Governor Christie balanced New Jersey's budget without passing new taxes. The cuts included an $848 million property tax relief package, the capping of local spending and property tax growth at 2 percent per year, and maintaining spending limits on counties, towns, and school districts. The law was applied to each entity beginning with the budget drafts for fiscal year 2012. Additional cuts to the 2011 budget included a reduction of $820 million in school aid and cuts of $407 million to municipal aid. These deep cuts, along with property-tax cap limits, forced municipalities and schools to make their own cuts to services at the local level. Tax credits to film studios were eliminated, and tax credits for high-tech businesses were drastically reduced as well.

These actions have polarized opinion on Governor Christie; his constituents

Figure 1.5 **FY2012 Projected State Budget Gaps: Percent of FY2011 Budget**

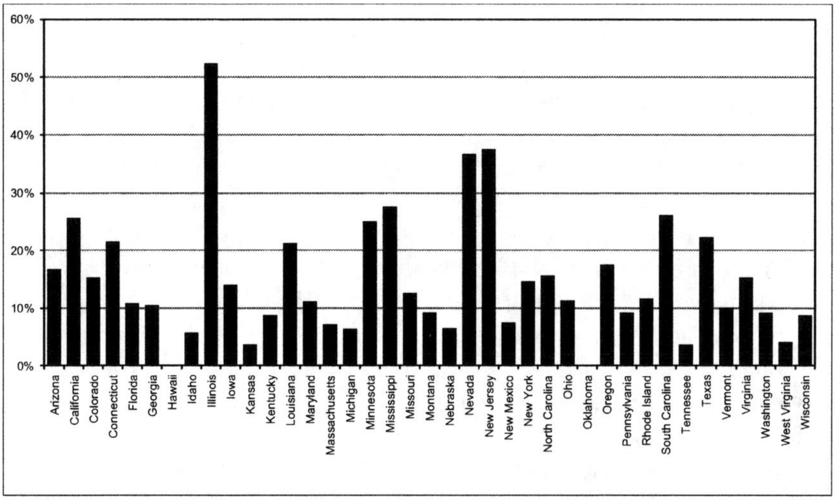

Source: McNichol, Oliff, and Johnson, 2011.

either love him or hate him. He is reviled by three-quarters of a million government employees and retired New Jersey workers after having signed a bill that increases their employee-paid pension contributions and health-care costs. The changes are significant. The age at which public employees can retire with full benefits was hiked to 65 from 62. Additionally, retirees will have to pay for their own health care once they retire. Former workers, who were largely protected from the harshest cutbacks thanks to grandfather clauses, nonetheless will immediately have their cost-of-living adjustments suspended. Lastly, current teachers and government employees immediately had their pension contributions increased by 1 percent, and that contribution will be adjusted upward by an additional 1 percent over the next seven years. Police and firefighters paid an additional 1.5 percent upon the budget's passage (Brogan 2011).

Going forward, public employee health-care premiums in New Jersey will be assessed on a sliding scale based on salary, with employee-contribution increases being implemented over a four-year period. It is estimated that out-of-pocket health-care premiums paid by employees will more than double, even for individual coverage. Premiums will triple for family plans. New Jersey estimates the cost savings to be $132 billion over the next thirty years. The new law also bans the issue of pension and health-care contributions from being part of collective bargaining agreements over the next four years.

To simply blame overspending or state and local governments' failure to save during the boom period of the last decade would be unfair. The dire straits in which New Jersey finds itself today were largely caused by former governor Christine Todd Whitman, who planted the seeds for New Jersey's fiscal failure nearly fifteen years ago. A popular Republican, Whitman captured national attention as a governor who fought hard to balance a budget while also broadly reducing taxes. Although the real cost of doing so would come to haunt nearly every New Jersey governor thereafter, Whitman was seen as a hero at the time, even if she was essentially mortgaging the state's contractual obligations.

Sworn into office as the fiftieth governor of New Jersey, Christine Todd Whitman had run on a pledge to reduce taxes, and over her two terms, she largely stuck to and enacted that promise. To begin with, she cut state income tax by 10 percent every year for three years, enacted a $1 billion property tax rebate program, cut utility taxes by 45 percent over a five-year period, and lowered the corporate business tax to 9 percent. While there was some uproar as many residents believed that local property taxes would increase to simply fill shortfalls at those levels, protests were few and far between. However, it is what Governor Whitman didn't do that contributed to the state's long-term fiscal crisis. As the stock market climbed during the mid-1990s, so did the value of New Jersey's pension funds, so that Governor Whitman chose to forgo $2.5 billion worth of payments into the system. Being able to essentially "borrow" from the pension fund at the expense of tax breaks seemed viable as long as the stock market kept rising (although some commentators characterized Whitman's actions as theft). No harm, no foul. By 1997, Governor Whitman was still standing tall on her anti-tax soapbox and instead of having to make a pension fund payment, she proposed and won approval for putting a borrowed $2.75 billion in bonds at a 7.6 percent interest rate into the pension system.

Governor Whitman did briefly appear to be a winner, but as the saying goes, what goes up must come down. The high-interest borrowing against pension funds and additional tax cuts through her second term set the state up for a disaster when the tech bubble burst in 2000 (Herbert 1995; Preston 1997). Between June of 2000 and the fall of 2002, the state's pension fund fell nearly $25 billion to $57 billion. While the bondholders who loaned the state $2.75 billion are contractually obligated to get paid, today, it is at the expense of the state's middle-class public employees, who also believed that they would be paid what was promised. Over the decade, New Jersey made strides to recover from the debacle, but the Great Recession proved to be too much, largely forcing New Jersey to make the significant cuts to benefits and services now being enacted by current Governor Chris Christie.

The City of San Diego as an Example

The rampant mismanagement of pension funds did not take place only in state chambers. The City of San Diego is still suffering the consequences of its pension scandal, which came to light in 2002. Intentional changes to actuarial tables and accounting methods led to a slow demise of the city's pension fund, which is not part of the state's fund (California Public Employees' Retirement System, or CalPERS). What started with a series of bad judgments beginning in the 1980s veered toward malfeasance and criminality in the 1990s (*CQ Researcher* 2006).

In 1995, City Manager Jack McGrory worked out a deal with the pension fund trustees to contribute less to the pension fund than what the actuaries required. In return, the majority of the trustees, who happened to also be city employees, received increases in their benefits. The benefits piled on. In 1996, senior employees could begin collecting pension checks up to five years before they actually retired through a program called Deferred Retirement Option Plans (DROP). Additionally, the city transferred its health-care obligations for retirees to the retirement system, but with minimal funding. As payments were lowered and benefits rose, the City of San Diego's pension fund was becoming more and more of a house of cards. Like New Jersey, financial amnesia took hold as the stock markets soared higher, hiding the shaky ground on which the pension system was already standing.

To make matters worse, the city passed additional measures providing new benefits without requiring additional contributions from employees. These included the ability to collect retirement pay in excess of the salary employees earned during their employment, the ability to collect higher benefits than had originally been budgeted for, and the permanent implementation of the DROP program. When the bottom fell out of the market, the city clearly had a problem, as its actuarial models had not predicted a pop in the bubble. For the year ending in August 2001, the city's pension fund assets dropped 71 percent, to nearly $15 million. This was immediately prior to the terrorist attacks of September 11, 2001.

Both city management and city elected officials knew that the underfunded pension levels could fall below its 82.3 percent funding threshold, forcing it to make a $150 million balloon payment for which it did not have the money. The scandal came to light later as city administrators and council members tried to hide the fact that they did not have the necessary money and worked out a deal to increase employee benefits as long as the pension trustees, again city employees, agreed to forgo the $150 million funding requirement. The negotiation and a persistent whistleblower led to Securities and Exchange Commission subpoenas and numerous resignations from the city's management team. By 2004, while other local and state governments were entering the housing boom, the City of San Diego was still facing a $1.7 billion shortfall in its pension fund and retiree medical benefits. Local and state jurisdictions like San Diego and New Jersey, which mismanaged funds well before the latest boom-bust cycle, will take years, if not decades, to recover from the budget downfall left in the wake of the Great Recession.

State Approaches to Public Employee Unions and Budget Cuts

New Jersey and San Diego are not the only jurisdictions attacking public employee unions or blaming them for today's budget shortfalls in an effort to rein in costs and future obligations that have spiraled out of control. State legislatures in Massachusetts, Michigan, and Ohio have passed measures to reduce the strength of public employee unions or have them contribute more to health insurance and pension benefits (NASBO 2011).

The actions of Wisconsin and its governor, Scott Walker, made national headlines as well when Walker attempted to reduce state deficits with a bill that would end up being challenged in court. For what was considered a relatively small budget shortfall, Wisconsin Republicans fought for months to eradicate public employee unions. In February 2011, Wisconsin lawmakers were poised to vote on the governor's so-called Budget Repair Bill, which would remove collective bargaining for public employees. In an attempt to stall the vote, which was assured of passage by the Republican majority in the State Senate, 14 Democrats left the Capitol and drove to Illinois. While the Republicans left behind were able to bring the measure to the floor and pass it, 20 lawmakers were needed to have a quorum and vote on any measure that involved spending. After thousands of protestors flooded the Capital, lawmakers on both sides did their politicking in the national spotlight only to have Republicans sneak in a vote that stripped most of Wisconsin's public employee unions of their collective bargaining rights. After legal wrangling and judicial rulings, the Wisconsin State Supreme Court decided in favor of the law. Except for fire and police workers, public employees no longer have the right to collectively bargain in the state of Wisconsin. The bill also requires public employees to pay more toward their health benefits and pensions. Consequently, unions successfully collected enough signatures to force a recall election of the governor and several senators.

Approaches to Cutting Pay and Benefits

Not every state can act like New Jersey or Wisconsin and force cuts by a majority vote. Through collective bargaining agreements, many public employee unions concede to cuts in pay or benefits. That said, with such a widespread downturn, many public employees feel that their hands are tied. If their unions do not concede to cuts, they face a potential backlash and a public relations nightmare from the private sector, who largely feel that they bear the brunt of the recession most and have sacrificed enough, yet without the same level of job security, bargaining agreements, and pensions as government workers. Additionally, if the public unions are unwilling to compromise, they have the power to inflict more damage by exacerbating the existing crisis and negatively impacting the ability of governments to provide essential services.

Yet, with the attention that states like Wisconsin and New Jersey are receiving, public employee unions now feel like their promises of future benefits are being retracted and redefined as the culprit for budget shortfalls and cuts to services. While middle ground is often eventually reached, several government entities faced significant challenges reaching this point. In an effort to close a $1.6 billion budget gap in June 2011, Connecticut governor Dannel Malloy and the state asked fifteen public employee unions to agree to a two-year wage freeze, pay higher health-care contributions, and take nine furlough days. Many workers were behind the concessions as opposed to layoffs, but by law, 14 out of the 15 unions must agree to any deal negotiated with the state. When four of the union boards rejected the state's plan, it appeared to leave the state with only one option: anywhere from 4,300 to 7,500 layoffs could have occurred statewide, affecting services through the reduction in state troopers, closings of respite centers, and many other cutbacks to community-based needs. Eventually, Connecticut's state employee unions were able to modify their bylaws in order to accept the state's plan.

While Connecticut residents might have been wondering what would have happened if a significant portion of the state's labor force were eliminated, residents in Vallejo, California, have already found out. More than one-third of Vallejo's unionized public safety employees were laid off after rejecting bargaining agreements on concessions. They were the beneficiaries of generous employee and retirement packages put in place over many years. By 2008, the average police officer earned $122,000 per year and the average firefighter $130,000, excluding overtime. These high salaries, coupled with pensions equal to 90 percent of the employee's final salary after 30 years of service and annual cost-of-living adjustments, meant that the city could simply no longer fulfill its obligation to retirees. Public safety jobs were not the only problem. City employees had their annual pensions increased to 80 percent of final pay after age 55 and 30 years of service. With its tax base declining, little economic development, and a heavy dependency on property tax for revenues, the city of Vallejo was forced to file Chapter 9 bankruptcy on May 9, 2008, close to the outset of the recession and its accompanying downturn in property values. Despite $200 million in outstanding bonds, the city had relatively little debt, but because it was forced to pay police and firefighters higher salaries and pensions, it could not meet its operating expenses.

Toward a Full Recovery

These two examples from the east and west coasts are simply that—two examples. Many more municipalities are still at risk. And because the majority of tax revenue is paid annually, local and state governments historically lag behind any sustained economic recovery nationwide. As of the first quarter of 2011, state and local government spending accounted for 11.0 percent of gross domestic product. If subnational government spending continues to erode, it could undermine a national recovery and cause further damage.

In essence, a ripple effect takes place throughout the broader economy each time spending is reduced, even in the public sector. The Economic Policy Institute estimates that 100 layoffs in the public sector cause approximately 30 layoffs in the private sector (Pollack 2010). Nearly half of the states do not expect their revenue collections to return to peak levels until sometime between fiscal years 2013 and 2016 (National Conference of State Legislatures 2011). Some states may believe they can get to prerecession levels in the next five years; however, it is highly doubtful that states that relied upon growth as an industry will see a return to prerecession revenue levels in this time period. The Great Recession's effect on state and local finances will continue to reverberate throughout much of the nation in the near term.

This does not mean that all states are taking hatchets to public employee unions. Alabama cut its spending obligations with across-the-board tax cuts to a variety of entities, and many other states have used a plethora of tools to cut waste from their budgets while minimizing cuts to state services and programs.

It was not just budget cutting that state legislatures engaged in around the country. For example, Arizona voters went to the polls in May of 2010 and approved Proposition 100 with 64 percent of the vote, temporarily raising the sales tax 1 percentage point for three years, to 6.6 percent. Two-thirds of the additional sales tax revenue goes to primary and secondary education, with the balance of funds being used for public safety and health and human services. It is estimated that the temporary one-cent increase in sales tax saved 13,000 jobs and preserved more than $442 million in federal matching funds for the state. However, after a year of paying the additional tax, residents and the governor admit, cuts to education and other services remain on the table. Proposition 100 directed additional tax revenues into specific areas like education, health care, and public safety, but there were no other laws passed by legislature or the voters that required a maintenance of effort from existing sources of funding. That said, the Arizona FY2012 budget projects cuts to education and health care by $454 million and $564 million, respectively.

It is difficult to say what the budget shortfall in Arizona would have been if its voters had not passed Proposition 100, but uncertainty still lies in what happens when the tax hike expires on May 31, 2013, taking nearly $1 billion out of government spending, or 12.7 percent of the state's general fund expenditures. That is quite a deep tax source hole, especially when it was passed to originally help fill a $2.6 billion budget gap.

There are two principal ways to fill a budget gap: raise revenue (taxes) or cut spending. However, there is a third option more favored by certain lawmakers and governors. It includes lowering specific tax rates or providing economic incentives for businesses to move or expand operations in their state. Between 2009 and 2010, eighteen states proposed laws to essentially fund a state carrot-on-a-stick stimulus package. Arizona took the initiative with Senate Bill 1403, designed to provide tax credits to individuals and corporations for new and expanded investments in renewable energy options. Colorado enacted a plan in 2009 to provide $50 million for a loan program to encourage private lending to small businesses and tax credits for creating new jobs. Florida passed a similar stimulus package, but with only $10 million in loans and support services. Illinois authorized a capital construction plan with $31 billion in spending over the next six years for improvements to roads, bridges, and schools. It also included green projects like the weatherization of buildings, water improvements, and high-speed rail efforts. When passed on July 13, 2009, Illinois estimated the bill would create 439,000 new jobs within six years. North Carolina enacted a similar stimulus package with the intention to distribute dollars used for construction projects at state education and corrections facilities more quickly. The $744 million allotted for this project is estimated to generate up to 26,000 jobs. While Iowa passed its I-JOBS program in 2009 as a way of stimulating the state's economy, Iowa governor Terry Branstad recently said that to create a more favorable economic climate to compete for new businesses and jobs would be "best accomplished by reducing our commercial property taxes which are second highest in the nation." The only exemption to his "no new taxes" pledge was the tax on gambling, which was increased to 36 percent.

While Iowa's governor focuses his attention on a single source of taxes like gaming, Governor Christie is perhaps the largest proponent of what he calls "pro-growth tax reforms." These reforms were laid out in his fiscal year 2012 plan, which included a reduction in the minimum S corporation tax to 25 percent, exempting "nonexempt" agricultural cooperatives, and increasing research and development tax credits to 100 percent. These incentives were strictly for corporations and businesses. Christie also wanted to exempt installation and support of electronically delivered business software, and raise the exemption on the estate tax to $1 million. However, the Democratic controlled legislature largely passed its own plan, which didn't look anything like his original one. The annoyed governor, with the ability to veto line items within a budget, gladly did so to muster up and pass a "constitutionally balanced budget," in his words.

After stripping benefits and passing additional costs on to public employees in his fiscal year 2011 budget, Governor Christie slashed budgets from municipalities, education, and social services for fiscal year 2012. The veto pen removed $55 million in higher education scholarships, further reducing access to many of the state's public colleges. The removal of $37.5 in state funding for nursing homes meant that nursing homes lost a total of $75 million since state contributions are matched by the federal government's Medicaid program. In addition to the loss of revenue, Medicaid copays at adult day-care centers will increase. In the end, fiscal year 2012 is projected to end with a surplus of $640 million, which is the highest that New Jersey has reported in the last decade.

The trickle-down effect, or lack thereof, when it comes to state revenues flowing to local governments will likely worsen in fiscal years 2012 and 2013. At least 20 states have recommended that aid to local governments be reduced as part of their 2012 budget plans. Arizona is requiring its two largest counties, Maricopa and Pima, to transfer a total of $21 million to the state's General Fund. Lottery money selected to provide funds for local services and the State Parks Heritage fund will be redirected to the General Fund. Similarly hit by the downturn, Florida has recommended reducing its tax distribution to local municipalities by $350.2 million due to increased pension contribution requirements. The state of Michigan recommended one of the broadest cuts to local governments, which became permanent beginning October 1, 2011. The cuts include a 4.1 percent decrease (–$452.2 million) in per pupil funding for K–12 education, abolishing statutory revenue-sharing payments to counties and, among other items, a reduction of 40 percent (–$2.3 million) to libraries. Nebraska is simply cutting all aid to counties, cities, and natural resource districts. The only local aid left in fiscal 2012, albeit 20 percent less, will be educational service units. Totaling nearly $1.8 billion, the State of New York has the largest dollar reduction to local governments. Approximately $1.5 billion will be taken funding for school districts. In Ohio, for fiscal year 2012, local funds from the state will be reduced to 75 percent of the fiscal year 2011 levels, and to 50 percent of 2011 levels in 2013. This is expected to draw a savings to the state of $167.1 million in 2012 and $388.2 million in 2013. The Lone Star State of Texas is removing aid to numerous programs. State dollars distributed for county road repair and maintenance, underage tobacco enforcement programs, county essential services grants, and renewable energy programs will be completely eliminated, for a total state savings of $62.7 million.

Significant reductions in programs and services, and a lessening in aid to local governments alone, is not enough to fill the deep budget gaps still expected to arise in a number of states. States have thus proposed a mixture of revenue changes for fiscal year 2012. California expects to raise an additional $4.5 billion annually by extending a 1.0 percent sales tax rate. Connecticut lifted its tax exemption on clothing and footwear under $50 and increased the sales tax rate on certain products and services, including yoga instruction, to 6.35 percent (State of Connecticut 2011). Connecticut has also proposed adding a 0.10 percent sales tax on products and services sold through retail establishments, and an additional 1 percent tax on car rentals and hotels. Minnesota has a laundry list of new revenue streams that include taxing digital video recorders and direct satellites, taxing hotel rooms at the full price paid online, expanding the definition of taxable admissions, and extending a tax to software hosted by application service providers. Minnesota spawned a new top bracket for personal income taxes estimated to raise state revenue by $1.1 billion. These are a few extreme or noteworthy examples of actions taken across the country.

Filling the Budget Shortfall into the Future

The severity and length of the Great Recession accentuated the strain that many local and state governments were already likely feeling in trying to fill budget shortfalls. Governments like consumers, believe that the good times will last forever. Yet, with increased health-care costs and pension obligations, it was likely inevitable that certain funding obligations would be unsustainable and would eventually be exposed. Since the national economy and many states are not out of the woods yet, a concern that was unfathomable a few years ago is now a reality for a few and a warning to us all.

Prichard, Alabama, is a small city on the gulf coast near Mobile Bay. Like many municipalities, Prichard created pensions for its public employees when the population and tax base were growing. It never adjusted those pensions, and in the 1970s, the city began to see tax revenues decline largely due to the out-migration of its population. Although the pension obligations were modest, workers were able to retire in their fifties, and this continued even as the outlook for the pension plan looked grim. Warnings about insolvency loomed. The monthly liabilities for pension checks hovered near $150,000, by September 2009, the pension fund had run dry. The town's tax revenue had declined to a level that if funds from the city's operating budget were used, current workers could not be paid. At the end of the day, there was no money for the remaining retired workers still living and the checks stopped coming. Lawsuits have ensued, and while the outcome of the cases varied, the Prichard case is not that far removed from the fiscal reality of an overall system that is fundamentally unsustainable. It should be a warning for lawmakers, pension-earning workers, retirees, and every taxpayer. With many cities and states strained by the Great Recession and unable to keep their pension plans funded, the question that must be asked and answered is what other city or state is likely to go down the same path as Prichard?

2

Seniority Rules

The Civil Service System

In describing the public sector personnel system for teachers in the United States, billionaire philanthropist Bill Gates recently pointed out, "In the U.S. we have one of the most predictive personnel systems ever invented—try and remember how many years you've worked, and you will know your salary" (Lyons 2011, 53). To begin to understand the issue of public sector employment, it is essential to understand both the history of collective bargaining in the public sector and how the civil service system has evolved in the United States. This chapter will briefly highlight the emergence of the civil service system and how we ended up with processes that are widely viewed as ineffective and overly bureaucratic.

The public interest in public employment is the provision of effective and efficient government services. The role of government is to provide and/or facilitate the delivery of these services to the public in the same responsive manner. Making this happen has proved to be challenging for a host of reasons, including the bureaucratic organizational structure that government operates within as well as the host of civil service systems and personnel rules that govern public sector employment. The effectiveness of these public services often depends on the quality, competence, and motivation of the employees who manage these services. The question that always arises for public sector organizations is, which personnel issues and structural barriers are creating barriers to productive performance and how can these be overcome (Elling and Thompson 2006).

The public sector personnel system is governed by a legally established merit system that establishes procedures for recruitment, selection, promotion, retention, and compensation of employees (Kearney 2009). Often, the current personnel and compensation system in the public sector rewards employees in many of the wrong ways. The system places too much emphasis on longevity rather than merit, and has difficulty rewarding high achievers and entrepreneurial thinking. I am uncertain what the original intent of these regulations was; however, like many well-intentioned reforms, things seem to have gone awry.

The Merit Principle

The power of political parties to determine who works for government predominated the public sector personnel system in the United States up until the early twentieth century. The corruption that was often associated with these practices led to a series of civil service reforms in the late nineteenth and early twentieth centuries. These reforms focused on two primary areas: the need to ensure the political neutrality of civil servants by removing them from partisan political pressure; and the need to ensure that the selection, promotion, and retention of public employees are done objectively and in accordance with the merit principle. The merit principle seeks to make employee competence the primary criterion for hiring and promoting public employees (Kearney 2009).

Essential elements of the civil services system as outlined by the federal Intergovernmental Personnel Act of 1970 include:

1. Recruitment, selection, and advancement of employees on the basis of relative ability, knowledge, and skills, including open consideration of qualified applicants for initial appointments.
2. Equitable and adequate compensation.
3. Training to ensure high-quality performance.
4. Correction of inadequate performance or separation of those whose inadequate performance cannot be corrected.
5. Fair treatment of all employees in all aspects of personnel administration without regard to political affiliation, race, color, national origin, sex, or religion.
6. Protection of employees against partisan coercion. (Kearney 2009, 181).

The nation's first presidents set the precedence for early civil service appointment and the character that would define a government worker. Although there is clear evidence that ability was the chief concern for Presidents Washington and Adams, there was a hint of benign patronage that would later evolve into the spoils system. As political parties grew in size and power, they looked to fill as many public positions with their party members as possible. When a new party gained control, it would supplant the previous party's appointments with its own partisans. The public sector personnel were shifting after elections to such a degree that administrative policies were often difficult to carry out (U.S. Office of Personnel Management [OPM] 2003).

Adams left his mark on early civil service through his "midnight appointments" at the end of his presidential term. Thomas Jefferson was the first president to enter office with hostile members of the opposing party making up the public bureaucracy (Shafritz, Russell, and Borick 2011). He felt it was necessary to appoint only individuals from his party, the Democratic-Republicans, until there was more party balance in the public sector. The Tenure of Office Act of 1820 limited many of the positions in the civil service to four years so as to coincide with presidential terms. The act was intended as a source of accountability for public officials' control of funding, and required accounts to be submitted at the end of each term. The Tenure of Office Act and the policy of rotation-in-office are often thought to be essential elements in the development of the spoils system.

The Spoils System

The spoils system got its name in 1832 when Senator William L. Marc asserted in a U.S. Senate debate that "politicians of the United States boldly preach what they practice. When they are contending for victory, they avow their intention of enjoying the fruits of it. If they are defeated, they expect to retire from office. If they are successful, they claim, as a matter of right, the advantages of success. They see nothing wrong in the rule that to the victor belong the spoils of the enemy" (Shafritz 2004, 272).

The spoils system ushered in an era of government where a change in the federal administration brought the dismissal of government employees so that the supporters of the new administration could be appointed to those positions. A change in administration would result in a mob of office seekers traveling to the Capitol with conflicting claims to public office, and these would often take a month or more to sort out. Lower-level public positions, such as clerical work, were used to give jobs for constituents who had difficulty finding employment. This form of patronage filled public offices with individuals who were not selected based on their ability or fitness for the position, but for their political loyalty. In return for public appointments, public officials were required to devote their time, money, and votes to the political party. The spoils system was not only used to remove members of rival parties during administration change but also to remove appointees from the same party for their allegiance to a rival within the party. This process of appointment in exchange for political support led to a lack of experience, weak appointments, and the appointees' discretionary use of public funds to pay back the cost of receiving and keeping the appointment.

The spoils system that evolved out of the noble intentions of our early presidents began to take shape during the presidency of Andrew Jackson (OPM 2003; Van Riper 1958). In 1990, the U.S. Supreme Court ruled traditional patronage in public employment to be unconstitutional in the case of *Rutan v. Republican Party*. The Court stated, "to the victor belong only those spoils that may be constitutionally obtained." The Court was also asked to decide "whether promotion, transfer, recall and hiring decisions involving low-level public employees may be constitutionally based on party affiliation and support," and they voted "that they may not" (Shafritz 2004, 216).

The spoils system was also well established in many states, including New York. Prominent members of Jackson's administration, including Aaron Burr, Martin Van Buren, and William L. Marcy, used patronage to create and maintain strong party support and as a weapon in political elections. Jackson's supporters sought to bring the system that they had designed in New York to the federal government. There was also an urge from the U.S. population at large, which thought it was time to appoint to government positions individuals from all levels of society from around the country, not just from the well-educated classes. During Jackson's term in office, many individuals were dismissed from civil service positions to make room for his allies and the leaders of his party so as to increase support for his policies. Jackson believed that longevity in office would generate a feeling of office dominion in appointees. An appointment in the Jackson administration often required partisan activity or the understanding that partisan activity was expected in the future.

In 1863, the American Consul General in Paris, John Bigelow, recommended competitive exams for the civil service after conducting a State Department report of the French customs service. Abraham Lincoln was aware of the dangers of the spoils system and despite his dislike for the system needed to utilize it to obtain and maintain congressional support during the Civil War. In his second term, Lincoln ushered the demise of the rotation policy when he decided not to remove the experienced officials he had appointed in his first term to reward a new group of supporters. The citizens were now starting to grow cynical about the spoils system and its increasing costs and scandals. The Joint Select Committee on Retrenchment was developed to explore the possibility of examinations for appointments. The final report of the committee was delivered in 1868. It evaluated the public personnel systems in Great Britain, France, Prussia, and China, detailed the issues of the American system in place, and recommended competitive examinations. In 1870, Ulysses Grant's secretary of the interior, Jacob D. Cox, introduced the merit system to the Interior Department, where competitive examinations were to be used for appointments to the Patent Office, the Census Bureau, and the Indian Office. In 1871, President Grant created the Advisory Board of the

Civil Service, which was later renamed the Civil Service Commission. This commission established the first central personnel organization for the federal government and instituted the first attempt to provide personnel advice and assistance to the president (OPM 2003; Van Riper 1958).

Political patronage and the spoils system were also alive and well in local governments. Tammany Hall and the notorious Boss Tweed best exemplified these practices. Tammany Hall was an organization based in New York City that became famous for the extent of its political corruption. Between 1854 and 1934, Tammany Hall essentially controlled Democratic Party politics in New York City and had a huge influence over the city's policies. One of the most iconic figures in the history of Tammany Hall was Boss William Tweed, a leader of the organization. Attempts by the city to reform Tammany Hall were thwarted because the organization was so powerful. The ward-based, patronage-driven form of local government is commonly thought of today in criminal terms and, in that sense, so are Boss Tweed and Tammany Hall.

As a political organization, Tammany Hall has perhaps never known an equal. It was a product of a nineteenth-century New York City in which there coexisted extreme wealth and devastating poverty. Tammany Hall supervised it all, reigning supreme over city politics from the end of the Civil War to the beginning of the Great Depression. There is also little question that members of the Tweed Ring were outright thieves. Between 1865 and 1871, at the height of its power under Boss Tweed, countless millions of dollars were stolen. In April of 1870, Tweed succeeded in changing the city charter to consolidate absolute power over the city's finances and politics. As an organization, Tammany wedded the Democratic Party and the Society of St. Tammany (started in 1789 for patriotic and fraternal purposes) into an operation that made the two entities interchangeable. City politics during that time could best be described as a triangulation of the mayor's office, the Democratic Party and the social club organization.

Pendleton Act

The assassination of President James Garfield in 1881 by a disgruntled office seeker had a significant impact on the reform of the spoils system by creating an environment more open and committed to civil service reform. The midterm elections that followed in 1882 had an important and more direct impact on reform legislation. Congress was more moderate in its opposition to reform than it had been previously, but was still reluctant to develop legislation until the citizenry took action. In 1883, Congress enacted the Civil Service Act, better known as the Pendleton Act after the name of its sponsor. The act created a bipartisan civil service commission that was responsible to the president to fill government positions by a process of open competitive exams, probationary periods, and protection against political pressure. Its main focus was to eliminate the use of patronage as part of the federal government's hiring process. Initially, only 10 percent of federal employees were covered. Over the years, Congress expanded coverage to other employee groups so that by the end of World War I, 70 percent of all federal employees were covered (Shafritz, Russell, and Borick 2011; Van Riper 1958).

The Retirement Act of 1920 was the first civil service retirement legislation that sought to reward employees for loyalty and address the issue of aging employees. The Classification Act of 1923 set the standard that equal work deserved equal pay, enabled the classification of public positions based upon tasks and responsibilities involved in the work, and ascribed a salary to the position classifications. Political activity by classified employees had already been restricted, but the Hatch Act of 1939 extended these restrictions to unclassified staff (Van Riper 1958). At the end of World War II, the Civil Service Commission was presented with the challenge of reducing the public sector workforce that had expanded during the war. Truman appointed the Commission on Organization of the Executive Branch of the Government (the first Hoover Commission) and their report in 1949 detailed guidelines for the personnel functions for each agency's personnel plan, including position classifications, recruitment and selection, performance evaluation, promotions, incentives, processing and storage of personnel records, and discipline. President John Kennedy created the President's Commission on the Status of Women in a move toward equal opportunity in the merit system. President Richard Nixon shifted the responsibility of personnel compliance with legislation and personnel evaluation procedures to the leaders of the departments and agencies (OPM 2003).

Civil Service Reform of 1978

In 1978, the Civil Service Reform Act separated the Civil Service Commission into two organizations, the Office of Personnel Management and the Merit Systems Protection Board. The U.S. Office of Personnel Management (OPM) was created to be the president's chief advisor on personnel issues. The office was empowered to handle all the issues involving career employment in a competitive service: examination and selection, merit promotion, compensation, training, employee relations, awards and incentives, development, and benefits. The Merit Systems Protection Board would assume the responsibility of safeguarding the merit system from political interference and formally overseeing and judging the appeal process for federal employees. The Civil Service Reform Act designated, for the first time in civil service history, personnel practices that were prohibited, and enshrined the basic principles of the merit system in law. The act intended to give more control over public personnel to the president by developing career employees who were involved with policy making (Maranto and Schultz 1991; OPM 2003).

State and Local Government Merit Systems

The merit system is now a standard feature of public sector human resource systems in the United States. At the federal level, the U.S. Office of Personnel Management and Merit Systems Protection Board oversee personnel processes in accordance with merit principles. In state and local governments, the responsibility is given to independent civil service commissions or a central human resource agency in the executive branch. When the federal civil service system was instituted, many state and local governments were slow to follow. The primary motivator for state and local governments to adopt merit systems has been the number of federal laws requiring them in order to receive federal funding (Denhardt and Denhardt 2006; Kearney 2003).

There is little accurate information on employment during the early history of state and local governments. It is unlikely that state and local personnel positions were filled through the spoils system because of the small number of public positions initially available (Lee 1979). The Pendleton Act of 1883 brought the merit system to the federal government and was also effective in facilitating the transition of the state and local systems. That same year the first state merit system was implemented in New York State (Selden 2009). The initial legislation that brought the merit system to New York was developed from a bill introduced in the New York State legislature by Teddy Roosevelt and later signed into law by another future president, New York governor Grover Cleveland. The legislation that brought the merit system to the state government in New York also extended to all of the cities in the state. The Commonwealth of Massachusetts soon followed with the development of its own merit system, introduced into the state government the following year. A year after implementation of the merit system in Massachusetts, twenty-four cities were covered under the state's merit system law. In 1895, the merit system expanded to the cities of Chicago and Evanston, Illinois, making them the first cities in the Midwest with merit system laws. The merit system reached the West Coast cities of San Francisco in 1900 and Los Angeles in 1903 (OPM 2003).

Despite the initial adoption of the merit system in these influential states, it took twenty more years for another state, Wisconsin, to implement a merit system (Selden 2009), which it passed in 1905, along with Illinois. These early state merit systems were based on the federal example, with three-member central commissions that carried out the personnel function (OPM 2003). By 1935, state-level merit systems existed in only twelve states. Some early efforts by states to introduce merit into their governments were unsuccessful, including the repeal of Connecticut's first civil service legislation (Shafritz, Russell, and Borick 2011).

Many states waited until the passage of the Social Security Act of 1939 to finally adopt merit systems (Selden 2009). The Social Security Act required all state agencies receiving federal grants-in-aid through the act to convert their employees to the merit system. For the first time, workers in every state were a part of the merit system. The "Second" Hatch Act extended the Hatch Act's political restrictions to the state and local agencies that were financed partially or totally by federal grants and loans. Excluded from this extension were governors, lieutenant governors, mayors, all elected officials, and positions not under the merit system. The 1940 census claimed that at least 850 cities had implemented a merit system that covered some portion of their employees, but there was much dissimilarity and variance in approach among the cities that developed merit systems on their own, except in regard to the use of competitive examinations.

By 1958, competitive examinations and formal merit system laws had spread to twenty-four states. During Richard Nixon's presidency, state and local governments were encouraged to develop merit systems by the federal government through the Intergovernmental Personnel Act of 1970, which required that organizations at the state and local level that received any federal grants-in-aid to introduce merit systems that would meet the guidelines established by the Civil Service Commission. The commission would oversee, give advice, set principles, and investigate state and local compliance along with other new responsibilities. It had the power to withhold federal grants for noncompliance at the state or local level. The National Commission on the State and Local Public Service recommended in 1993 the decentralization of the state and local merit systems, a decrease in job classifications, and less dependence on competitive examinations (Riccucci 2007). These recommendations were intended to repair the image of government and public officials in the eyes of citizens (Nigro and Kellough 2008; OPM 2003).

Traditional state merit systems involved a central personnel organization that would administer competitive examinations and other public personnel functions. The centralized personnel organization approach was intended to be more equitable for employees and in service delivery (Selden 2009). As the state and local systems grew and evolved, the technical aspects of public personnel positions helped to secure the merit system's place in state and local personnel systems. The federal government also threw its weight behind the merit system through legislation and grant funding. Today the merit system is implemented and functional in the majority of public personnel systems (Shafritz, Russell, and Borick 2011).

Organizational management in the state and local public sector has witnessed personnel professionals who are more active in developing flexibility and efficiency in their personnel systems, which also align with the organization's goals. Some modern state and local personnel systems consist of elaborate structures of merit system rules and regulations. Improving government performance is a significant factor and force in attempts to reform state personnel systems. As the federal government has been pushing the implementation of merit systems in the state and local systems, the centralized personnel system has begun to decentralize its power (Shafritz, Russell, and Borick 2011). The current basis for this decentralization is that the fundamental aspects of the merit system have been established in the public sector and that decentralization will increase efficiency and effectiveness (Klinger 2006).

Performance-Based Pay

The civil service system was established to combat the spoils system but has come under fire itself for being the problem instead of the solution. The protections set up through the civil service system such as free speech, free association, liberty rights, and social equity have often been viewed as impeding managers' ability to do their job (Elling and Thompson 2006). Elling and Thompson utilized a survey of managers in ten states in 1982 and a similar survey in 2000 to identify the most significant hindrances to effective management, which included problems recruiting proficient employees because of low compensation, an inability in rewarding exceptional performance, concerns over recruitment and selection, and difficulty retaining quality employees. Many of these issues encompass some of the main problems associated with the civil service system in public organizations.

Merit pay was introduced to address some of the hindrances to effective management, and is a system for motivating employees that usually involves performance-based rewards given to individuals that compensate different performance with varying levels of raises in base pay or salary (Risher, Fay, and Perry 1997). Merit pay is easy to understand from a theoretical perspective but often very difficult to implement effectively in the public sector. As with any other policy, the utilization of merit pay can be analyzed and understood by looking at the internal and external environment in which the organization operates. Performance-based and merit pay systems are often opposed by unions and employee groups, who favor more compressed wage systems and are often concerned that raises would be used by managers as blatant displays of power or administered in an unequal and/or inconsistent manner.

Often, management and unions have worked together to avoid implementing a performance-based reward system because of the work needed to do so effectively.

In 2001, after returning to county government in Clark County, Nevada (the Las Vegas Valley), to be chief executive after a few years at the University of Nevada, Las Vegas, I was disappointed to learn that the county's performance-based reward system had been dismantled. After years of tense discussions and debate, management and the union had jointly adopted the merit system in place at the time. The system included an annual evaluation of all employees that featured a performance-based evaluation, resulting in a 0 to 6 percent increase in base pay. That system was eliminated and replaced by 0 or 4 percent increase so that, in essence, nearly everyone received a 4 percent increase yearly on top of their step increase (for those who had not topped out of their salary range), as well as negotiated cost-of-living increases. In essence, the organization had moved from an agency that valued high performance and rewarded high performers to one that treated everyone in the organization in the same manner. County management and the head of the local union had adopted the change as a "side bar" agreement, meaning that it did not have to come back to the vote of members. Both sides had decided that that the performance-based evaluation was more of a headache to administer. Instead of implementing the necessary training needed to conduct evaluations in a fair and consistent manner, they had chosen to take the easy way out, as well as one that minimized grievances.

Yet there are numerous tools available to assist in evaluations. The 360-degree review, an assessment used by individuals inside and outside the organization with whom the employee interacts is one such tool. The 360 evaluation does not rely solely on the assessment of the supervisor and thus more accurately captures how the employee is performing. This tool can help eliminate the distrust many unions have about the fairness of supervisory evaluations. Upon my return, I was successful in implementing a management plan that was focused 100 percent on performance (no annual cost-of-living raise, no longevity pay, and the ability to award sizable bonuses), but was only partially successful in getting the union to agree to a return to the same type of performance-based pay.

With the significant restraints involved in managing public organizations, including limited resources and diminishing budgets, the merit increase system needs to innovate or develop alternatives in order to be effective. One-time bonuses, with little or no raise in base pay, is one feasible alternative. Other alternatives include creating a distinct budget line that provides funds for exceptional employee performance, setting a cap on merit pay at pay range midpoint, and lump sum increases (Risher, Fay, and Perry 1997). A good part of the blame for the failure to properly enforce the principles of the merit system rests not only with executive management but with departmental management, who fail to recognize their responsibility to the public trust and avoid conflict by giving out undeserved merit increases—with zero accountability.

Barriers to Reform

While some public sector agencies have shown a growing interest in revising their personnel compensation programs and implementing a more streamlined, entrepreneurial, and responsive governance system, true reform has been slow to materialize and has been inconsistently delivered. Some reforms have focused efforts on attempting to have the public sector operate like the private sector because the private sector fosters performance and efficiency. For example, the mayor of Indianapolis from 1992 to 1999, Stephan Goldsmith, required city departments to compete for contracts with the private sector. Privatization efforts in Phoenix, Arizona, in the 1990s gained nationwide acclaim when the city enhanced competition among service providers and significantly raised performance standards.

The 1992 book *Reinventing Government*, by David Osborne and Ted Gaebler, spawned a movement that paralleled international trends and focused on competition, innovation, customer service, and performance management in the public sector. While Osborne and Gaebler's seminal work did not go as far as stating that government should act more like a business, it began a nationwide reform effort focused on the ineffectiveness of government organizations. This work and subsequent dialogue was credited with President Clinton's National Performance Review (NPR) initiative headed by Vice President Al Gore. NPR focused on increasing the trust of the American people in their government through a broad range of improvements in the accountability and productivity of government as well as reductions in bureaucracy and the size of government. Overall, the recommendations aimed to create an environment where employees, who were restrained by regulations and oversight, could now utilize their creativity and innovation in solving problems and providing services. The National Performance Review recommended reforming all aspects of the personnel system, including recruitment, selection, position classification, wages, promotion, and rewards (Shafritz, Russell, and Borick 2011).

Like many reform initiatives, the long-term durability of the NPR movement at the federal level and reforms at the local levels are mixed. While examples can be found at all levels of government—federal, state, and local—that have made significant progress toward creating a more responsive, entrepreneurial, and results-based system of governance, these clearly do not yet dominate the practice in government today.

Reforming the personnel system within government has also proven problematic. The Nixon, Carter, Clinton, and George W. Bush administrations all attempted to make the civil service system more efficient, effective, and economical. President Jimmy Carter made reform of the personnel system one of his administration's central focuses and ushered in one of the most comprehensive reforms of the federal personnel system since its inception in 1883. His administration targeted five areas: (1) technical overkill; (2) excessive protection of employees; (3) lack of management flexibility; (4) inadequate incentives to eliminate inefficiencies; and (5) discrimination. While Congress enacted most of Carter's proposals, a lack of funding and follow-through diminished their impact.

Under Clinton's NPR, Vice President Gore focused on administrative initiatives such as reducing red tape by streamlining processes, eliminating unnecessary regulation, improving customer service, creating marketplace dynamics, decentralizing decision making, and empowering employees. Specific emphasis was on personnel management in governmental agencies in an attempt to: (1) create a flexible and responsive hiring system; (2) reform the general classification and basic pay scheme; (3) authorize agencies to develop programs for improvement of individual and organizational performance; (4) authorize agencies to develop incentive award and bonus systems; and (5) strengthen systems to support management in dealing with poor performers. President George W. Bush felt that NPR did not make government more efficient and did not encourage formal evaluations that could be used in making budget decisions. Under Bush, the President's Management Agenda (PMA) attempted to create a "whole of government" approach linking program performance, evaluation, management, and budgeting in the same system.

Ingraham (1995) best summarizes much of the criticism of civil service systems, describing them as having excessive and constraining rules and regulations; a slow unimaginative recruitment process; a rigid classification system; and isolation of public employees from elected officials and citizens. Despite all of these federal efforts, observations, and criticisms, civil service reform efforts at all levels of government has been spotty at best over the years (Denhardt and Denhardt 2006).

Key components of virtually all state and local governmental civil service and personnel systems are practices such as seniority, "bumping rights" for senior workers, and across-the-board wage increases. Collective bargaining agreements have often codified these practices even more deeply within the organizational culture of most public agencies. Yet these features were not established to promote the public interest. They were put in place solely for the benefit and protection of public employees.

Seniority involves granting preference in certain personnel actions based on how long an employee has been with the organization. In the public sector, it is often a key component of collective bargaining agreements or a practice embedded through statute or civil service rules (Kearney 2009). Sullivan (2011) suggests that seniority is not the same as performance and may prohibit many assignments from going to top-performing employees. Promoting the most senior, rather than the most qualified, into management jobs also is likely to lower productivity. Newer employees often possess the latest skills, knowledge of technology, and the ability to innovate. While senior people might turn out to be the best performers, they should have to prove their superior performance each and every time. Civil service system laws protect public sector employees and make it very difficult to terminate them.

Job bumping is a practice whereby employees losing their jobs can literally take any job beneath them and the employee that they "bump" can then, in turn, bump someone below him. The practice is always disruptive but can be particularly damaging in the public sector, where training budgets are limited. As a result, each "bumper" is forced to learn his or her new job painfully, through trial and error. Bumping also does not allow the organization to utilize the best individuals for the job. Kearney (2009) argues that when layoffs are based on last hired, first fired, "a perverse sort of self-seeking logic can arise . . . in which more senior union members opt to exchange jobs of less senior members of the bargaining unit for their own security and well being. Thus the majority gives up nothing, while a small minority loses their livelihood" (188).

Across-the-board rewards also limit performance. The practice is routinely pushed by union and employee groups, but eliminates a manager's ability to provide incentives to, and/or monetarily reward, individual performance and innovation. Governments, instead, need to develop a performance-based culture, one in which those who produce dramatic results are rewarded more generously than those who simply show up. Government often has trouble rewarding top performers, which can create an exodus of high achievers and innovators.

Job Security

The heavy emphasis on job security versus performance can also have a chilling effect on service delivery. The long, tedious, and elaborate steps needed to terminate poor performers often results in managers giving up and leaving many of these individuals on the payroll. Too much emphasis on job security and not enough on job performance creates a status quo atmosphere and breeds mediocrity. The organizational culture in many public agencies seems to reflect the notion that once an employee passes the required probationary period, she is with the organization for life. A long-term practice that persists in some public agencies is longevity pay, which rewards employees simply for staying on the job for a period of time. While clearly there is a need to retain employees for institutional knowledge, too much emphasis on longevity creates a culture in which job security dominates daily work.

Historically, longevity pay was implemented in order to retain public workers so that they would not leave and go into the private sector. With wage and benefits between the private sector and public sector at least equal, if not higher in the public sector (depending how one calculates the cost of public employees' deferred benefits), the need for longevity pay can be seriously questioned. These dollars, it is often suggested, should be replaced with performance-based bonuses and/or merit pay that reward innovative and high performers.

New Public Wage Management Systems

Traditional public compensation systems operate under the assumption that organizations and jobs change gradually. The traditional system has operated with centralized control and very detailed job descriptions, and was based originally on the principles of scientific management and the work of early industrial engineers. The goals of many of these traditional models do not align well with the needs of the current public personnel environment, which is constantly changing, and where organizational problem solving occurs across jurisdictional boundaries (Goldsmith and Eggers 2004; Reilly 2007; Risher 1997). Risher and Fay (1997) offer a new system for wage management that focuses on broadbanding, making pay levels consistent with the current trends in the labor market, pay-for-performance, relegating personnel accountability to line managers, and the elimination of entitlement.

Many of these concepts for new public wage management systems have previously been used in the private sector (Lawler 2000). The employment needs in both the public and private sector have shifted toward employees who possess complex knowledge and skills. These employees do not have traditional concrete job activities; instead they have roles with general duties that they carry out in a flexible manner. The challenge to organizations in general, which can be translated to the public sector, is to create compensation systems that are able to adapt to the changing environment (Lawler 2000).

Lawler argues that to implement a successful pay system in the modern personnel arena, organizations should compensate individuals according to their individual worth in the job market, including the skills and knowledge that they possess, and not the worth of their job. To create a pay system that compensates individuals in line with their market value, organizations must develop a system to measure an employee's knowledge and skills that can be translated and compared in the external market. A successful pay system must reward excellence, through policies such as pay-for-performance so as to attract and retain superior performance. No single pay-for-performance plan fits every organization, so an organization's mission, framework, and management style must be considered when creating a pay-for-performance policy that will work for it. One recommendation for organizations that want to compensate for performance is to have multiple pay-for-performance plans to reward employees. Offering multiple performance plans could provide the opportunity for employees to choose the way in which they wish to be compensated, which may have an effect on future motivation and performance (Lawler 2000).

There are many perspectives on how the public sector should approach the challenge of civil service reform. Unlike the private sector's ability to adapt to new systems and policies, the public sector often has to wait and see what the impact of a particular policy will be before they attempt its large-scale implementation. That is why it is often the public risk takers and the manner in which they implement the policy that ultimately determines which reforms are instituted.

Some states have made some progressive and experimental moves to step away from the traditional or a tenure-based system of civil service. The argument for doing away with one of the central job-security components established under the civil service system and requiring employees to operate under an at-will policy is being advanced in some state and local jurisdictions.

Civil Service Reforms in Georgia, Florida, and Texas

The state of Texas has the most experience with public at-will employment policies and personnel reforms such as decentralization and deregulation. These reforms have been expected to impact public personnel through greater productivity, expanding the flexibility of managers, and allowing managers more control in their work environment. The State Classification Office within the Texas State Auditor's Office requires that unless specifically stated otherwise through recorded contract, law, or policy, all state employees are employed at will, meaning that either the employer or the employee can break the employment relationship at any time. State agencies may have the ability to establish certain personnel policies for their organization but are instructed to retain their at-will status (Coggburn 2006).

A 2005 survey of Texas human resources managers revealed that at-will employment ensured that employees were responsive to agency administrative goals, yet the same impact was not seen in regard to personnel efficiency, managerial flexibility, or employee motivation. According to the respondents, employee terminations through at-will employment were used to combat performance issues and to a lesser extent respond to budget issues and the need for reductions in workforce. Respondents to the survey reported that employees were more likely to feel insecure about their job stability in at-will employment, but that this insecurity did not necessarily lead to increased productivity. Coggburn (2006) argues that at-will employment increases administrative control in a public setting but does not significantly affect the ability to lure new employees to the public sector or increase employee motivation.

Several other states, including Georgia and Florida, have made significant strides to convert large portions of their state's employees to at-will employment. In 1996, the state of Georgia passed legislation to reform the civil service system by making all new public employees at-will employees and allowing many of the essential personnel functions to be performed at the department or agency level (Condrey 2002). Also in 1996, Georgia governor Zell Miller proposed at-will employment to remove job positions from the authority of the State Personnel Board and its expansive rules and regulations regarding personnel practices. Due to the decentralization of many of the personnel functions from the Georgia State Merit System of Personnel Administration, many of the state agencies in Georgia had to prepare to execute the recruitment and selection of applicants, define and assign pay grades to agency-unique jobs, and ensure compliance with personnel laws and regulations. Organizations had the ability to execute the functions in-house, utilize the state personnel department, or contract out the services to an outside consulting firm. The state personnel agency would remain responsible for classification and pay scales for positions that are prevalent in the majority of public organizations, including administrative clerks and secretaries (Condrey 2002).

A significant part of the personnel reform in Georgia involved a new method of compensation for public employee called GeorgiaGain (Kellough and Nigro 2002). GeorgiaGain and its focus on pay-for-performance was a departure from the traditional approach of merit pay and the performance-based annual salary increases associated with it. Research on public pay-for-performance policies has shown that employees' and managers' acceptance of these policies is affected by job satisfaction and confidence in organizational management. GeorgiaGain was implemented to furnish managers with progressive performance management tools to motivate employees and enhance efficiency (Kellough and Nigro 2002).

Under GeorgiaGain, employee performance ratings were connected to increases in pay and new methods of performance appraisal that were linked to the performance guidelines. Public organizations were required to have clearly stated performance goals, objectives, and plans to achieve these goals and objectives. GeorgiaGain insisted upon the creation of new job descriptions with the ability to continually adjust the descriptions in the future. The program sought to diminish the number of public pay grades and allow the public sector to compete in the labor market with competitive midpoints and entry-level wages. Instilling confidence in public employees about the integrity and equity of the public personnel system was an essential objective of GeorgiaGain (Kellough and Nigro 2002).

Civil service reforms in Georgia had a significant impact on public agencies in the state, including Georgia's Department of Human Resources and that organization's human resource management program. These reforms gave agencies the power to create new job positions and define their pay ranges; provided agencies with greater control over disciplinary actions; created a new dynamic between the agencies and the merit system; and provided more agency control over recruitment and selection processes (Lasseter 2002). However, state employees' perception of the program was mixed. Kellough and Nigro (2002) sought state employees' impressions of evaluation, pay-for-performance, training, and the implementation of GeorgiaGain through a survey. The findings indicated that respondents felt GeorgiaGain had not been implemented fairly or consistently, that GeorgiaGain was not able to recognize and reward outstanding employee performance, and that pay-for-performance in their organizations had been undermined by biases. The respondents agreed that the standards of performance closely resembled job content and that employees realized the expectations of their jobs. Respondents claimed that under GerorgiaGain the recruitment of competent applicants was problematic, that the benefits were not comparable to those in the private sector, and that resources intended for training and development were not made available. One of the more interesting findings was that greater job satisfaction existed among unclassified employees—those considered at-will—rather than among classified employees. Overall, respondents were skeptical about GeorgiaGain, agreeing that the program was a way for organizations to increase productivity without substantial raises and benefits, and that the state would benefit from the program by securing control over payroll expenses (Kellough and Nigro 2002).

According to Condrey (2002), civil service reform in Georgia occurred due to several factors, including a governor with knowledge and experience in personnel management, disapproval of the vast human resource rules and regulations, ineffective employee unions, and agency bureaucrats looking for more discretion over personnel matters. Condrey noted that reforms in Georgia could prove difficult to replicate in other states.

In 2000, the state of Florida attempted civil service reforms similar to those undertaken in Georgia (West 2002). The Service First legislation was introduced by Republican governor Jeb Bush and bolstered by Florida business leaders, the Florida Council of 100, and Florida Tax Watch. The Service First legislation shared similarities with Georgia's reform including the conversion of civil service employees to at-will employment and the creation of a job classification and payment structure. The factors that many pointed to as hindrances to performance in the previous system included protected status for employees, seniority, across-the-board salary increases, lack of planning, insufficient implementation of technology, and enormous amounts of paperwork. With Service First, Florida looked to the private sector and its flexibility to assist in the reforms. Opponents of Service First felt that scrapping the whole system was not the right approach and that the civil service system should be repaired. Critics claimed that reformers had not provided enough evidence to support Service First and that private sector cures were not always successful in the public sector (West 2002).

Broadbanding

Broadbanding is another method of state civil service reform that has been attempted by states such as Florida, South Carolina, and Virginia. Broadbanding refers to the process of substituting large pay bands for the narrow job classification system usually used in public organizations (Whalen and Guy 2008). It has been implemented to combat the use of a narrow job classification system tied to individual pay ranges and to pay-for-performance in the public sector.

The job classification system set up to bring innovative improvements over 100 years ago has led to a decreased flexibility for managers to develop workers outside of their job tasks and pay grades as well as an inability among managers to distinguish superior performance or hire more experienced individuals at greater than entry-level salaries. The wider pay bands encompass many pay grades so that managers have greater flexibility in the hiring and promotion of employees, in facilitating agency restructuring and job mobility, and in developing organizations centered on performance as opposed to duration or rank. Critics of broadbanding claim that the process allows managers excessive discretion, creates favoritism and wage disparity, expands the range of tasks asked of employees, and is used as excuse for downsizing (Whalen and Guy 2008).

South Carolina instituted broadbanding in public organizations in 1996. The state's main objective was to reduce the number of pay grades from 50 to 10 and to restrict job classes to 800. Under the new job classification system, all employment positions in the state were reclassified and the state organizations were now responsible for regulating the movement within pay bands. The new system gave the state legislature the power to decide when to link pay with performance. Cost-of-living increases were provided in the new system on a yearly percentage basis and any exceptions to these rules needed the approval of South Carolina's Office of Human Resources Management (Whalen and Guy 2008).

The state of Virginia initiated its reform in 2000 by implementing broadbanding in the public sector. Although the main objective was to utilize pay-for-performance in the civil service systems, the reforms also sought to decrease the number of job classifications and to reclassify outdated job positions. Through broadbanding, Virginia intended to decrease the number of job descriptions from 1,650 to 275 and to reduce pay bands from 23 to 8 so that employees had the opportunity to earn higher wages without switching positions. Pay-for-performance under the new system was determined by formula and the intention was that state managers would decide which employees would be rewarded. The reform was endorsed by elected officials, organization heads, and state managers, but a failure to teach managers how to properly implement the formula severed the connection between performance and pay in the implementation of the policy. A large portion of the implementation costs of the pay-for-performance program was used for technological updates, with little going to wage increases for employees (Whalen and Guy 2008).

Broadbanding was also one of the chief objectives of the previously mentioned Service First Initiative reform in Florida. Like the reforms in Virginia and South Carolina, broadbanding in Florida intended to connect performance with pay, increase managerial flexibility, and terminate obsolete job positions. The design of the framework for the pay structure was based on private organizations including Suntrust Banks, Inc., and Tropicana Products, Inc. Pay bands and pay ranges were established, but unlike Virginia, a formula was not provided to determine performance increases for Florida's state workers. Much like in Virginia, the funds for budget increases were principally utilized for technological system updates (Whalen and Guy 2008).

New Governance-Shared Delivery

For the better part of the twentieth century, hierarchical government organizations were the predominant service delivery model for distributing local and regional public services and executing public policy goals and objectives (Goldsmith and Eggers 2004). These traditional structures were typified by their pyramid shape and top-down configuration, and could be characterized in two ways. In the first, the lower levels of the pyramid are fully included in the higher levels. In the second, the lower levels are superseded by the higher levels (top-down) (Van Dijk and Winters-van Beek 2009). Increasingly, traditional city and county governments are being replaced by new collaborative approaches to governance: regional structures with complex networks of local governments, limited-purpose regional authorities and taxing districts, and private, civic, faith-based, and nonprofit organizations participating in local governance (Foster 2000). Over the last couple of decades, there has been a proliferation of these regional governance structures and arrangements both to provide a region-wide platform for economic development and regional planning (Luger 2007; Ye 2009), and to address the ever-growing number of cross-boundary, complex, and large-scale problems affecting local communities (Frahm and Martin 2009; Kettl 2000; Laslo and Judd 2006).

Near the turn of the century, researchers began to view shared service systems or "networks" as the new organizing model for the delivery of public goods and services (Agranoff and McGuire 2001; Frederickson and Smith 2003). In many respects, the new framework associated with the term "networks" embodies the contemporary analyses and practices of public administration (Heinrich, Hill, and Lynn 2004). One reason for the recent focus on networks is the newfound relationship between public service providers and the populations that they serve (Kettl 2000). This contemporary view of networks suggests that governmental institutions will no longer act in the role of direct service providers; instead, they will become producers of public value within the web of multigovernmental relationships that increasingly characterizes modern government (Goldsmith and Eggers 2004). This new perspective also suggests that the idea of hierarchical government structures being best suited to the delivery of public services is falling by the wayside. Networks—public service providers operating within a setting of multiple, shared forces—are taking their place (Stoker 1998).

Contracting out, outsourcing, and privatization are realties of public sector life. Much of the polarizing debates on these topics are pointless and irrelevant. Practically, all government services include a degree of contracting out. For most public managers, the question is not so much whether to contract out or outsource a service or program. Rather, it is how much of the program or project to contract out or outsource (Brown and Brudney 1998), and how to minimize opportunism and weak contract management capacity (Morriss 2001).

With the relationships developing between different levels of government and private and nonprofit organizations, the government must be concerned with the tradition vertical hierarchical structure as well as the developing horizontal interactions defined by governmental and nongovernmental partners. One issue that evolves from these horizontal interactions involves the question of who is accountable if there is a failure to deliver, or if goods and services delivered are of low quality. Other issues developing from the new environment of governance include adapting traditional systems to the new environment, the incorporation of horizontal systems into existing vertical systems, and the ability to effectively manage in the new environment (Kettl 2000).

As the environment around government continues to change, the public sector must concern itself with making public employment opportunities appealing (Perry and Buckwalter 2010). Perry and Buckwalter argue that the sustainability of infrastructures in the changing governmental environment will depend upon the ability to rejuvenate interest in public employment, successful reform of compensation structures, the overhaul of the public retirement systems, enhanced public service values in and among organizations, and make training and development an essential feature of public employment.

To be effective at cross-jurisdictional problem solving, government needs a new breed of leaders at the local and regional levels who promote collective action so as to advance the public good by engaging government, general-purpose entities, quasi-public and nonprofit organizations, private industry, and citizens. Instead of delivering the service themselves, local and regional government managers need to become facilitators, conveners, and brokers who engage the community's talents to solve difficult and complex problems (Goldsmith and Eggers 2004; Laslo and Judd 2006; Reilly 2007).

Government needs an array of employees who not only perform traditional duties, such as planning, budgeting, and deploying staff, but are also trained in boundary-scanning skills, such as facilitation and negotiation, contract negotiation, contract management, risk analysis, and the ability to manage across boundaries (Goldsmith and Eggers 2004; Salamon 2002; Thomas 2007). Frahm and Martin (2009) have additionally suggested a need for activation/enabling skills to bring public, private, nonprofit, and other agencies to the table to jointly address issues; framing skills to arrange and facilitate agreement on respective roles; orchestration skills to keep everyone working cooperatively; mobilization skills to build and maintain support; synthesizing skills to create cooperative environments; and modulation skills to successfully use rewards and penalties to solicit and maintain cooperative interactions between various players.

Public managers must not only effectively manage people inside government, but also focus outward by negotiating shared purposes, coordinating services, mobilizing resources, and forging political coalitions that benefit the entire community. The key is to be able to influence the strategic actions of other actors, as well as to effectively manage resources that belong to others. It is critical that universities include these skills in their undergraduate and graduate curricula and broaden the curriculum's perspective to include the emerging tools of collective action. Additionally, public, private, and nonprofit agencies need to build these competencies into their recruitment and hiring practices, in-house training courses, and job performance standards.

State and local governments are dominated by organizational structures that still operate under the assumption that they will deliver services directly, even though services are increasingly being delivered through multiple and often nongovernmental partners. The challenge is to build an organization that can structure itself hierarchically for some problems and nonhierarchically for others (Nalbandian and Nalbandian 2003). According to Kettl (2000), "government's structure is function-based, at a time when more of its problems are area-based" (495). As a number of regional network systems and shared service delivery models are emerging across the United States in an attempt to be more creative and responsive to boundary-spanning problems, functional budgeting and personnel systems that dominate state and local governments often prevent the cross-jurisdictional problem solving that is needed. Traditional budgeting systems seldom have the ability to track community-wide expenditures and capture the number and dollar volume of contracts awarded. They tend to be single agency–focused. Likewise, the civil service system is organization-focused, hierarchical, and built on the assumption of direct service delivery (Kettl 2000).

Increased unionization of the public sector has produced labor agreements and rigid job classifications focused on single governmental entities. Collective bargaining units differ from local government to local government, making it difficult to craft job classifications and performance rewards that allow cross-boundary work with multiple actors. New regional institutional arrangements are needed with their own fiscal and administrative powers that are focused on the community or region. Involvement of the private and nonprofit sectors may contribute to or facilitate these institutional arrangements and offer additional accountability measures, along with flexible and creative tools for collective action.

Summary

There are numerous barriers to the ability of governments to perform in effective, efficient, and responsive ways. Reforming the civil service system has been recognized as a necessity at all levels of government; however, implementation has been inconsistent and short-lived. Governmental reforms tend to be incremental, yet it may now be time for some bolder action. For the most part, the current public employment system rewards employees in many of the wrong ways. The system places too much emphasis on security and longevity rather than on performance. It has difficulty rewarding high performers and entrepreneurial thinking. A system that grants raises according to longevity rather than performance, and that makes raises and promotions appear to be automatic, encourages mediocrity and inefficiency. Rigid personnel systems that discourage flexibility and innovation and raise costs must be restructured to balance employee costs with service demands.

While civil service protections reduce political interference, the public sector must restructure public employment so as to connect government to an increasingly complex, dynamic, and networked environment (Mintzberg 2004) and increase the attractiveness of public sector work to young employees. Given the need to respond to the ever growing number of cross-boundary, complex, and large-scale problems, state and local personnel and compensation systems, with their rigid job classifications and horizontal reporting relationships, make it exceedingly difficult to attract and manage employees with a skill set necessary to work within the interconnected network of cities, counties, and suburbs. In short, present-day governance work has bypassed the era when traditional civil service systems functioned fully and were practicable.

Statewide reforms are needed to increase accountability and to promote the effective and efficient delivery of services while encouraging entrepreneurial thinking. Laws implemented at the state level will ensure legal barriers are removed and that expectations are established for governmental work. Likewise, the federal government needs to allow flexibility at the state and local government level to implement bold initiatives without the threat of losing federal dollars. State laws need to establish broad frameworks for reform, including the upholding of strong employee protections in areas such as whistleblowing, and prohibitions against political patronage.

At the local level, the "council-manager" form of government, where an elected body appoints a chief executive to run regional or municipal operations, as opposed to the "strong mayor" form, in which the mayor runs city operations, already has many checks and balances that protect employees against political interference from elected officials. Yet even at the state level and within strong mayor types of government, reasonable protections can be built into the personnel system to protect employees instead of maintaining the current systems, which often tilt the balance in favor of worker rights at the expense of the public interest and hinder the ability to deliver effective and efficient services. Anti-discrimination laws are already on the books in all fifty states.

One approach is to build upon the reforms dealing with at-will employment of governmental workers. Despite fears that the mandating of at-will status for public employees in Florida, Georgia, and Texas would lead to the return of the spoils system, this has not occurred. At-will status provides governmental agencies with powerful tools to ensure employee productivity and flexibility, and the ability to control and eliminate many of the excessive protections of employees while better equipping agencies to deal with poor performers.

Components of these statewide legal frameworks should include mandatory pay-for-performance systems. There are a plethora of reliable approaches in both the public and private systems that can ensure the fair and objective evaluation of employees while rewarding high performers and/or those employees who are contributing positively to organizational and/or community-wide goals. There is solid evidence that performance-based pay can improve performance. Research also shows that employees prefer to be rewarded for their performance (Risher and Fay 1997). However, the reformers need to recognize that institutional factors affect performance as well. Pay-for-performance programs operate most effectively when employees know what to do and whom they serve. Yet a clear understanding of organizational objectives may not be possible as a result of multiple and/or changing leaders with different goals. This problem is especially evident when staff members serve many masters: chief executives, political appointees, legislators, judges, and senior career managers. This does not make pay-for-performance ineffective, but simply means that in today's working world, ideal conditions are seldom present in organizations.

Implementing broadbanding and more flexible classification systems is another component that should be included in this broad statewide framework. Wider pay bands allow greater flexibility in the hiring and promotion of employees, in facilitating agency restructuring and job mobility, and in developing organizations centered on performance and not on duration or rank.

Granting preference based on seniority and bumping or last-hired-first-fired practices is a vestige of outdated personnel policies that are not in the public interest and should not be allowed in public employment. While these practices may be preferable to many managers and employees because they make decisions more measurable and quantifiable, they prevent agencies from employing the best, brightest, and most appropriate employees for needed tasks.

Finally, new institutional arrangements are needed, with their own fiscal and administrative powers that are focused on the community or region. Performance evaluations need to reflect the reality that most government work requires working and managing across boundaries. Rigid job classifications and accountability to only one agency often prevent innovative performance. New arrangements that can craft job classifications and performance rewards so as to allow and provide for cross-boundary work with multiple actors is required. Involvement of the private and nonprofit sectors may contribute to or facilitate these institutional arrangements and offer additional accountability measures, along with more flexible and creative tools for governance.

In the final analysis, public service is more than simply the application of business economics. It is an obligation of public duty. The integrity of civil service systems is a matter of utmost importance for citizens. If these systems don't work, then neither does government.

3

(Public) Workers of the United States Unite!

Collective Bargaining in the Public Sector

There has been a remarkable reversal of union membership in the United States. In the 1950s, private sector unions were a powerful force in the economy. Union density (i.e., the proportion of workers who belong to unions) was at 35 percent. Public sector unions were barely on the radar, with minimal bargaining rights outside the postal service and density around 10 percent (Hurd and Pinnock 2004; Kearney 2009).

Figure 3.1 shows membership trends of unions in the public and private sectors. While union membership has been declining in the private sector for the past several decades, public sector union membership has been rising steadily. Government workers are nearly five times more likely to belong to a union than private workers are. The number of union workers employed by government for the first time outnumbered union ranks in the private sector in 2009 as a result of massive layoffs that plunged the rate of private sector union membership to a record low of 6.8 percent (Bureau of Labor Statistics [BLS] 2011e). The union membership rate for public sector workers is 36 percent, which is substantially higher than the rate for private industry workers (BLS 2011a) and higher than it was in the private sector during the union's glory days in the 1950s. Local, state and federal government workers made up 51.5 percent of all union members in 2009. Within the public sector, local government workers had the highest union membership at 42.2 percent (BLS 2011e).

Hurd and Pinnock (2004) suggest that the decline of private sector unionization is a result of several factors, including globalization, technological innovation, changing labor markets, deregulation of key sectors of the economy, a pro-employer National Labor Relations Board during Republican administrations starting with Reagan, and the increased resistance to unions in the business community. Kearney (2009) contends that the growth of unions

Figure 3.1 **Union Membership: Public vs. Private as Percent of Employment**

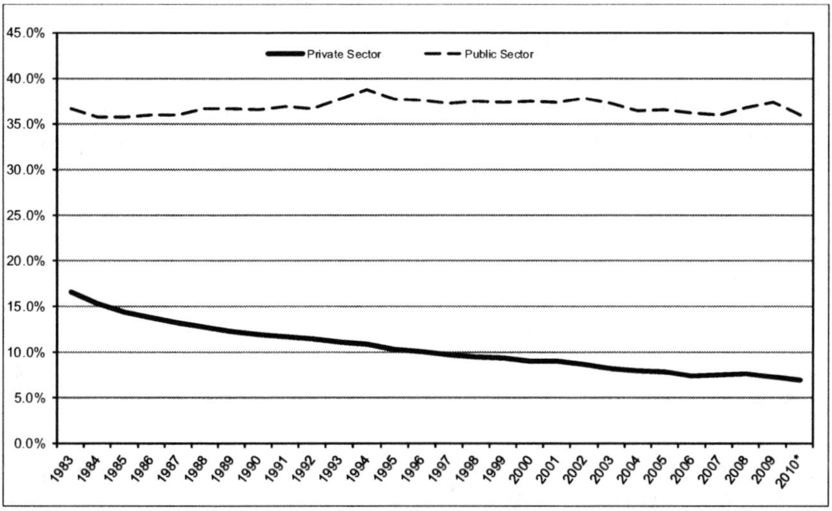

[Chart showing Private Sector and Public Sector union membership from 1983 to 2010. Public Sector remains around 35-40%. Private Sector declines from about 16% in 1983 to about 7% in 2010.]

Source: Hirsch and Macpherson, 2011.

in government was due to the significant growth of government, especially during the 1960s and 1970s; the success of the private sector in winning wage and benefit increases and improved working conditions; the changes in the legal environment, particularly the executive order signed by President Kennedy in 1962 that guaranteed unionization and bargaining rights for federal employees, discussed later in this chapter; and an era of social change and turmoil that witnessed a massive infusion of young people and racial minorities into the public workforce during the 1960s.

Philip Dray (2011), author of *There Is Power in a Union*, attributes the severe drop in private sector union membership in large part to globalization. Dray argues that continually sending manufacturing jobs overseas creates less demand stateside for industrial workers, who have traditionally made up the bulk of private sector union membership. This sort of practice also occurred inside U.S. borders as companies transferred production to anti-union southern states (Lind 2011). The present lack of dominance over industrial jobs by domestic workers, as compared to those overseas, has significantly weakened the unions' power. This ties in to another factor reducing union membership—the rise of technology, which has eliminated many traditional blue-collar jobs. Even in 1984, this view was shared by Jack Barbash, who wrote, "The basic problem in the long-term decline in relative union membership has been union inability to penetrate private sector white-collar technical and professional employment at a rate anything like the rate of growth in that sector" (1984, 12). Barbash goes on to assert that corporations have contributed to reduced interest in union membership in the private sector by granting their employees similar protections. The basic assumption that seems to be borne out by these circumstances is that employees will see unions as unnecessary if companies have good management. In a recent article, Susan Berry (2011) reports that the decline is due to the fact that unionization stifles competition, which leads to higher costs and, ultimately, job destruction.

The public-private shift has also had a radical impact on the economic status of union members. In the 1950s, unions were solidly working class. Today, public union membership is much more middle class, and more than one-third of union workers have at least a four-year degree (Butcher 2011).

As the labor movement membership has moved toward encompassing more government employees, its priorities have shifted. Early trade unions in the private sector focused on redistributing profits from business owners to workers and to improving private sector working conditions. Governments make no profit, so the focus has shifted toward increasing government pay and benefits. Most civil service protections for public sector workers are enshrined under federal, state, and local civil service systems. The frequency of strikes, a main economic tool that unions used to win concessions from private employers, is now exceedingly low. Unions used to launch hundreds of strikes every year, over 470 in 1952. In 2009, both public and private unions initiated only five major strikes. Strikes by government workers in many jurisdictions are prohibited and would interrupt vital functions such as police, fire protection, and education. Figure 3.2 shows work stoppage trends from 1947 to 2010, and Figure 3.3 details the days idle from work stoppage during the same period. Sherk (2010) argues that the decreased frequency of strikes in the private sector is proof that unions have reframed their focus to the public sector. He maintains that this reduction in strikes cannot be explained by the current recession, as in 2007, the last year before the recession, there were a mere twenty-one strikes in the private sector.

Public sector unions are some of the most powerful interest groups in the United States and have evolved into formidable political machines, especially in electing local politicians who end up sitting on the other side of the bargaining table. There is little dispute that public sector unions, via collective bargaining processes, positively inflate employee wages and benefits (Belman, Heywood, and Lund 1997; Johnston and Hancke 2009; Kearney 2003; Llorens 2008; McKethan et al. 2006; Reilly, Schoener, and Bolin 2007). Public sector unions actually raise nonwage benefits for their employees more than wages because these benefits are less transparent and the cost can be spread out over time (Freeman 1986; Kearney and Carnevale 2001).

Historians usually date the origins of secure public unionization back to

(PUBLIC) WORKERS OF THE UNITED STATES UNITE! 45

Figure 3.2 **Work Stoppage Involving 1,000 Workers or More, 1947–2010**

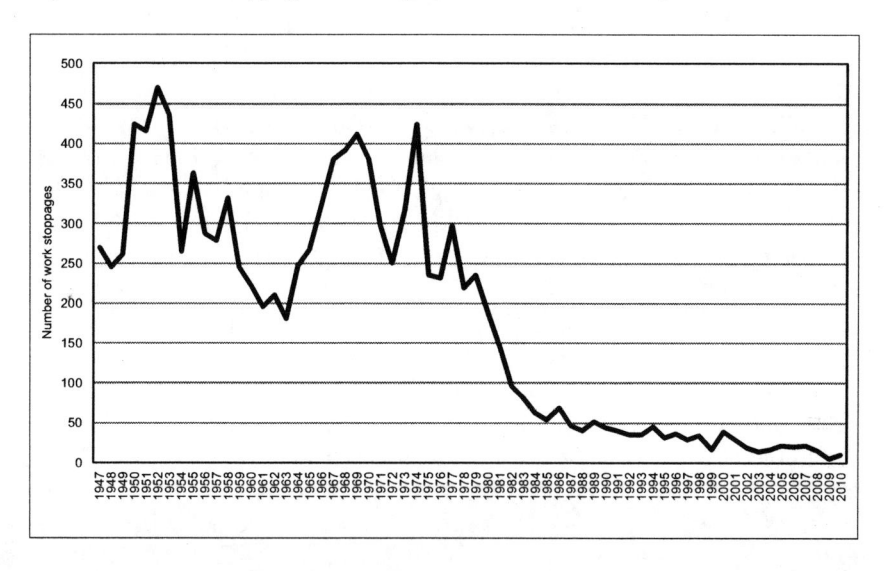

Source: Bureau of Labor Statistics, 2011b.

Figure 3.3 **Days Idle from Work Stoppage (Thousands), 1947–2010**

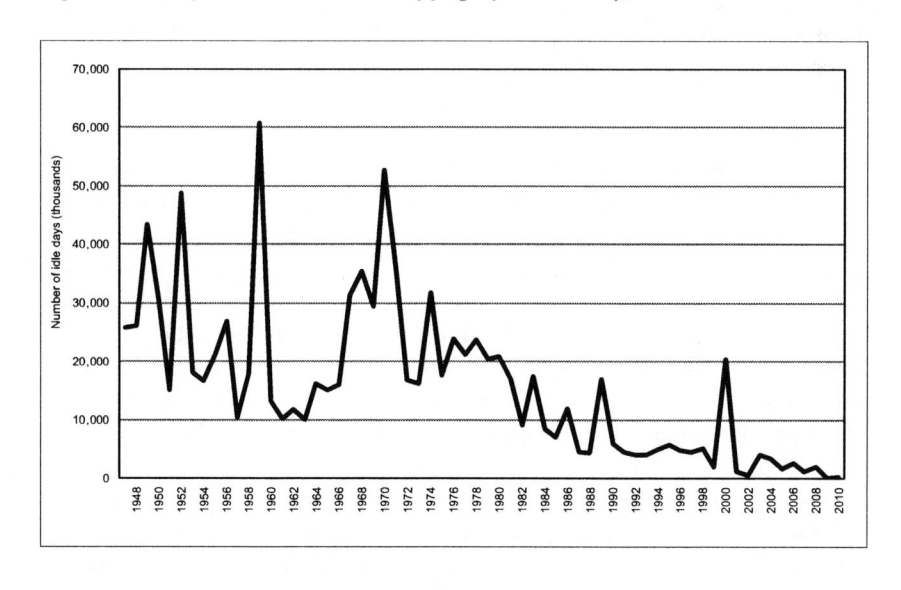

Source: Bureau of Labor Statistics, 2011b.

when Presidents Theodore Roosevelt (1902) and William Howard Taft (1909) put a gag order on federal postal workers, preventing them from speaking with Congress on all matters without approval from their supervisors. In response, Republican Senator Robert La Follette spearheaded the passage of the Loyd-La Follette Act of 1912, legislation that made the process of firing public employees more difficult. For the first time, federal workers gained the formal right to organize, which marked the beginning of the union movement in the public sector. Prior to the act's passage, there was no statutory prohibition against the government's discharging federal employees. An employee could be discharged with or without cause for conduct, which was not protected under the First Amendment to Constitution. The 1912 act was also the first federal law to specifically protect whistleblowers.

Another significant event occurred in 1919 when Boston police officers decided to strike in order to take a stand for increased rights and working conditions. Boston police experienced major backlash from the American Federation of Labor (AFL) and other associations representing police officers, as these groups severed ties with the officers after the incident. Prior to the strike, a charter was granted to the Boston Social Club, representing police officers, from the AFL on the grounds that those represented would never strike. All police officers who participated in the strike were fired. Calvin Coolidge, then Massachusetts governor, made a statement that became legend, declaring, "there is no right to strike against the public safety by anybody, anywhere, anytime" (Shlaes 2010). Though the strike set back the unionization of police officers for decades to come, it also proved to be a historic precursor to public sector employees' eventually gaining the right to bargain collectively (Shlaes 2010; Slater 2004).

President Franklin Roosevelt echoed Coolidge's assertion that inadequacy of response by cities to poor working conditions can "justify the wrong of leaving the city unguarded" in a letter he wrote during the summer of 1937 to Luther Steward, president of the National Federation of Federal Employees (Shlaes 2010). In this letter, FDR stated, "government employees should realize that the process of collective bargaining, as usually understood, cannot be transplanted into the public service" (Shlaes 2010). Roosevelt did provide legal rights for collective bargaining in the private sector with the passage of the Wagner Act in 1935. His contention was that the employer is the whole of the people and that it is, therefore, impossible for administrative officials to be fully representative and bind the employer in mutual discussions with employee organizations. This was his justification for not supporting the same mechanism of collective bargaining in the public sector. What is clear from Roosevelt's letter was his greater concern that militant action on behalf of public employees would leave the public unsafe:

Particularly, I want to emphasize my conviction that militant tactics have no place in the functions of any organization of Government employees. Upon employees in the Federal service, rests the obligation to serve the whole people, whose interests and welfare require orderliness and continuity in the conduct of Government activities. This obligation is paramount. Since their own services have to do with the functioning of the Government, a strike of public employees manifests nothing less than an intent on their part to prevent or obstruct the operations of Government until their demands are satisfied. (Spero 1948, 2)

While it is clear that Roosevelt initially opposed collective bargaining in the public sector, he, like many politicians who like to tell voters what they want to hear, later appeared to hedge on public sector collective bargaining. In 1940, the Tennessee Valley Authority (TVA) signed a number of agreements with fifteen unions representing the TVA construction and operating employees. At this point, Roosevelt had nothing but praise for the arrangement, calling it a "splendid new agreement between organized labor and the TVA" (Spero 1948, 346). Roosevelt went on to say, "collective bargaining and efficiency have proceeded hand in hand" (346). Additionally, the Inland Waterways Corporation, the Alaska Railways, the Bonneville Power Administration, the Securities and Exchange Commission, the National Labor Relations Board, the National War Labor Board, and the Federal Public Housing Authority all entered into agreements with their employees after Roosevelt's letter to Steward. These agreements seem to indicate that Roosevelt had a change of heart and was not totally opposed to nonmilitant organizing and bargaining among public sector employees.

Resistance to Public Sector Bargaining

In 1941, the National Institute of Municipal Law Officers published *Power of Municipalities to Enter into Labor Union Contracts.* This report effectively stated that no city had ever signed a collective bargaining agreement like those commonly used in the private sector. It further stated that the agreements that had been made between the relatively few cities and representatives of labor unions were symbolic, only containing declarations of good will or positive intentions to take employee concerns seriously. The document concluded that "legal opinions of the courts, city attorneys and state attorney generals are unanimous in their decisions that cities do not have the power to sign collective bargaining agreements" (Spero 1948, 343).

Six years later, the strength of this assertion was modified by Charles S. Rhyne, general counsel of the institute, stating that "any contract between a municipality and a labor union covering terms and conditions of employment of public employees is void as a delegation of public power to a private group, i.e., the union, but there is a minority view to the effect that all such agreements are not in and of themselves illegal, but each agreement must be considered separately upon its specific terms" (Spero 1948, 343). At that time, the legality of collective bargaining remained unclear in most states. Cleveland, Ohio, was an example of this. In 1945, a court contended that the Transit Board was not permitted to enter into a contract with organizations representing the employees of the transit system, even though the city had acquired the transit system from private owners. Months later, a law was passed allowing the authorities of publicly owned utilities to uphold and recognize contracts with labor unions for those utilities that were previously privately owned. In 1935, the state of Washington passed a law that authorized collective bargaining contracts between cities that owned public utilities and the employees of these utilities.

Conversely, in 1946, Virginia passed a law prohibiting collective bargaining in the public sector. It was declared to be against public policy for the state and subdivisions to recognize labor unions as representative of its employees and to negotiate with them. Carefully scripted, the same law permits organizations to form that do not strike or have outside labor affiliations with which work conditions can be discussed with employers.

The very next year, Texas passed a law with the same prohibitions. The state of Florida also held out on accepting collective bargaining, as its Supreme Court ruled in 1946 that the constitutional amendment allowing collective bargaining for employees did not apply to municipal workers. This ruling saved Miami from having to come to the table with employee organizations. The Court of Appeals in Maryland upheld the same standard, banning the city of Baltimore from entering into agreements that would recognize a union as the sole representative of city employees in bargaining. The ruling made clear that no representative organization could wield the power to bind city authorities to determine conditions, wages, and hours. A district court of appeals ruled similarly in California, absolving the city of Santa Monica of the obligation to recognize sole bargaining rights to a union representing the majority of city bus employees.

The Essence of Collective Bargaining Appears in the Public Sector

In 1945, the city council in Reading, Pennsylvania, created an ordinance that recognized the American Federation of State, County and Municipal Employees and the International Brotherhood of Teamsters, Chauffeurs, Warehousemen and Helpers of America as representative unions. The ordinance specified agreements with regard to voluntary check-off of union dues, pay, hours, vacation time, grievance procedures, strikes, and wage negotiations. This ordinance, though not collective bargaining in the normal sense, represents a legislative form of agreement arrived at between representative unions of public sector employees and their employer.

Similarly, in 1944, the Philadelphia city council passed an ordinance "authorizing the Mayor to execute and deliver an agreement between the City of Philadelphia and the American Federation of State, County and Municipal Employees . . . for the purpose of avoiding industrial disputes of bargaining collectively with regard to wages, hours and working conditions of certain employees of the City" (Spero 1948, 349). The ordinance specified that wages would be agreed upon in accordance with the terms of the budget ordinance. This meant that the developers of the budget would bargain with the unions to determine wages. As specified in this ordinance, the mayor and city council met with the union to discuss requested wages ninety days prior to adoption of new budgets. Though put forth through legal action, this form of agreement relied on direct negotiation with unions over worker wages—the essence of collective bargaining (Spero 1948).

Unions Begin to Grow Through the Legislative Process

In the 1960s, union membership more than doubled among public employees. By 1968, there were 2.2 million members, up from 1 million in 1960. The American Federation of State, City and Municipal Employees (AFSCME) membership reached to 460,000 in 1970, from 185,000 in 1960. In this same period, the American Federation of Government Employees (AFGE) saw membership increase from 70,000 to 325,000.

Many judicial changes took place between 1960 and 1970. Prior to 1960, most courts maintained that public employees did have the right to join or form unions. Even in 1963, the Michigan Supreme Court upheld the constitutionality of *AFSCME, Local 201 v. City of Muskegon*, in which a police chief prohibited police officers from joining any organization identified with any labor union or federation that admitted members who were not Muskegon Police Officers.

But by 1968, the U.S. Court of Appeals for the Seventh Circuit ruled that "an individual's right to form and join a union is protected by the First Amendment" (Shaw 1972, 21). In this ruling, involving two teachers claiming that their contracts were not renewed due to activities related to the American Federation of Teachers, the court further stated that "the Civil Rights Act of 1871 gives them a remedy if their contracts were not renewed because of their exercise of constitutional rights" (21). This began a trend in the judicial system of defending the constitutional right of public workers to join unions. Nevertheless, the courts remained firm that the Constitution cannot force public employers to bargain collectively without legislation present. This was clearly declared by the U.S. Court of Appeals for the Seventh Circuit in stating, "there is no constitutional duty to bargain collectively with an exclusive bargaining agent. Such duty when imposed is imposed by statute" (*Indianapolis Education Association v. Lewallen*, 1969, as cited in Shaw 1972, 22).

Though public employers could not be constitutionally forced to enter collective bargaining, many courts upheld that it was legally permitted should they decide to do so. This was illustrated by the Illinois Appellate Court in 1966, which stated that the Chicago Board of Education did "not require legislative authority to enter into a collective bargaining agreement with a sole collective bargaining agency selected by its teachers and . . . that such an agreement is not against public policy" (Shaw 1972, 22).

The issue of a right to strike was taken up by some public employees at the federal level. The courts remained clear that public employees do not have the right to strike, due to the special circumstances of their employment being in the service of the public. In 1971, this precedent was upheld in the case of *Postal Clerks v. Blount* by the U.S. District Court for the District of Columbia, which stated that "it is not irrational or arbitrary for the Government to condition employment on a promise not to withhold labor collectively, and to prohibit strikes by the public employment, whether because of the prerogatives of the sovereign, some sense of higher obligation associated with public service, to assure the continuing functioning of the Government without interruption, to protect public health and safety, or other reasons" (Shaw 1972, 22). This ruling continues the agreement of the courts with FDR's concern about public organizing activities having the potential to undermine government and public safety if public employees are given the option to strike.

Prior to 1960, only one state, Wisconsin, had enacted legislation that protected public workers' right to collectively bargain. During the 1960s, however, there was a great deal of legislation concerning relations between public employers and their workers, thus solidifying much of what would occur with regard to public labor relations for the decades that would follow.

While federal employees first gained the right to organize under the Lloyd-LaFollette Act of 1912, President John F. Kennedy's 1962 Executive Order 10988 recognized for the first time the right of the federal government's employees to join and form unions and bargain collectively (Thompson 2007). Codified in this order were three types of recognition. These were exclusive, formal, and informal, depending upon the percentage of employees represented by the labor organization. For those organizations given exclusive recognition, the agency was required to "meet at reasonable times and confer with respect to personnel policy and practices and matters affecting working conditions, so far as may be appropriate subject to law and policy requirements" (Shaw 1972, 24). However, it is important to note that the scope of issues over which employees could bargain was extremely limited. Pay and benefits were excluded from negotiation and instead delegated to Congress and the president (Thompson 2007).

President Richard Nixon's Executive Order 11491 in 1969 replaced Kennedy's Executive Order 10988 and created an administrative structure for the bargaining process. A major change that Nixon made to Kennedy's initial executive order was to do away with formal and informal representation, allowing for all labor organizations to enjoy the bargaining rights previously reserved only for those with exclusive representation. This was seen as a way to expand labor organizations' rights, though the limited parameters of collective bargaining in Kennedy's order were left unchanged. Nixon's order also established a Federal Labor Relations Council for the purpose of deciding policy questions. To oversee mediation and resolve disputes during negotiations, a Federal Services Impasse Panel was created. The Secretary of Labor for Labor–Management Relations also gained more oversight, including the authority to resolve representation matters and to decide unfair labor practice charges in accordance with the standards of conduct listed in the executive order.

In 1970, the postal workers gained more bargaining power with the passage of the Postal Reorganization Act, which gave unions the power to bargain over hours, wages, conditions, and other terms of employment. Though bound by the same restriction of strikes, and containing binding arbitration for collective bargaining impasses, the Postal Reorganization Act provided a larger scope for bargaining than Executive Order 11491 did because it did not have an attached statutory management rights provision. Further, the act made mandatory that proposals to restrict technological changes and subcontracts be subject to bargaining. This act was the most comprehensive coverage up to that point of topics in which federal employees could bargain, and it became the goal of the American Federation of Labor and Congress of Industry Organizations (AFL-CIO) that these full bargaining rights be extended to all federal government employees (Shaw 1972).

Federal organizing and bargaining legislation was soon followed by similar legislation in many states. Kennedy's Executive Order 10988 seemed to be interpreted by many states and municipalities not as a mandate to give limited bargaining power to federal employees, but rather as the first step in overturning the long-standing denial of rights, long overdue, to public workers. By 1971, twenty-one states had enacted far-reaching statutes for public employees. Fifteen states had enacted further statutes covering teachers and ten states enacted statutes for firefighters and/or police. Despite continued illegality, strikes began to occur with more frequency in the public sector. Initially, many of these strikes were supported by the general public, which empathized with the plight of underpaid public workers in comparison to those in the private sector. By 1972, public support had substantially dropped for public workers such as teachers, firefighters and police. However, in many big cities these workers had bargained successfully, eradicating most wage inequalities (Shaw 1972).

Public employers began to suffer, caught between the demand for more services and the fiscal reality of inflation. In local and state governments, the ability to pay for robust services began to look infeasible, especially given the public's unwillingness to pass referenda for larger school and government budgets. As the budgets of governments did not seem able to pay for the services public unions had bargained for, public employers resorted to reducing other programs to make money available for negotiations (Zack 1972).

Public Unions Experience Government Backlash

In 1973, the proportion of public sector employees who were union members surpassed the rate of union membership from the private sector. By 1979, the rate of union membership among public sector workers rose to 39 percent. During the 1980s, however, public sector membership suffered a setback. The country was in a recession. Federal aid money was cut, and tax limits, beginning with Proposition 13 in California, were beginning to be imposed. President Ronald Reagan stood up to the striking Professional Air Traffic Controllers (PATCO), firing 11,000 of them for the being public workers on strike. At the same time, PATCO was decertified as a bargaining agent. Most of the fired union members were henceforth barred from going back to work. During this period, the unions prioritized retaining membership, salaries, and benefits. Though this was a low point for unions representing public employees, membership did not go below 35 percent (Adler 2006).

Kennedy's Executive Order 10988 was followed by a steady increase of federal union membership and likely sent the message to state and local employees to unionize. The executive order was seen by many as an act of appreciation on JFK's part for AFL-CIO union head George Meany, who had helped Kennedy win the presidency.

While President Reagan fired the striking air-traffic controllers of the Federal Aviation Administration in 1981, it was during his administration as well as those of George H.W. Bush, Bill Clinton, and George W. Bush that the generous compensation packages, pay schedules, and tenure rules of today were signed into law. Union sentimentalism and the demand by public workers to be treated on par with private sector workers continues to be rhetoric that protects collective bargaining, job security, and pensions for public sector workers (Shlaes 2010).

The Contemporary Status

Though union membership remains relatively stable across all levels of government, membership and representation rates have dropped steadily, from their peak of 44.7 percent and 38.7 percent, respectively, in 1994, to 40.7 percent and 36.8 percent in 2008. Membership and representation rates are quite different between states. As illustrated in Table 3.1, New York State has the highest rate of membership while Mississippi has the lowest. According to Kearney (2009), this strong differential mirrors the variance in legal environments between states for collective bargaining. The states with robust bargaining laws for state and local employees have higher rates of membership and representation than those states with partial or no legal bargaining. North Carolina, Virginia, and Georgia fall into the latter category, while New York and Connecticut fall into the former.

Upon review of the research, Kearney (2009) found that the relation between collective bargaining laws and union density is mutually reciprocal, rather than one being consistently caused by the other. Not only can growing union membership influence legislators to adopt new bargaining laws, but Burton (1978), Farber (1987), Hindman and Patton (1994), Ichniowski (1988), and others have found evidence that bargaining laws also stimulate continued growth in union membership.

When it comes to the states that have adopted bargaining laws, geography cannot be overlooked. Historically, most of the areas that adopted laws permitting bargaining were urbanized, industrialized, and had high levels of private sector unionization. The states that did not adopt specific bargaining laws were largely south of the Mason-Dixon Line. As citizens in the southern and southwestern states are generally more conservative in political and social matters, it follows that these states have a history of aversion to organized labor. In many southern states, only partial bargaining laws are in place. Only firefighters and transit workers in Georgia, police and firefighters in Texas, and teachers in Utah have formal bargaining rights. Other states, such as Maryland, Nevada, Alabama, and Oklahoma allow local, but not state, workers to collectively bargain. State workers continue to advocate for legislation that would give them all the same bargaining rights, as occurred with Washington State's Personnel Reform Act of 2002, which granted bargaining rights to state employees after decades of pressure (Kearney 2009).

Mareschal (2006) has found unions such as AFSCME, Service Employees International Union (SEIU), and the Office and Professional Employees International Union (OPEIU) are focusing on new sectors for membership growth. Day-care centers, cultural entities, schools, churches, social service organizations, and health-care workers are newer areas of representation for

Table 3.1

Union Membership, Coverage, Density, and Employment by State, 2010

Code	State	Sector	Obs	Employment	Members	Covered	% Members	% Covered
63	Alabama	Public	334	345,485	99,776	111,617	28.9	32.3
94	Alaska	Public	614	78,205	43,311	45,994	55.4	58.8
86	Arizona	Public	333	441,192	87,060	116,603	19.7	26.4
71	Arkansas	Public	279	185,164	19,552	25,806	10.6	13.9
93	California	Public	2,332	2,405,816	1,362,553	1,432,833	56.6	59.6
84	Colorado	Public	573	325,700	70,985	83,818	21.8	25.7
16	Connecticut	Public	619	230,602	148,415	153,129	64.4	66.4
51	Delaware	Public	440	59,718	23,221	25,224	38.9	42.2
53	D.C.	Public	725	81,497	13,609	16,245	16.7	19.9
59	Florida	Public	943	1,081,317	252,445	300,652	23.3	27.8
58	Georgia	Public	624	666,034	73,752	96,906	11.1	14.5
95	Hawaii	Public	514	103,330	51,868	53,866	50.2	52.1
82	Idaho	Public	334	112,318	24,409	29,653	21.7	26.4
33	Illinois	Public	795	802,749	402,758	422,006	50.2	52.6
32	Indiana	Public	377	373,017	99,798	119,684	26.8	32.1
42	Iowa	Public	627	248,331	77,210	101,397	31.1	40.8
47	Kansas	Public	511	246,166	39,454	54,115	16.0	22.0
61	Kentucky	Public	379	264,855	47,978	56,563	18.1	21.4
72	Louisiana	Public	288	322,647	30,115	37,773	9.3	11.7
11	Maine	Public	476	79,828	39,067	44,520	48.9	55.8
52	Maryland	Public	1,032	612,194	178,331	198,622	29.1	32.4
14	Massachusetts	Public	374	389,899	242,201	251,065	62.1	64.4
34	Michigan	Public	539	541,558	264,684	280,245	48.9	51.7
41	Minnesota	Public	690	365,042	208,161	215,981	57.0	59.2
64	Mississippi	Public	296	214,359	15,819	24,040	7.4	11.2
43	Missouri	Public	410	346,671	63,198	82,513	18.2	23.8

Obs	State	Sector	Employment	Members	Covered	%Mem	%Cov
81	Montana	Public	273	71,703	29,663	41.4	46.5
46	Nebraska	Public	547	153,906	43,529	28.3	36.3
88	Nevada	Public	355	145,577	58,068	39.9	45.7
12	New Hampshire	Public	604	92,848	39,913	43.0	50.3
22	New Jersey	Public	592	604,347	356,649	59.0	60.6
85	New Mexico	Public	394	219,182	41,207	18.8	24.5
21	New York	Public	1,357	1,503,358	1,059,643	70.5	72.9
56	North Carolina	Public	589	663,513	62,920	9.5	15.7
44	North Dakota	Public	527	67,034	11,687	17.4	23.1
31	Ohio	Public	719	725,058	312,559	43.1	46.2
73	Oklahoma	Public	398	280,928	37,203	13.2	16.2
92	Oregon	Public	388	251,834	130,248	51.7	56.9
23	Pennsylvania	Public	688	696,936	347,492	49.9	53.4
15	Rhode Island	Public	441	66,171	42,153	63.7	66.6
57	South Carolina	Public	378	316,140	41,369	13.1	16.3
45	South Dakota	Public	523	63,201	11,293	17.9	20.9
62	Tennessee	Public	346	393,175	69,162	17.6	20.2
74	Texas	Public	1,468	1,640,448	276,479	16.9	21.0
87	Utah	Public	395	222,223	38,903	17.5	24.0
13	Vermont	Public	457	46,734	21,447	45.9	53.7
54	Virginia	Public	836	749,001	80,844	10.8	14.4
91	Washington	Public	552	535,691	304,444	56.8	61.2
55	West Virginia	Public	402	160,470	41,944	26.1	28.8
35	Wisconsin	Public	532	376,605	175,366	46.6	49.6
83	Wyoming	Public	629	62,881	9,207	14.6	16.4

Source: Hirsch and Macpherson, 2011.

Note: Data sources: Estimates are complied from the Current Population Survey (CPS). Variable definitions: Obs = CPS sample size; Employment = employment, in thousands; Members = union membership, in thousands; Covered = workers covered by a collective bargaining agreement, in thousands; %Mem = percentage of wage and salary workers who are union members; %Cov = percentage of wage and salary workers who are covered by a collective bargaining agreement.

these unions. Unions have pushed for new legislation to protect the bargaining rights of these groups in states such as California, Oregon, and Washington. In these three states, SEIU successfully pushed through "policy interventions that created public authorities as employers of record for home care aides," for collective bargaining purposes (Mareschal 2006, 27).

Management for employees previously considered nontraditional workers was resolved by legislation such as this. Another example of this sort of legislation is Eliot Spitzer's executive order for New York State in 2007, which gave federally subsidized, home-based child-care providers the right to unionize and engage in collective bargaining. This did away with the previous categorization of these workers as independent contractors. Also in 2007, the United Federation of Teachers gained representation rights for 28,000 providers (Greenhouse 2007). The states of California and Washington, however, held out on granting such rights to these workers in 2008 as legislation failed in Washington and Governor Arnold Schwarzenegger vetoed a bill to grant collective bargaining to subsidized child-care providers and their family members in California (Sanders 2008). These two state actions were among the few that resisted union pressure.

Unions have utilized influence over governors to gain further bargaining rights in exchange for political support. The efficiency of this design is that it is cheaper and easier to influence one person, resulting in governors creating executive orders rather than persuading the majorities in both houses of the legislature to pass similar legislation.

This was the case in Arizona as Governor Janet Napolitano issued an executive order late in 2008 that granted state employees the right to meet and confer. Colorado governor Bill Ritter issued a similar executive order in 2007 that allowed for "partnership agreements," essentially allowing unions to represent classified state workers in negotiations on issues such as wages, staffing, health care, training, efficiency, and workplace safety. Though not explicitly called collective bargaining, it seemed to carry the same effect. Within seven months of the order, 22,500 state employees that were represented by unions such as AFSCME, SEIU, and the American Federation of Teachers (AFT) and were protected by union contracts (Fender 2008). Similarly, in 2001, unions persuaded Missouri and Kentucky governors to issue executive orders that would permit collective bargaining. The order was quickly undone in Kentucky the following year, when Governor Ernie Fletcher annulled it. The original order was restored in 2008 by Kentucky governor Steve Beshear.

State supreme courts are another avenue utilized by unions to gain bargaining rights. The first instance of this occurred in 1968 in the case of *Dade County Classroom Teachers Association v. Ryan*. The court ordered the state of Florida to set up a specific law that would specify standards and regulations for public sector bargaining. More recently, the states of Missouri and Florida have gained constitutional rights to collective bargaining for state workers as the result of state supreme court decisions (Lieb 2007).

Virginia and South Carolina are the two southern states that clearly prohibit collective bargaining between state agencies, local governments, and unions. In Virginia, there is a statute as well as a Supreme Court ruling, in the case of *Commonwealth of Virginia v. The County Board of Arlington et al.* (1977), prohibiting collective bargaining. In North Carolina, Statute 95–98 was signed into law in 1959, effectively prohibiting collective bargaining. Nonetheless, some meet-and-confer relationships exist in certain North Carolina municipalities in which topics such as pay, benefits, and working conditions are discussed between city managers/council members and union representatives (Honeycutt 2007). In 2008, an attempt to overturn the ban on collective bargaining in North Carolina was introduced. It passed the House judiciary committee but died soon after. In 2008, public sector union membership rates went up to 11 percent from 8.2 percent the previous year. This was largely due to the affiliation of State Employees Association of North Carolina with SEIU, and to large contributions to the 2006 and 2008 legislative elections (Hirsch and Macpherson 2011).

In 2002, with the creation of the Department of Homeland Security (DHS), union representation and collective bargaining was restricted as special provisions were introduced that proved even more limiting than Title VII of the Civil Service Reform Act (1978), which governs most federal collective bargaining. Ferris and Hyde (2004) found that parts of the provisions excluded about 175,000 federal workers from collective bargaining rights altogether. Under the establishing statute of DHS, management had the right to make null and void any part of an existing collective bargaining agreement.

In 2003, the Department of Defense (DOD) gained the power to eliminate civil service protection for over 700,000 civilian employees. Furthermore, DOD gained the right to create its own pay, classification, performance evaluation, labor relations, and employee appeals system. The National Security Personnel System (NSPS) was created to oversee these changes. Many of these new provisions were overturned in 2008 due to strong union and Democratic opposition. Ballenstedt (2008) notes that labor–management relations in DOD were largely restored to standard procedures and regulations for the civil service at the close of the Bush administration.

The George W. Bush administration clearly opposed many collective bargaining rights earned by public sector employees. Bush revoked President Clinton's Executive Order 12933, which mandated labor–management partnerships in all federal agencies, shortly after taking office. Recorded by Tobias (2004), the Bush administration attempted to send 425,000 federal civil service positions to private sector firms in effort to boost the doctrine of freedom to manage.

The year 2008 saw a push for federal legislation to cover state and local employees by outlining standards for labor relations and collective bargaining. H.R. 980, the Public Safety Employer-Employee Cooperation Act, passed the House of Representatives in 2007 by an overwhelming majority vote, 314–97. The bill's major support in the Senate rested on Edward Kennedy's backing, though when he was hospitalized with a brain tumor the bill lost momentum. The attention of the Senate moved to the national financial crisis, and its adjournment for the New Year in anticipation of the Obama administration left H.R. 980 unfinished at the close of Congress in 2008.

Anti-Union Push?

The recent push to either strip or scale back collective bargaining rights at the state level is seen by some as the Republican effort to move forward their agenda to cut spending and maintain tax cuts; however, some Democratic governors have also pushed for changes in pension program operations, upsetting public sector unions. Scott Walker, Republican governor of Wisconsin, has led the way in his efforts to curb collective bargaining. A law he signed bars public sector unions, except those representing police officers and firefighters, from bargaining over health benefits and pensions. It allows bargaining over wages, but does not permit raises higher than the inflation rate unless they are approved in a public referendum. Similarly, Republican governors in Michigan, New Jersey, Ohio, and Oklahoma passed laws in 2011 eliminating or curtailing collective bargaining of wages and/or benefits.

In Ohio, Governor John Kasich signed a bill on March 31, 2011, limiting collective bargaining in the public sector to an even greater extent than Wisconsin's bill, signed by Governor Walker on March 11, 2011. Unlike the Wisconsin bill, the Ohio bill also limits collective bargaining power for police and firefighters. Both bills, however, prohibit any bargaining over health coverage and pensions. Argument for the bill's utility came from State Senator Shannon Jones, a Republican, among others. He purported that limiting collective bargaining makes sense in the wake of budget deficits across the board of states, counties, and cities. Jones points to the fact that this bill will help reign in growing health-care and pension costs in favor of minimizing layoffs (Greenhouse 2011).

William Leibensperger, vice president of the Ohio Education Association, sees the state's efforts in a different light. Leibensperger states, "It's a politically motivated effort to weaken and destroy the unions that the leaders of the Republican Party perceive as their biggest political opponents" (Greenhouse

2011, para. 8). William Even, a professor of economics at Miami University of Ohio, agrees that the roots of this push have grown out of a difference in philosophical views between Republicans and Democrats with regard to the unions' effect on the efficiency of government. All of the bill's supporters in Ohio's Senate and House were Republicans, giving some credence to Even's claim.

In both Ohio and Wisconsin, unions have moved quickly to battle back. A lawsuit was filed in Wisconsin temporarily suspending the law for violating the open meetings act; however, it was overturned by the state's Supreme Court. Unions have since failed in their federal lawsuits to overturn the legislation. In addition, unions have successfully gathered signatures in an effort to recall the governor and impeach several state senators. In Ohio, rank-and-file union members are gathering signatures to hold a referendum on the law. As to the question of why there was such a disproportionately larger protest in Wisconsin as compared to Ohio to rally against these laws, observers believe it is due to the fact that the Wisconsin legislation came first. Furthermore, with Madison's liberal university and Wisconsin being the birthplace of the progressive movement, a greater number of protestors were to be expected.

Though both laws allow government employees to opt out of paying union dues or fees, the Wisconsin law goes further in prohibiting any public employer from deducting workers' dues from their paychecks to forward to union treasuries. Further, the Wisconsin law requires public employees to vote every year in order to keep their union. In Ohio, however, the taxpayers now have the right to pass a referendum that would overturn any contract a public employer signs that requires a raise in taxes to pay for it. Governor Kasich has repeatedly said that this law will allow for fewer layoffs by limiting labor costs, saving the state $75 million and local governments $393 million annually by switching from statutory step-pay increases to merit pay. However, Ohio House Democratic leader Armond Budish maintains, "This bill is an effort to camouflage the pain that the governor's huge budget cuts are going to cause" (Greenhouse 2011, para. 19).

In New Jersey, Governor Chris Christie signed a bill that imposes new terms for health insurance on the unions, stripping them of the power to address the issue in collective bargaining. Christie insists that he is not trying to eliminate collective bargaining, but union leaders say the New Jersey bill would have that effect. Under current state law, in a contract impasse, a governor or mayor can go through a series of steps and impose terms on most employee groups on every issue except health care. Most public employees now contribute 1.5 percent of their salaries to health insurance, or $975 yearly for a person earning $65,000. Under the new law, low-income government workers could pay as little as 3 percent of their current salary for full family coverage, while high-paid employees could pay up to 5.5 percent. For the $65,000-a-year employee, that would mean about $3,600 at today's rates, but the increase would phase in over four years. The bill would also increase what most employees contribute to their pensions, from 5.5 percent of salary to 6.5 percent right away, and in stages, to 7.5 percent.

On June 1, 2011, Tennessee joined the ranks of Wisconsin, Ohio, Indiana, Idaho, and Michigan in passing a bill to limit union power in public schools. "Tennessee Governor Bill Haslam affixed his signature on House Bill 130 and Senate Bill 113, ending collective bargaining and giving local school boards the full authority to operate their districts in the manner they choose" (Olsen 2011). This new law, however, also allows for the signing of binding memorandums of understanding, should both sides agree on an issue, which essentially is similar to collective bargaining. The difference is that for unsettled issues, the unions won't have the right to appeal decisions made by the school board. Further, school boards will now have the option of passing on making agreements with the unions in favor of unilaterally deciding on changes. Arguably, one of the most significant changes of this new law is that the union concept of seniority as applied to payroll structure and layoff processes will no longer exist (Olsen 2011).

Some cast this debate as part of the Republican–Democrat divide. However, some of those seeking union givebacks include Democratic governors Andrew Cuomo of New York, Martin O'Malley of Maryland, and John Lynch of New Hampshire. Governor Cuomo has announced that his approach to scaling back state pensions would save taxpayers $93 billion over 30 years. Among the proposed changes: raising the standard retirement age from 62 to 65; eliminating early retirement; requiring a 6 percent employee contribution for a workers' entire career rather than a limited period of time; excluding the use of overtime when calculating retirement pay; and banning the cashing in of unused sick days or vacation time. The retirement age for teacher would be raised from 57 to 62. Cuomo has commented on several occasions that the current pension system is unsustainable. Wage cuts and increased employee pension contributions being proposed in California, Maryland, and New York are actually greater, on a per capita basis, than those being proposed by Republicans Scott Walker, John Kasich, Rick Scott, and Chris Christie.

Public Sector Union Influence in California

The disproportional influence of public sector unions in the State of California has been chronicled by many sources. California public workers gained collective bargaining rights in 1968, as did local government workers; in the 1970s, state workers and teachers did so as well. Malanga (2010) believes the onset of this trend was a result of workers quickly learning how to elect their own bosses, which would lead to sympathetic politicians granting them outsize pay and benefits in exchange for their support. Likewise, Greenhut (2009) suggests that many legislators are beholden to one special interest group—public sector unions. While he maintains that this is due to organized labor wielding an immense amount of influence over Democratic lawmakers, who are heavily dependent on the unions for campaign donations, Greenhut also points out the close alliance between Republican lawmakers and law enforcement unions.

From the 1960s to the 1980s, population and job growth boomed in California. Government jobs grew from 874,000 in 1960 to 1.76 million in 1980 to 2.1 million in 1990. In 1978, California taxpayers passed Proposition 13, capping property taxes in order, in part, to slow the growth of government. Organized labor strongly opposed this measure, and through increased union efforts led a series of strikes—40 times in 1980 alone. Beyond strikes, unions began to invest more in political activity, becoming one of the most powerful lobbying factions in Sacramento.

This power proved to be effective as the California Teachers Association (CTA) successfully passed Proposition 98, requiring 40 percent of the state budget to fund local education. Much of this budgeted money was in the form of discretionary funds, resulting in higher teacher salaries and making California's teachers the highest paid in the country. Though teacher wages went up, California's per-student state spending rose to only slightly higher than the national average, raising questions about the true motives of Proposition 98.

California's teachers continued to benefit in 1996 after the CTA spent more than $1 million on a campaign for smaller class sizes. Governor Pete Wilson responded by earmarking three-quarters of a billion dollars to the cause. Student performance did not change, though a wave of new teachers were hired, further bolstering CTA union membership. When Governor Wilson offered more funds in 1998 to continue reducing class size but with oversight mechanisms attached, the CTA strongly opposed the measure.

A second public sector union group gaining considerable power in the state was law enforcement, including police, prison guards, and highway-patrol officers. Politicians treasure the political endorsement from these industries, as California has some of the strongest criminal laws in the country and the endorsements make candidates look tough on crime. Public unions representing these workers tend to back candidates who will be sympathetic to granting higher benefits for public-safety workers. Unlike many of the other public sector unions representing teachers and civil servants that are closely aligned with Democratic lawmakers, law enforcement unions also have the backing of many Republican lawmakers. State Assemblyman E. Richard Barnes lost reelection in 1972 in California largely due to opposition from police and firefighters. His record showed that he was tough on crime but also aimed to fight pension and fringe benefit enhancements for government workers.

The state prison guards' union has also exhibited strong political influence. With California's building of a multitude of new prisons beginning in the 1980s, union membership rose from 1,600 in 1980 to 17,000 in 1988, 25,000 by 1997, and it currently stands at 31,000. The California Correctional Peace Officers Association (CCPOA) spent $200,000 in 2004 on a campaign to unseat Assemblyman Phil Wyman of Tehachapi for advocating for privatization of state prisons (Malanga 2010). CCPOA's protection of its own interests through political influence can also be seen in their support for Governor Gray Davis in 1998. When Governor Davis ran for reelection four years later, he also raised the pay of CCPOA 34 percent over the next five years. This effectively raised the base salary of prison guards from $50,000 to $65,000 a year. This was also a time when the state was facing a budget crisis, unemployment had been rising steadily over the prior year, and government revenues were diminishing. Davis's wage increase resulted in a $1 million donation to his reelection campaign from CCPOA. Police and sheriffs' unions have similarly been involved politically in California and have benefited as a result. In California, most police officers receive 90 percent of their pay upon retiring at age 50, as compared to a pension of about half their final salary in other states at the same retirement age (Greenhut 2009).

California governor Schwarzenegger also experienced the wrath of the state prison guards' union in 2006 when he came under severe criticism for his attempts to reform prisons. Schwarzenegger's plan involved building new prisons and expanding the already existing prisons to house more prisoners rather than releasing low-level drug offenders or sending illegal immigrant prisoners back to their home countries (Thompson 2006). In response, the state prison guards' union launched a two-week campaign, running two television ads against the governor. One ad criticized his preference for building more housing for more prisoners and the other accused him of ignoring California's mismanaged prison system. That year, the union was expected to have $15 million to spend on the upcoming November election; by August, they had already committed $5 million in television advertising for October. This kind of power clearly demonstrates the significant potential of unions to affect political decisions.

Schwarzenegger came under fire once more from the CCPOA in 2008. This time the union was seeking the recall of Schwarzenegger as governor in response to their not receiving a new labor contract for the previous two years and not being granted an exemption from pay reductions for state employees to deal with the budget deficit. Without an exemption from pay cuts, guards could no longer significantly increase their salaries by working excess overtime (Associated Press 2008). Although Governor Schwarzenegger brushed off the threat of recall as merely an intimidation tactic, it brought significant public attention to his performance and once again demonstrated the power that unions wield over politics.

California's third big public-union player is the state chapter of the SEIU the nation's fastest-growing union, whose chief, Andy Stern, earned notoriety by visiting the White House over twenty times during the first six months of the Obama administration (Malanga 2010). The California SEIU currently represents 700,000 workers, half of whom are government employees. The number of California employees represented by SEIU is more than one-third of its nationwide membership, which has risen dramatically due to some key victories for the union. In the 1980s, for example, the SEIU engaged in a lengthy legal battle to have home health-care workers paid by county Medicaid programs switched from independent contractor status to government employees. After winning this battle, SEIU was able to organize these workers, effectively gaining representation for 74,000 of them in Los Angeles County alone. No other membership drive had been so successful since that of the United Auto Workers' unionization of General Motors in 1937. As a result, home health-care workers added a great deal to the budget of Los Angeles County. This proved to be a successful tactic for increasing SEIU membership. Applying the same strategy in other California counties added 130,000 new members to the number of home health-care workers in California (Malanga 2010).

California's fiscal deficit grew drastically with the Democratic Party in control of the State Senate and as Governor Davis continued to increase benefits for the union workers who had helped him get elected. In 1999, extremely costly legislation was passed increasing the pension benefits for state employees. In this plan, a retroactive cost-of-living adjustment for already retired employees was included. It also replaced an older, less expensive pension plan that Governor Pete Wilson had instituted in 1991. Further, this legislation allowed public safety workers to retire at age 50 with 90 percent of their salaries. The California Public Employee Retirement System (CalPERS), whose board consisted mainly of union reps and members appointed directly by state officials supported by unions, backed Governor Davis and the legislation by issuing a statement declaring that it was affordable to enact this pension plan due to the pension systems' surplus and coupled with projected stock market gains. Most state municipalities followed suit, likewise increasing pension benefits for their workers.

In 2000, repercussions from this legislation began. State and local governments both faced having to deliver on paying pensions that they could not afford. The state's annual share of pension payments reached $3 billion by 2010, originally estimated to be only a few hundred million by CalPERS in 1999. Municipalities were also in over their heads: Orange County's payouts jumped to $410 million in 2009, up from $140 million in 1999.

Also in 2000, Governor Davis negotiated favorably with the California Teachers Association (CTA), eventually agreeing to increase spending to $1.84 billion on education. As noted by *Sacramento Bee* columnist Dan Walters, this deal locked in higher baseline spending for education and used up the state's surplus (Malanga 2010). Davis finally announced the huge deficit that the state faced after reelection in 2002 and was soon thereafter recalled. Despite the unions' shift of support from Davis to Lieutenant Governor Cruz Bustamante, Arnold Schwarzenegger was elected California's next governor. With a Democratic state legislature, Schwarzenegger was unable to push through a series of initiatives in 2005 aimed at reducing government size and union power.

Today, California's municipalities continue to suffer from pension promises they cannot afford. Unable to afford inflated employee salaries and pensions, the city of Vallejo filed for bankruptcy in 2008. A report issued by the Little Hoover Commission (2011), charged with studying the state's pension crisis, found that the state's ten largest pension funds, encompassing over 90 percent of all public employees, are overextended in their promises to current workers and retirees. In the cities of San Diego, Los Angeles, San Jose, and San Francisco, over one-third of the operating budgets are going to retiree costs. Even the City of Orange, located in conservative Orange County, spent $13 million of its $88 million budget on pensions alone in 2009. In the next three years, the City of Orange projects that spending will rise to $23 million on pensions. A similar budget crisis has plagued Contra Costa County, with pension costs growing from $70 million to $200 million between 2000 and 2010. The City of Los Angeles spends almost half of its $7 billion budget on payroll and faces budget shortfalls predicted to climb to $1 billion annually in coming years. This was only exacerbated in 2007, when 23 percent raises were given to public workers despite the current revenue decline. Presently, California seems unable to rely on its economy to dig out of its budget deficits, as even major companies such as Google and Intel are choosing to expand out of state.

Current Views of Unions

A recent poll by the Pew Research Center for the People and the Press found that public discontent with organized labor and public pensions and benefits is on the rise. The poll found overwhelming support for cutting pension plans for government employees as the favored route for closing the budget deficit by more than 16 percentage points in California (Rutten 2011). The poll further reported that the American people's opinion of unions was divided almost 50–50 between favorable and unfavorable. Among those indicating an unfavorable view, there is even more discontent with public sector unions than private, 40 percent to 37 percent, respectively.

The Pew study found that despite the fact that the majority of Americans acknowledge that unions have increased employees' salaries and working conditions, they see unions as crippling global competition, productivity, and the creation of good jobs (Butcher 2011). Public support for unions has dropped a dramatic 17 percent since 2007, when it stood at 58 percent. Interestingly, the Pew report found that more Americans would side with business over unions than government over unions in cases of labor disputes. The figures were close, though, with 43 percent supporting business over 40 percent supporting unions, and 44 percent supporting unions over 38 percent supporting government in their initial reaction (Pew Research Center for the People and the Press 2011). A Gallup poll in August of 2010 found a mere 52 percent approval rating for unions by Americans, the lowest in Gallup history. A recent poll by *USA Today* and Gallup found that despite low support for labor unions, Americans still support the right to collective bargaining by a margin 61 percent to 33 percent.

The Difference Between Public Sector and Private Sector Unions

Public sector collective bargaining is a fairly recent phenomenon that only became common starting in the 1960s and began to gain momentum while the slow decline of the private sector unionism was under way. A change in both the legal environment and government policy paved the way for the rise in public sector unionism. During much of the national policy debate, there has been a tendency to lump together private and public sector unions as if they were the same; however, Troy (2003) asserts that public sector bargaining is not an extension of collective bargaining in the private sector despite conventional wisdom and assertions in the academic literature. One factor that makes public bargaining unique is that municipal leaders are elected, inserting political considerations into the bargaining process. The government model differs from the private sector in the way that collective bargaining is performed and in its consequences for consumers in the private and public economies.

There are also significant historical differences between the two. Despite clear similarities, such as a shared interest in improved working conditions and wages and a link to some history and institutional structure, the distinct differences center on goals, approaches to bargaining, and philosophies (Troy

1994). Many have deemed the use of the private sector model for public sector bargaining laws problematic. A common belief that favors unions in the private sector is that unions were initially created to redistribute profits from business owners to workers and, therefore, workers need protection to ensure that this happens. Those opposed to public sector unions subscribe to this belief and maintain that unions do not belong in the public sector, as government does not make profits. Eileen Norcross (2011) summarizes the key differences when she states, "Private unionism operates as a labor cartel within the market economy and thus affects the profitability of firms, economic growth, the supply of labor, and consumer process. Public sector unions function as a monopoly provider of labor within a bureaucratic-political realm" (1).

In fact, tensions between private and public unions date back to George Meany, the first president of the AFL-CIO, who opposed collective bargaining for the public sector (Crane 2011). In 1955, Meany stated, "it is impossible to bargain collectively with the government" (Sherk 2010, 11). As recently as 1959, the AFL-CIO executive council stated, "government workers have no right to collectively bargain beyond the authority to petition Congress—a right available to every citizen" (Kramer 1962). Some of the key distinctions between private and public sector unions are explained below.

State Sovereignty and Democratic Governance

Some of the early objections to the formation of unions by public workers centered on concerns about state sovereignty and democratic governance (Slater 2004). Public sector unionism creates a uniquely powerful interest group. In theory, bureaucrats are supposed to work for and be accountable to the elected representatives of the people. The argument is that public sector unionism introduces an unelected body into policymaking, thereby undermining the sovereignty of the state (Troy 1994). Government (i.e., the public sector) is sovereign, unlike any other institution in our society. Under the U.S. democratic system, governmental sovereignty is derived from popular sovereignty, which we as citizens give to government, within constitutional limits, in the interest of security and the public good. In the issuing of sovereignty, the ultimate power to decide issues of public policy in a democracy rests with the people or their elected representatives, and cannot be properly delegated to nongovernmental groups such as unions (Kearney and Carnevale 2001). The essence of the sovereignty argument against public sector unionism is that collective bargaining undercuts the inherent power of the state as a sovereign representative of the people, and therefore is anti-democratic. When elected representatives cannot carry out their business due to public sector unions, sovereignty has broken down. While the sovereignty argument still surfaces from time to time, for the most part, sovereignty objections to public unionism have diminished.

Strikes

Another difference between public and private sector unionism centers on the threat of strike and how this would impact public safety and the general welfare. In the private sector, if a union goes on strike, there are often many alternative products and service suppliers available to customers. Since most government agencies operate as a monopoly, work slowdowns, sickouts, and strikes can really damage a community. Faced with this severe damage, government officials might give in to demands that would not be agreed to in a nonmonopoly environment. It is argued that strikes pose unacceptable threats to public health, safety, and well-being, and thus, public officials tend to concede to public pressure to settle with the unions.

In the private sector, workers' right to strike is legally protected by the National Labor Relations Act. In the public sector, federal employees are prohibited from striking under the Taft-Harley Act and the 1978 Civil Service Reform Act. Most state statutes preclude essential employees such as police, firefighters, corrections officers, and hospital workers from striking. When there have been bans on strikes for nonessential workers, they have not been particularly effective (Kearney 2009). However, this has been somewhat ameliorated by the emergence of arbitration procedures that can limit the need for strikes and have also contributed to a corresponding decrease in private sector strikes.

Civil Service Protections

A further difference with public sector unions is that unlike their counterparts in the private sector, public workers already have civil service protections codified in law at the federal, state, and local levels. In addition, there are state and local civil service protections that govern the employment of public workers and provide a host of protections, rules, and regulations to ensure that public workers are treated in a fair and equitable manner and freed from managerial abuses. There is no corresponding body that exists for the protection of workers in the private sector.

The Market Economy Versus Political Decision Making

Collective bargaining is also fundamentally different in the private sector than in the public sector because of competition, profits, and the lack of market constraints. Public sector decisions are political no matter how important their economic impact. The decisions made by government are based on political considerations, not economic ones. Private sector decision making is based on economic considerations, not their political impact. In the public sector, politically popular but economically devastating decisions can get individuals elected and/or keep them in office. In the private sector, politically popular decisions with negative economic consequences can put individuals and companies out of business (Denholm 2001).

Since the public sector has neither competition nor profits to consider when making decisions, there is little to limit its demands. Unlike their counterparts in the private sector, government unions are largely free from market discipline. There is no profit incentive to keep costs down because businesses are driven to make industry-leading quarterly and yearly profits. Most labor relations executives learn quickly not to give away the farm. Without that profit incentive, in the public sector there is a tendency for managers to grant greater concessions. Those concessions are primarily in nonpay areas (work rules and benefits), where the public and the press are not nearly as likely to notice and create an uproar. While the private sector unions push against the interests of shareholders and management, public sector unions push against the interests of taxpayers. Private sector union members know that their employers could go out of business, so they have an incentive to mitigate their demands; public sector union members work for state monopolies and have no such interest. There is only one fire department, one police department, and one system of public education. A monopoly on essential services gives government unions tremendous leverage to force concessions from the public.

Unions as a Political Machine

As the strength of public sector unionism rose, its formal role of collective bargaining expanded to encompass a much more powerful role as a political machine that enabled it to affect election outcomes and larger policy and spending issues. When it comes to advancing their interests, public sector unions are some of the most powerful interest groups in the United States, with significant advantages over traditional unions. For one thing, using the political process, they can exert far greater influence over their members' employers—that is, government—than private sector unions can. Through their extensive political activity, they help elect the very politicians who will act as "management" in their contract negotiations. They thus hand pick those who will sit across the bargaining table from them, again, in a way that workers in a private corporation cannot. Government labor unions can also reward politicians who give them what they want and punish those who do not. Vast quantities of campaign cash, coupled with volunteer workers, have assisted public sector unions in developing alliances with various candidates and political parties. As a result, negotiations in the public sector have an inherent bias toward higher salaries, more generous benefits, and more inflexible work rules.

There has been ongoing criticism of compulsory union membership and the use of members' dues for political contributions. Many would argue that individuals should have a right to decide whether or not they want to join a union, and that forcing individuals to join unions is undemocratic. Others argue that without compulsory membership, "free-rider" workers can enjoy the benefits of union membership (wages and benefits are always better in a union company) without joining the union or paying dues. The right-to-work laws enacted in some states prohibit collective bargaining agreements that make union membership a condition of employment. Other states have implemented paycheck protection measures that allow union members to withhold dues payments that are used for political purposes.

Through their political activism, public sector unions have been able to affect larger policy and spending issues at the state and local level. Their political muscle is well known. The AFL-CIO consists of a federation of 55 labor unions representing more than 12 million members; the American Federation of State, County and Municipal Employees has about 1.5 million members, and the Service Employees International Union stands at about 2 million members. AFSCME was the biggest contributor to political campaigns in 1998–2004 (*The Economist* 2011a). In many state and local elections, spending by public employee unions far outpaces that of other industries, as well as what candidates themselves spend. For example, in 2010, public sector unions spent $45.4 million on state-level races in California, far outpacing the next big industry spenders such as health care and real estate, at $18 million and $10.3 million, respectively. At the national level, political action committee spending by public sector unions totaled $17.6 million. The insurance industry spends $21.2 million, while the pharmaceutical and health product industry, lawyers and law firms, and military contractors spend $15.1, $14.9, and $14.3 million respectively (Duhigg 2011).

Public sector unions have traditionally been more aligned with the Democratic Party. The AFL-CIO made more than $2.8 million in campaign contributions during the past two national election cycles, with the vast majority going to Democrats, according to the Center for Responsive Politics. In the 2010 election cycle, 99.5 percent of contributions made by the AFSCME went to Democrats. Similarly, the National Education Association donated 96 percent and the American Federation of Teachers 99.7 percent to Democrats.

However, public sector unions have also developed strategic alliances with the Republican Party, especially those unions dealing with public safety. The incestuous relationship between California's state prison guards and the state Republican Party has been well documented. The prison guards' union has been one of the leading advocates of getting tough on crime the most famous example being their support for a 1994 ballot measure known as the "Three Strikes and You're Out" law. The union sponsored the measure, working closely with the state's Republicans. The law doubles the length of a criminal's sentence if it is a second conviction and slaps a sentence of 25 years to life on a third conviction, even in cases of nonviolent or trivial offenses. The result of this measure becoming policy has been a dramatic increase in both the size of the state's prison-industrial complex (from 12 prisons in 1980 to 33 in 2000) and the pay of the people who run it (prison guards in 2006 made $70,000 a year in base salary and $100,000 with overtime). Wisconsin's Republican governor Scott Walker excluded public safety unions from his "reforms" to balance the budget because many of their members and leaders were loyal soldiers for the Republican Party.

Counter to Big Business

One argument being advanced on behalf of public sector unionism is, ironically, not focused on their formal role of collective bargaining but on their role as political power broker. The reason given for the need to support public sector unionism through such requirements as compulsory membership in unions and paying union dues that are used for political activity has been to counteract the special interest of corporate America. It has been argued that public sector unions serve as an important vehicle for the promotion of the middle class and therefore advocacy on larger policy issues impacting this group is needed. Jeannette Wicks-Lim (2009) of the Political Economy Research Institute suggests in a recent paper that collective bargaining presents a powerful way to turn the tide on declining workers' pay and benefits, that a union worker has a 20 percent greater chance of having a decent job than a similar nonunion worker, and that there is no strong evidence that higher unionization rates lead to higher unemployment rates.

The concern has been expressed that corporate America will dominate with the demise of the union movement. This alarm has escalated as a result of the Supreme Court's *Citizens United* decision, which struck down any restraint on political spending by corporations, unions, and wealthy individuals wishing to influence the political process. Many liberal and progressive groups fear that without a counterbalance, there will be no effective check on the power of well-heeled corporations in either party. Public sector unions have served as an important force of this counterbalance.

There is credence to the argument that without the muscle of public sector unions, there will be little counterbalance to big business and its ability to influence elections and public policy. However, the solution should not be to utilize public employment and the provision of responsive and efficient services to the public as a counteroffensive to big business's special interests. The focus needs to be more on curbing the undue influence of these special interests—both from corporations and from unions that have sought to influence policy outcomes and elections by pouring in excessive amounts of money during elections. This should not be done at the expense of the overall public interest in public employment—which is to provide effective and efficient government services.

Justice Elena Kagan summed up the problem with special interest money influencing elections and public policy in the beginning of her dissent to *McComish v. Bennett* (the Arizona public financing measure):

> Imagine two States, each plagued by a corrupt political system. In both States, candidates for public office accept large campaign contributions in exchange for the promise that, after assuming office, they will rank the donors' interests ahead of all others. As a result of these bargains, politicians ignore the public interest, sound public policy languishes, and the citizens lose confidence in their government. (Froomkin 2011, para. 19)

Summary

Unions were first created in the private sector to prevent employers from exploiting their employees. They have done much to improve working conditions, end exploitative child labor, establish the eight-hour work day, ensure that workplace safety measures were put in place, and successfully raise wages for millions of Americans. But the municipal and state governments that employed them never exploited public employees, mainly due to the existence of civil service protections. Collective bargaining is a good thing when it is needed to equalize power, but when public employees already have much of this equality due to built-in civil service protections, collective bargaining in the public sector can serve to reduce benefits for citizens and raise costs for taxpayers.

There has been a tendency in national policy debates to lump public and private sector unions together. This does not make sense. There are important historical differences as well as approaches to bargaining that make transplanting the private sector model in its entirety, as well as the guarantees to organize, to bargain collectively with their employees, and to strike, problematic when applied to the public sector. Private sector bargaining operates within a market economy and public sector bargaining functions as a monopoly. Due to their extensive political activity, public sector unions help elect and remove the very individuals with whom they negotiate. Their political power, employed in their capacity as special interest groups, has not always promoted the public interest.

This is not to suggest that public sector unions should be abolished. The most important thing unions do is to give an important constituency a voice, an ability to protect themselves from unfair treatment, and a way to articulate grievances. Consideration should be given to a more open and alternative approach to negotiations as it concerns delivery of public sector services. Different policies and practices might need to be utilized depending on whether one is working with public sector unions or ones in the private sector. As the economy grows, instead of negotiating higher wages for unions, governments should look at providing services in a different way. For example, managed competition should become the norm rather than the exception. Governments also need to operate in a more open and transparent manner (this will be addressed in later chapters).

While individuals should clearly be afforded the right to join a union, compulsory membership is undemocratic. The "free-rider" issue is a problem in terms of nonunion paying members reaping the benefits of pay increases negotiated by union officials, but it is hard to justify making individuals join a group that they do not wish to join or with which they have philosophical differences. Further, using membership fees to fund political activity without an opportunity to opt out is equally undemocratic. The notion that public sector unions are needed as special interest groups to counter the interests of big business is the wrong debate. The money that big businesses, unions, and wealthy individuals are using to influence elections and public policy is undermining our democracy. Instead, we should be attempting to remove the pressure to seek huge, potentially corrupting pots of money from big donors. Using public sector employment as an avenue to fund a counteroffensive to the special interests of big business undermines the purpose of public employment and adversely affects government's ability to provide useful services to citizens.

Furthermore, allowing strikes by any public sector employee is also problematic. Many states and local governments grapple with determining which are "essential" services and which are not; however, interrupting nonessential government services also impacts the public interest in significant ways. As has already been pointed out, since most government services are a monopoly, citizens cannot freely choose to get services elsewhere.

4
Public Versus Private

Who Really Makes More?

So who makes more—the public or private sector? The answer is not as simple as many commentators, researchers, and pundits would like you to believe. Historically, there has been a trade-off for working in the public sector—the promise of job security and solid health and retirement plans in compensation for forgoing higher wages in the private sector. Has the wage gap between the two sectors diminished? Has the cost of public sector benefits increased so much that the total compensation for public sector workers now dwarfs that of the private sector?

Principles for Determining Pay in the Public Sector

A well-designed compensation system includes economic and nonmonetary components, criteria for fair pay for fair work, and has important social and symbolic roles in an organization, such as employee commitment and performance (Bloom 2004). The public sector has traditionally relied on job tenure, cost-of-living increases, and average general increases for these compensation practices. In addition, benefit packages typically include health, pension, and other postretirement benefits (OPEBs) that are provided as a deferred form of compensation, vacation, disability insurance, sick leave, and paid time-off benefits. In some jurisdictions, longevity pay is still in existence, whereby employees are given a lump sum each year simply for remaining with the organization. Seniority plays a central role in a traditional compensation system, where movement though the pay scale is tied to rank. Performance-based pay and bonuses do exist but play a lesser role in public sector compensation practices. A new concept of skill-based and competency-based pay, which places greater emphasis on individual performance, is not a consistent feature.

It is important to consider generally accepted principles for determining pay in the public sector. The first is that public employees should be compensated in a manner comparable to their private sector counterparts (Kroncke and Long 1998). This is consistent with economic and efficiency principles and with the concepts of fairness and equity (Smith 1977; Venti 1987). But determining what is comparable is not always easy.

Another principal used in setting public sector wages and benefits considers the impact wages and benefits will have on future generations of elected officials, public administrators, and citizens. Utilizing the theory of intergenerational equity, Peng (2004) suggests, for example, that delaying pension payments in the context of structural or other budget problems, or granting wage and benefit increases that government cannot afford, simply shifts the financial obligation from the current taxpayers at an increasing cost to future taxpayers, thus violating the intergenerational equity principle. Some local governments increased pension benefits (either in flush economic times or as an alternative to wage increases in depressed economic times) in an attempt to be seen as partners with union and employee groups rather than as adversaries, or to defer the cost to a later period of time. Many elected officials have chosen to support increasing benefits over wages because the costs are less transparent to the public and can be spread out over time. These changes resulted in employees being able to retire earlier, to receive a larger percentage of their working salary, and/or to have a portion or all of their health care covered upon retirement. As the financial impact of these commitments became apparent, governments began turning to tax increases, service reductions, and/or borrowing to cover these costs.

Pay Differentials

Although there has been considerable research on the level of pay differences between public and private workers, there has been little consensus on what pay differentials actually exist and whether or not these differences are justified. Differences have emerged depending upon the type of methodology employed, including comparisons by occupational composition, education level, and experience of the two sectors, as well as compensation differences that exist between federal, state, and local governments (Borjas 2002; Llorens 2008; Miller 1996). Public-private comparisons can also prove challenging because of confounding factors, such as other workers' characteristics and wage dispersions. Additionally, certain methodological shortcomings in research further complicate this debate, among them the values and political ideology of the researcher and either neglecting to include benefits as a dependent variable or difficulty in determining a dollar value of benefits in the analysis (Kearney 2009). Ultimately, much of the public-private debate centers on elusive accounting and areas that are difficult to value, especially retirement benefits, retiree health care, and job security. Most public employees are guaranteed a

Figure 4.1 **Trends in Total Compensation: Public vs. Private Sector**

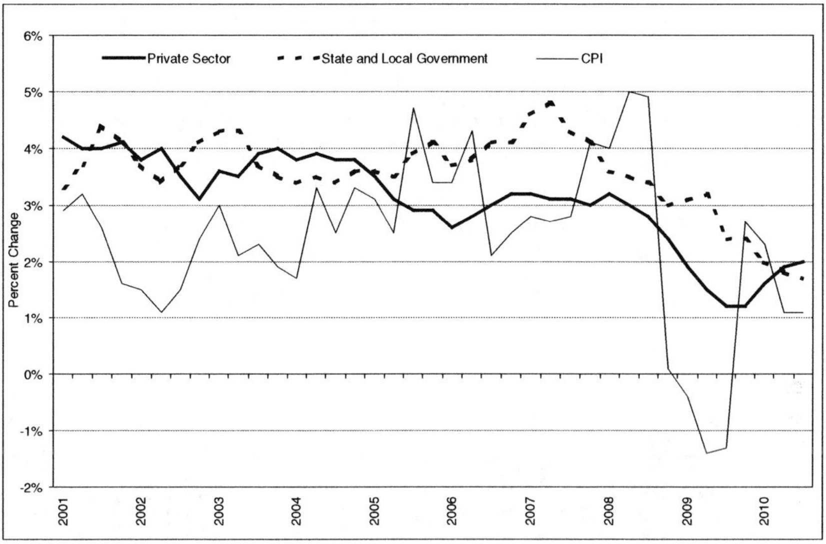

[Figure: Line chart showing Percent Change from 2001 to 2010 for Private Sector, State and Local Government, and CPI]

Source: Bureau of Labor Statistics, 2011b.

pension via a defined benefit package and have access to retiree health care. These benefits have been disappearing rapidly in the private sector. Determining the worth of these benefits is the subject of much debate.

More conservative analysts tend to want to use a straight comparison by simply comparing average salaries earned by private and public sector employees. Based on Bureau of Labor Statistics (BLS) data for this comparison, public sector employees on the average earn US$12 an hour more than their private sector counterparts (Bureau of Labor Statistics [BLS] 2011a).

Figure 4.1 shows the recent rates of change in compensation levels between the private sector and state and local governments. These data tend to suggest that the differences in compensation for state and local government employees do not appear to be a passing trend. Similarly, Bureau of Economic Analysis data show that average compensation in the public sector in 2008 was $67,812, including $52,051 in wages and $15,761 in benefits. Average compensation in the private sector that same year was $59,909, including $50,028 in wages and $9,881 in benefits. In this comparison, the public sector pay advantage is most pronounced in terms of benefit dollars.

The problem with these comparisons is that they fail to account for any differences in education (jobs in the public sector typically require more education than the private sector), or occupation (white collar versus blue collar).

On the other hand, liberal-leaning analysts want to control for multiple variables, including education, experience, occupation, race, gender, age. Additionally, they often neglect to include the value of deferred compensation such as defined benefit pension packages, health insurance, paid leave, and/or retiree health care, and they often undervalue the total dollar amount of these benefits. Additionally, pension payouts, growth in monthly retirement (from cost-of-living adjustments), and terminal payout amounts are rarely factored into these comparisons (Lewis and Galloway 2011).

Most studies report that the average federal payout is higher when compared to similar positions in private industry (Bureau of Economic Analysis 2009; Krueger 1988; Linneman and Wachter 1990; Moore and Raisin 1991; Perloff and Wachter 1984; Picard 2003; Smith 1976). This has not been the case at the state and local level, where differences in wage and salary payouts are less when compared to the private sector. Researchers generally have found either a smaller premium for state and local worker salaries or wage penalties when education, experience, and other factors are taken into consideration (Bender 2003; Borjas 2002; Branden and Hyland 1993; Lewis and Galloway, 2011; Miller 1996; Picard 2003; Thompson and Schmitt 2010). Using panel data from the BLS's Current Population Survey, Llorens (2008) found that, on average, state government employees enjoy a positive wage premium when compared to their private sector counterparts, and Barro (2011) found that state and local workers enjoyed a higher overall compensation (salary plus retirement and health benefits) than their private sector counterparts.

Others have found that public sector workers earn less than the private sector, especially when they controlled for education. Belman and Heywood (1995) compared private and public sector earnings in seven states, statistically controlling for occupation and various worker characteristics. They found that lower level workers earned more in the public sector than their private sector counterparts, while mid- to high-level employees in the public sector earned less than their private sector counterparts. Miller (1996) found a similar pattern. Data compiled by the *New York Times* (Luo and Cooper 2011) seem to support these findings as well. An analysis of recently released census data by demographers at Queens College of the City University of New York looked at wages and salaries of state workers and found the clearest pattern to emerge was an educational divide: without college degrees, workers do better working for government while state workers with degrees do worse. They also found that this divide has widened in recent decades. Since 1990, the median wage of state workers without college degrees has surpassed that of non-college-educated private workers, while college-educated state workers' median pay lagged further behind that of their peers in the private sector.

Keefe (2010) used national data and within a range of states found that public employees (state and local government) receive total compensation that is equal to or less than that of the private sector. Controlling for education and various human capital variables (such as age), he found public employees earn 11.5 percent less in terms of base pay than their private sector counterparts. When he added health and retirement benefits, the difference between public and private sector compensation is reduced to 3.7 percent, with private employees receiving the higher compensation.

Likewise, Bender and Heywood (2010) compared worker earnings across and between private, state, and local sectors over a twenty-year period and found wages and salaries of state and local employees to be lower than those for private sector workers with comparable earning determinants (e.g., education). They found that state employees typically earned 11 percent less and that local workers earned 12 percent less. When benefits such as pensions for state and local employees were factored in, on average, the total compensation was 6.8 percent lower for state employees and 7.4 percent lower for local workers when compared with comparable private sector employees. However, the study has been criticized for skewing the findings by excluding the cost of public employee retirement benefits such as retiree health care and for ignoring the cost of unfunded pension costs; for controlling for unionization and then removing it as a factor even though unionization has been found to be a driver of compensation costs; and for using the compensation practices of the school district for comparisons in college education. Almost one-half of the public workers in the study were educators, and teachers are paid less than other college graduates in the private sector (Miller 2010).

Determining the Cost of Deferred Benefits

Biggs and Richwine (2011) have been vocal critics of many of the studies that fail to properly account for the deferred benefits available to public employees. The authors claim that most of these studies omit or understate retiree health care and defined benefits and pensions when calculating overall compensation figures. For health care, the costs of coverage are generally calculated as the amount by which retiree coverage increases costs to the employer plan by increasing the average age of the covered population. They also contend that the increase in individual policy costs versus purchasing an individual health plan (25 percent more in general) are also not considered in most calculations and studies but that they should be since most private sector retirees are required to purchase their own policy, especially if they retire early. With regard to pensions, they argue that public sector workers will receive a guaranteed rate of return throughout their employment, while private sector employees receive a variable rate based on their contributions and holdings. The authors contend that this can increase total compensation by as much as 4 percent. Finally, on the topic of job security, they suggest a model to determine its cost advantage. Using the theory of "certainty equivalent," they estimate the additional compensation for job security to be 15 percent. In one study, the authors found that public workers in California earn 30 percent more than private sector workers once elements like retirement benefits, including pension and health care, and job security are taken into consideration.

Employee benefits and the ability of local governments to fund them are increasingly becoming a focus of public attention (Cooper 2009; *The Economist* 2009; Ginsberg and Horwitz 2009). The two most substantial public sector benefits are pensions and health care. The soundness of many state and local pension and retiree health-care plans is of particular concern (Coggburn and Kearney 2010; The Pew Center on the States 2007). Due to new accounting standards issued by the Governmental Accounting Standards Board (GASB), states and local governments are being forced to recognize unfunded pension and health-care liabilities that have grown substantially during the recession (Coggburn and Kearney 2010; The Pew Center on the States 2007).

While there is still a lack of consensus on what pay disparities exist and whether these differences are justified between public sector and private sector workers, there seems to be little dispute with regard to benefits. Public sector workers have traditionally received relatively generous benefit packages (Brady 2007; Fleet 2007; Munnell et al. 2011) as well as better benefits than their private sector counterparts (Lewin et al. 2011). As Figure 4.2 indicates, the average benefit cost to employers as a percentage of wages and salaries is 34 percent for state and local government employees and 29 percent for private sector employees (BLS 2009a).

According to the latest figures reported by the Bureau of Labor Statistics, retirement and saving costs are $3.23 per hour worked for state and local public sector employees versus 94 cents for private employers, and health benefit employer costs are $4.43 per hour worked for state and local government compared to $2.01 in private industry (BLS 2009a). Eighty-four percent of state and local government employees have access to a defined benefit plan versus 21 percent of private sector employees (BLS 2007, 2008). As a result, public employees do not assume the same investment risk for their pensions as workers in the private sector (Schneider 2005). This is in sharp contrast to the investment losses experienced by many private sector workers with individual plans during the current recession. In addition, public sector employees can retire on a full pension an average of five years earlier than their private sector counterparts (Clowes 2004; Edwards 2010).

Other benefits such as retiree health care and paid leave are much more generous in the public sector. Paid sick leave is available to 61 percent of

Figure 4.2 **Benefits Costs as Percentage of Total Compensation, Public vs. Private**

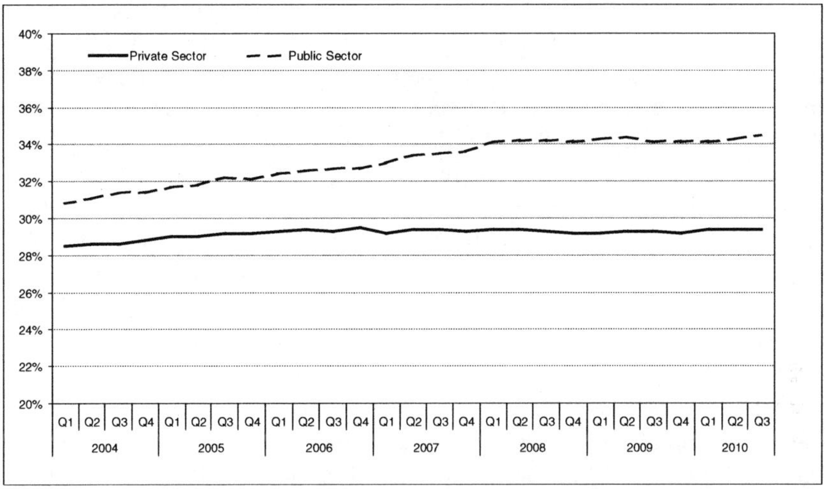

Source: Bureau of Labor Statistics, 2011a.

private sector employees as compared to 89 percent of public sector employees (BLS 2011a). Another difference in the public/private comparison of retiree health-care benefits is that the public sector allows employees to retire earlier and to enjoy health-care benefits before Medicare coverage at age 65. While subsidized retiree health care is common in the public sector, it is rare in the private sector (Edwards 2010).

A key nonmonetary difference between public and private employees is job security, which is much stronger in the public sector. Public sector workers quit less often and are fired less often than their private sector counterparts. Data from the BLS (2009a) confirm that layoffs and discharges in the public sector occur at one-third the rate of the private sector. Additionally, public sector workers are fired at much lower rates. By estimating the income lost before fired workers find new jobs, some economists argue that this is a benefit worth as much as 15 percent of their pay (Biggs and Richwine 2011).

The Impact of Unions

One major reason cited for the escalation in wages and benefits for public sector workers is the increase in public sector employee unions. Research has confirmed that public sector unions, via collective bargaining processes, positively inflate employee wages and benefits (Belman, Heywood, and Lund 1997; Johnston and Hancke 2009; Kearney 2003; Llorens 2008; McKethan et al. 2006; Reilly, Schoener, and Bolin 2007). Data from the BLS indicate that public employees who are union members earn a higher weekly salary than those who are not unionized. Unionized public sector employee's wages are 31 percent higher, on average, and their benefits are 68 percent higher than nonunionized public sector workers (Edwards 2010). Farber (2005) found that union workers' earnings were 10 percent higher where unionization was either permitted or compulsory. Where right-to-work laws prohibit the agency from having a union shop, earnings were lower. Keefe (2010) found that weaker public employee collective bargaining rights were associated with lower public employee compensation relative to the private sector. However, it is the ability of public sector unions to raise nonwage benefits for their employees more than raising wages that is key to understanding the current disparity in benefits between the public and private sectors (Freeman 1986).

The "union power" thesis advanced by Wellington and Winter (1971) holds that labor unions in the public sector have the ability to create government wage differentials through political action rather than through collective bargaining. Building on this thesis, Hunter and Rankin's (1988) compensation model suggests that public employees are compensated for providing two sets of services: public services and political services. Public services are those that the public expects employees to provide, and political services include activities such as endorsing candidates, raising money for them, giving them campaign donations, and/or providing staffing for particular elections.

Hunter and Rankin contended that this helps explain why fringe benefits have grown substantially in the public sector and are larger as a percentage of wages and salaries than in the private sector. Fringe benefits provide the perfect avenue for political payment because they are usually invisible or unknown to the public. The political power of public sector unions will have a greater impact on fringe benefits than on wages if compensation in that form is less likely to be subjected to public scrutiny (Hunter and Rankin 1988). Kearney and Carnevale (2001) also contend that public sector unions support increasing benefits over wages because the costs are less transparent to the community and can be spread out over time.

In their 1984 book *What Do Unions Do*, Freeman and Medoff posit that unions have two faces. One face is the undesirable monopoly, which enables unions to raise wages above the competitive level, resulting in a loss of economic efficiency. The inefficiency arises because employers adjust to the higher union wages by hiring too few workers for the organization. The other face is the more desirable one that allows employers to channel worker discontent into improved workplace conditions and productivity (Blanchflower and Bryson 2004). Under the undesirable monopoly premise, the financial flexibility of local and state government is compromised because of commitments to existing wage and benefit levels, and thus, they are unable to add more employees to meet service demands. There is some empirical evidence to support this thesis (Bryson 2001; Leonard 1992).

It may be that the political power of unions has a larger impact on wages, benefits, and spending than actual collective bargaining. Unions do influence public policy and spending (Norcross 2011). The tools used to influence budget outcomes include political activity. Public employee unions make considerable campaign contributions. After all, public sector unions through political campaigning and donations help elect the very political leaders with whom they negotiate wages and benefits. By influencing the political process, unions are able to sit on both sides of the negotiating table. The parties at the negotiating table share similar goals, and each benefits from the expansion of public spending.

The Iron Triangle

The Iron Triangle is a phrase used by political scientists to describe the linkage between elected officials, government bureaucracies, and interest groups such as employees' groups and labor unions. These relationships ultimately evolve into very tight-knit and closed policymaking circles. The term is frequently used in discussions having to do with "agency capture" or the cooptation of government agencies by special interests. The subgovernment interpretation of policymaking emphasizes a narrow set of participants, namely, bureaucrats, lobbyists, and legislators with jurisdiction over a selected policy area.

The Iron Triangle concept posits that the operations of the subgovernment are closed, cooperative, and can seldom be penetrated by outsiders. Members operate largely unchecked within their own spheres of influence and make routine decisions in selected, well-defined policy areas. Conflict is avoided because it would allow outsiders to intervene in policy affairs and alter the distribution of benefits (Johnson 1992). This can occur when conflict rises to the level of news media coverage. Iron Triangle proponents maintain that these relationships provide an important conduit for nongovernmental players to have input and a say in policy and program formation (Ripley and Franklin 1991). As Figure 4.3 indicates, the key drivers of the triangle are funding and oversight; legislating, donating and investing; and approving contracts.

A competing theory of policymaking that has emerged is that of the issue network. Issue networks are clusters of interdependent political actors (e.g., Congress, the administration, organized interests) who interact in an open and flexible system to exchange information, influence public policy, and attain mutual goals (Browne 1995; Marin and Mayntz 1991). Issue networks are characterized by their permeable boundaries (Berry 1989; Browne 1995;

Figure 4.3 **Iron Triangle**

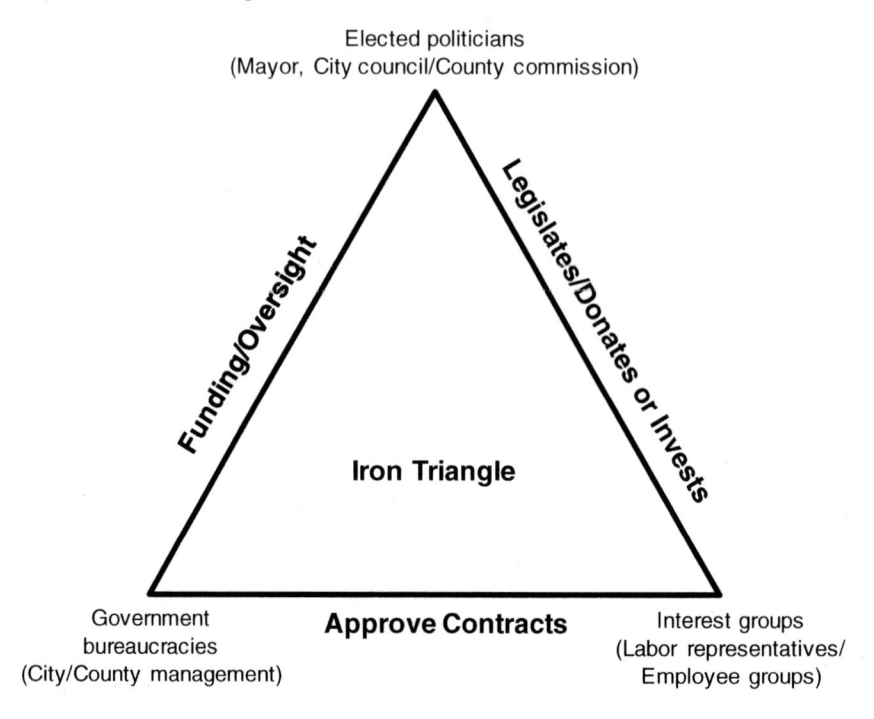

```
                    Elected politicians
          (Mayor, City council/County commission)
                            /\
                           /  \
                          /    \
              Funding/   /      \   Legislates/Donates or Invests
              Oversight /        \
                       /  Iron    \
                      /  Triangle  \
                     /_____\
         Government      Approve Contracts      Interest groups
         bureaucracies                          (Labor representatives/
         (City/County management)               Employee groups)
```

Heclo 1978; Johnson 1992) and are commonly lauded for the mechanism they provide to policy participants to exchange information and influence policy discussions (Johnson 1992).

The application of the Iron Triangle model to the discussion on public sector compensation is warranted. A triangle is formed among locally elected politicians, public sector management, and labor representatives or employee groups. These groups engage in public compensation discussions while outsiders (citizens and the media) are seldom informed as to the details, costs, and commitments stipulated by the agreements. Often, once an agreement is reached, only selected pieces of information are shared with the public, while many of the mundane and complicated portions are not publicly discussed even though they are costly and often contain future financial commitments. The political partnerships that elected officials forge with unions are particularly powerful. Public sector unions provide financial and in-kind contributions to elected officials. They also have the ability to elect whom they want and punish those who do not support them. City and county management often work closely with both union and employee groups to avoid conflict. They also often benefit from the same terms negotiated in the employee contracts.

All parties have a mutual interest in being cooperative with each other when adopting wage and benefit agreements.

The lack of transparency in adopting public worker wage and benefit decisions has led to the adoption of many unsustainable benefits and has been done within this tight circle of insiders without the press or the public taking much notice. Shortsighted politicians, union officials, and public managers have chosen to provide compensation via deferred benefits because it is less transparent and the cost can be spread out over time. The example of the pension scandal in San Diego previously discussed best illustrates how the theory of the iron triangle applies to public sector compensation. City administrators, elected officials, and union leaders worked closely and went to extraordinary efforts to conceal their self-dealing from the public as they decreased payments into the pension fund while increasing benefits to city employees.

The same "triangle" often applies at the state level. In some circumstances, pension benefits are established by the legislature rather than through collective bargaining and it is the government employees and their associations and unions that serve as "special interests."

To illustrate how wages, pensions, and post-retirement benefits can escalate under this model, let's look at a firefighter contract. Negotiating a firefighter, police, or other public safety contract involves specifying many costly terms, conditions, and elements that are often buried deep within the agreement. While public discussion may center on the cost of awarding a cost-of-living adjustment (COLA), there are additional personnel costs that are covered in the agreement. The following components make up a firefighter contract for Clark County in Nevada (also known as the Las Vegas Valley).

1. *Holidays.* Clark County Fire has 12 recognized holidays. Fifty-six-hour employees receive 16 hours of one-and-a-half their hourly rate (overtime). Eight- or ten-hour employees have the day off if the holiday falls during their scheduled shift. If it falls on their scheduled day off or the weekend, they receive one-and-a-half their hourly rate (overtime).
2. *Insurance.* Clark County contributes a negotiated monthly sum to the Insurance Trust Fund for each member of the fire department. The coverage includes hospitalization, major medical, dental, life, and disability. The county also makes a monthly contribution to the trust fund for the retiree's insurance coverage.
3. *Longevity.* Employees receive longevity pay equal to 2.85 percent of their gross salary after 5 years. The rate escalates 0.57 of 1 percent for each year of employment. Gross salary is defined as all wages earned. There is no cap on the yearly increases.

4. *Tuition Fees.* The county prepays tuition for all required courses necessary to obtain an associate or bachelor's degree in fire science, criminal justice, public administration, and fire administration. The courses may be taken either through the University of Nevada Las Vegas (UNLV) or through a correspondence program at an accredited university. There is no limit to credit or degree program costs.
5. *Bonus Leave.* Employees may receive up to four bonus shifts if less than one shift of sick leave is used. These hours can be used for vacation or paid in cash to the employee.
6. *Long-Term Disability.* An employee may receive two years of salary if awarded this benefit. To be deemed permanently disabled, an employee must be evaluated by two doctors, one selected by the employer and the other selected by the employee. If both agree that the employee is no longer able to perform the duties of his current position, disability benefits are provided.
7. *Uniform and Linen Allowance.* Employees receive an annual allowance to maintain their uniforms and bed linens. The amount of recent Collective Bargaining Agreements is approximately $2,200 annually.
8. *Premium Pay.* Employees receive premium pay for "specialty" certification, including emergency medical technician (paramedic, EMTI, and EMT), heavy rescue technician, hazardous material technician, and safety officer. The premium pays consist of 10 percent, 7 percent, and 5 percent of the base pay. These may be "stacked" or combined when the employee holds two separate certifications, such as paramedic with heavy rescue certification (15 percent).
9. *Shift Differential Pay.* If an employee, usually a fire inspector, works outside of a regularly scheduled shift, a 4 percent shift differential payment is awarded. A regular shift begins no earlier than 5 A.M. and ends no later than 7 P.M.

The aforementioned provisions do not include the agreed-upon cost-of-living increase, retiree health care provided by the county, or pension benefits, which are covered by the state. Even excluding the deferred retirement benefits, these components of the union contract, especially the additional premium and shift differential pay, increase the base salary of the average firefighter by a minimum of 25 percent.

With regard to retirement, firefighters earn the right to pension benefits from the state after 5 years of employment and this pension is based on the highest paid 36 consecutive months of employment. The formula is based on the number of years of service multiplied by the average compensation (highest 36 months) multiplied by 2.67 (retirement yearly multiplier). Firefighters can retire after 25 years at any age, at age 50 with 20 years, and age 55 with 10 years without penalty. Despite a state law passed in 1983 requiring that any increase to the retirement fund be equally shared by both the employer and employee, firefighters have successfully negotiated retirement provisions so that the county as employer pays the employee's (firefighter's) portion of the retirement contribution. This agreement has never been discussed in public when the firefighter union contract has been ratified by the County Commission, despite the fact that it contains a very costly deferred benefit for firefighters. Further, the collective bargaining agreement between the firefighter's union (Local 1909) and the county stated the agreement would not be published or released without a written request being submitted to the county. This provision obviously was included to prevent transparency and to limit the public's ability to review the agreed-upon terms of the contract.

Keep in mind that these collective bargaining agreements are cumulative—that is, gains realized during the last bargaining session become the baseline for the future and there is a constant need for union negotiators to gain new victories for their membership. When management and unions negotiate a new contract, the process doesn't begin with a blank piece of paper, nor are all items automatically renegotiated. Typically, except for cost-of-living increases, once a benefit is agreed upon, it remains as part of the contract in perpetuity unless one side opens it up as an item to negotiate during contract discussions. If a subsequent group of managers or elected officials wants to remove an existing benefit and the union does not concur, there is often an impasse, leading to several possibilities for resolution, such as mediation, fact-finding, and arbitration.

Upon expiration of a collective bargaining agreement, an employer is required by the National Labor Relations Act to "meet at reasonable times and to confer in good faith" with the bargaining representative for its employees "with respect to wages, hours, and other terms and conditions of employment." This is known as an employer's duty to bargain. A violation of an employer's duty to bargain may result in an unfair labor practice charge being filed at the National Labor Relations Board. Removing an existing benefit is known as a "take-away," and fact-finders and arbitrators are often loathe to carry this out. A major criticism of arbitration is that it rarely results in a decrease to the compensation being negotiated, so not much is ever lost by going to arbitration. In the worst-case scenario, the party retains its current position. In many states, such as Nevada, there is state law that requires collective bargaining agreements to operate under last-best-offer arbitration, where an arbitrator would accept one or the other party's offer in its entirety.

Norcross (2010, 2011) suggests that the current fiscal crisis in many state and local jurisdictions has prompted government negotiators to share the goals of unions to increase spending and conceal the full cost of the collective bargaining agreement with citizens in the form of current and deferred compensation (e.g., enhanced pension and benefits). She contends that governments often resort to spending deferrals, or intergovernmental aid, so the government can increase employment and wages (often deferred) for public sector workers while concealing the true cost of doing so from citizens. She says this can result in government officials' relying on accounting techniques of what she calls "fiscal illusion." Fiscal illusion occurs when the methods employed by government to finance spending cause citizens to perceive spending as less costly than it actually is. Examples cited include very complex revenue systems and the financing of debt.

The Iron Triangle phenomenon is also evident in the decisions made by suppliers of public services (i.e., locally elected politicians, city/county management, and labor representatives), who have every incentive to support and vote for large budgets and to delay costs. Elected officials, union leaders, employee groups, and public sector management have often decided that deferring costly benefits offers the easiest way to hold down spending and still satisfy employees. The result is that public sector pay is skewed too heavily toward pensions and other retirement costs, such as retiree health care. The Iron Triangle participants act in the political arena as single cohesive interest group that almost invariably ends up supporting an increase in the quantity and quality of public services. There is an inherent conflict of interest that elected officials encounter when they have the option of awarding pensions to special interest constituencies, including themselves, without citizens understanding what is involved and without the bills coming due until after they have left office (Schieber and Longman 2011).

The effect of public sector unionism (both collective bargaining and political activity) on state and local budgets and spending has also been long debated in academic literature. Research conducted by Benecki (1978), Vallenta (1989), and Zax and Ichniowski (1988) found that local government unionism increases department and city expenditures. However, O'Brien (1994) found that although increased union political activity leads to greater department expenditures, it did not necessarily lead to greater municipal expenditures or revenues.

Marlow and Orzechowski (1996) have also looked at the relationship between public sector unionism and public spending and found that unionization had a positive influence on government spending. Using Public Choice Theory, the authors contend that public employees are an interest group and have an incentive to express the need to expand public spending to elected officials. They do this by influencing the supply of goods, exerting pressure to expand their monopoly. The authors use examples such as the teachers' union opposition to school choice and privatization. Since public employees have been shown to vote more often than their public sector counterparts (Bush and Denzau 1977; Gramlich and Rubinfeld 1982), it is in their best interest to be politically active.

Summary

In summary, comparisons between public and private sector workers reveal that public sector workers at all levels (federal, state, and local) earn higher wages and benefits than their private sector counterparts. This is most pronounced at the federal level. However, when public and private sector workers at the state and local level are compared to workers in the private sector of similar education, age, and occupation, most studies show that public workers are either modestly over- or underpaid, depending upon the accounting assumptions used. The educational divide has emerged as one of the most significant factors: without college degrees, employees do better working for government, while public sector workers with college degrees do worse. However, since approximately one-half of the public workers at the state and local level in the United States are educators, and teachers and are paid less than other college graduates in the private sector, concern has been raised as to whether this fact skews the findings.

Notwithstanding, the main controversy centers on how much to value deferred benefits (pensions, retiree health care) and job security. Most studies that compare public versus private sector pay either neglect to include the value of deferred compensation such as defined benefit pension packages, health insurance, paid leave, and/or retiree health care, and they frequently undervalue the total dollar amount of these benefits. Additionally, pension payouts, growth in monthly retirement (from cost-of-living adjustments), and terminal payout amounts are rarely factored into these comparisons. While there is little dispute that public sector workers receive significantly better benefits than their private sector counterparts, researchers disagree on how best to assign a value to them.

In an effort to explore this controversy further, the next chapter includes a comparative analysis of public versus private compensation that was constructed by examining both active employment and post-retirement years. The question to be answered is, if one looks at total lifetime compensation, who is paid more: public or private sector workers?

5
Comparison of Lifetime Earnings

A Compensation Model

To address the impacts of any financial instrument, a good analysis creates a working model, parsing its components down to the smallest variables that have an impact. In a debate that has persistent off and on for decades—public versus private sector compensation—this exercise has occurred. The ongoing dispute over differences in pay has largely centered on "total compensation" and how to value deferred elements such as pensions, retiree health care, and job security. A response to this wage-earning gap often includes benefits and the fact that a public employee understands the difference in immediate earnings and still chooses to enter into a labor agreement knowing that benefits and, perhaps, job security, overcome any present wage gaps. The length and depth of the Great Recession has only intensified the light on this subject.

In an effort to assess the impact of different compensation tools beyond simple wage differences, a comparative model analyzing public versus private sector compensation was constructed to gauge the cost of lifetime compensation. It is important to note that the model only addresses compensation during active employment and post-retirement years. Other compensation tools such as disability and insurance are excluded from the model. It would be difficult to calculate the value of a health insurance plan and its benefits from one sector or another as employees often have the option to opt in to these programs. Understandably, a health insurance benefit has the potential to indirectly put more dollars into an employee's disposable income. Nevertheless, a separate, more complex benefit model would need to be constructed and it would still be difficult to compare apples to apples on a macro scale since many health-care plans are unique to the individual. That said, the model does account for health-care subsidies often received by public sector employees in retirement.

Compensation in real dollars goes beyond the biweekly paycheck. The model was designed to measure the total value of a person's employment throughout their entire life, including retirement. Over a lifetime, compensation variables incorporated into the model include cost-of-living adjustments, step increases, longevity pay, Social Security participation, individual retirement accounts with employee matches, public employee retirement systems, retirement age, and a post-retirement health-care subsidy. The model was constructed knowing that each job, jurisdiction, and bargaining agreement is different; therefore, it became its own working model. However, on a national scale, an average could be inserted into the different variables to understand how one payment tool impacts the employee's compensation over a lifetime. Only the input values would need to be modified to compare two employees in a single jurisdiction.

Using the model, two public-private comparisons were made: one comparing a typical blue-collar job, that of janitor; and the second, a white-collar job, a civil engineer. Data from the Bureau of Labor Statistics (BLS 2009b, 2009c, 2011c) were used for the modeling and to determine the starting salary of each occupation in both sectors, assuming each public and private employee was 24 years of age at the start of her career in 2008.

The Blue-Collar Model

Comparing janitors, the private sector janitor will receive a starting salary of $15,487 per year while the public sector janitor will earn $20,645 in annual compensation. Figures 5.1 and 5.2 provide the data graphically. The public sector employee will receive an annual 3.55 percent increase in the cost-of-living adjustment (COLA), while the public sector janitor's increase will be slightly less at 3.05 percent. The higher assumption is based on historical COLAs and the fact that collective bargaining in the public sector will typically add a 0.5 percent advantage. Similar gaps are witnessed in the model when it comes to step increases, where it is assumed that the private sector grants it janitor a 4.0 percent increase in salary for simply showing up and continuing to do the job. This is generally assumed over the first eight years of employment. The same goes for the public sector, but instead of 4.0 percent, the public sector janitor is rewarded an annual step increase of 5.0 percent. While longevity pay is built into the model, it is now being eliminated in many jurisdictions. Longevity pay or nonproduction bonuses are only available to 7 percent of full-time public sector employees. The model adjusts for longevity pay based on starting year, base pay rate, and incremental pay rates.

Moving into retirement compensation, the model assumes that the private sector janitor participates in Social Security, contributing 4.2 percent of their income, with the employer contributing 6.2 percent of salary. In addition, the model assumes that the employee can begin receiving Social Security payments at age 66. The public sector janitor also participates in Social Security.

Figure 5.1 **Comparative Analysis of Wage and Salary Levels: Hypothetical National Janitor**

Wage and Salary Compensation: Public Sector Employee

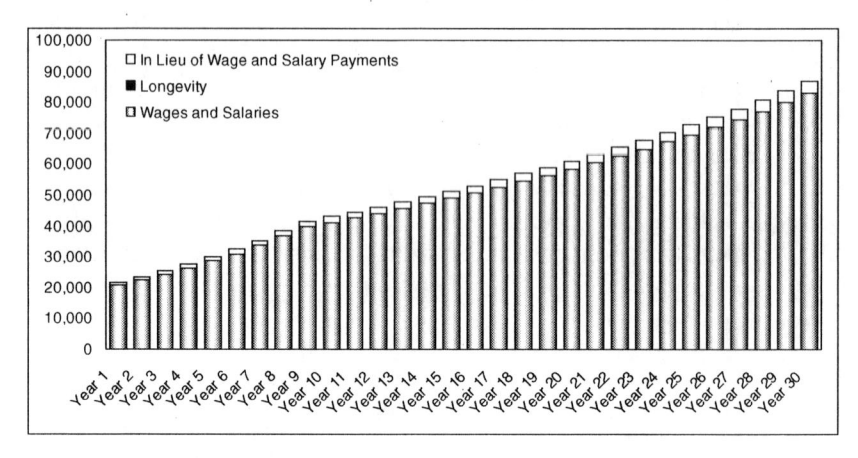

Note: Assumes public employee retires after 30 years of service.

Wage and Salary Compensation: Private Sector Employee

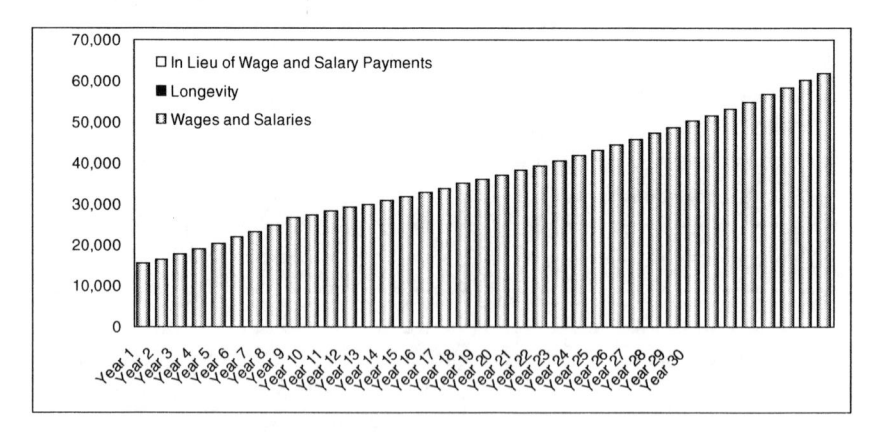

Wage and Salary Comparison

	Private Sector Employee	Public Sector Employee
Wages and Salaries		
General Wages and Salaries	$979,930	$1,604,602
Longevity Pay	$—	$—
In Lieu of Wage and Salary Payments	$—	$73,812
Total Wages and Salaries Paid	$979,930	$1,678,413
Average Annual Salary	$32,664	$52,955
Average Annual Increase	4.12%	4.89%
Age Eligible for Retirement	Age 60	Age 53

Note: For first 30 years of employment.

Wage and Salary Compensation Comparison Trend

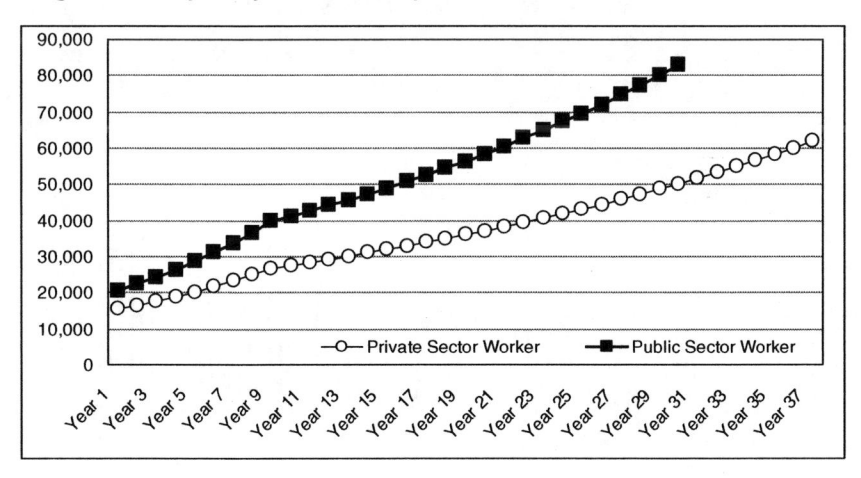

Figure 5.2 **Comparative Analysis of Combined Compensation: Hypothetical National Janitor**

Combined Compensation: Public Sector

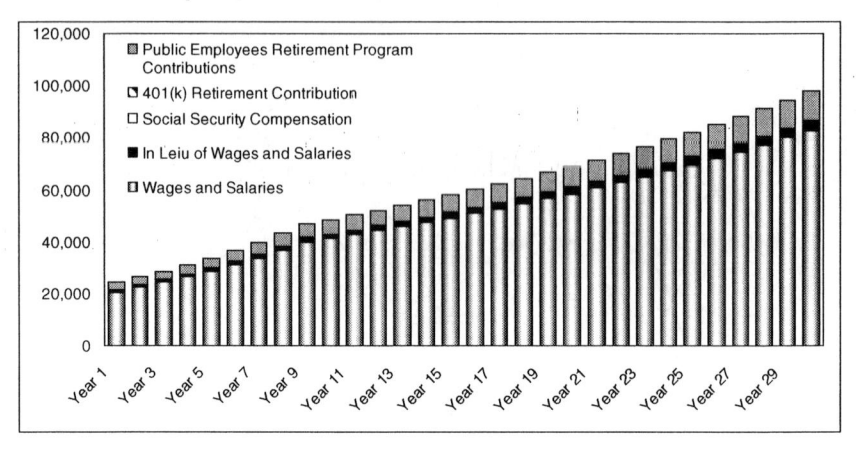

Note: Assumes public employee retires after 30 years of service.

Combined Compensation: Private Sector

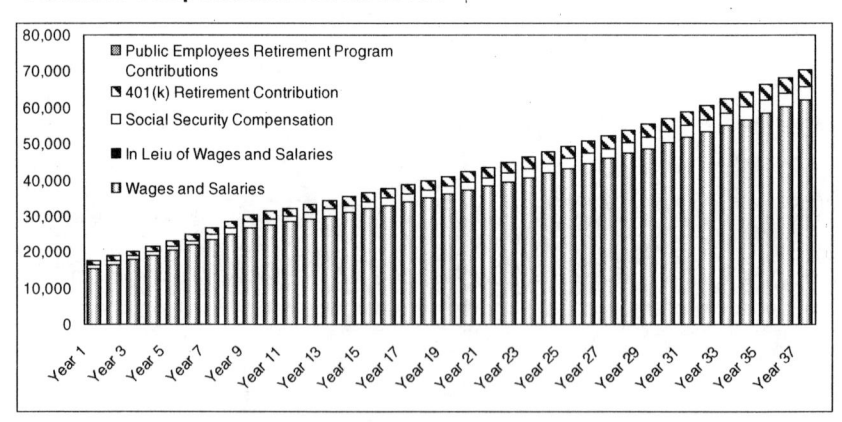

Note: Assumes public employee retires at age 60.

Total Compensation Comparison

	Private Sector Employee	Public Sector Employee
Wages and Salaries		
General Wages and Salaries	$979,930	$1,604,602
Longevity Pay	$—	$—
In Lieu of Wage and Salary Payments	$—	$73,812
Total Wages and Salaries Paid	$979,930	$1,678,413
Average Annual Salary	$32,664	$52,955
Average Annual Salary Increase	4.12%	4.89%
Retirement Benefits		
Employer-Paid Social Security	$60,756	$—
Employer Contributions to 401(k) Program	$20,579	$—
Employer PERS Contributions	$—	$136,691
Total Employer-Paid Retirement Benefits	$81,334	$136,691
Combined Compensation Levels	$1,061,264	$1,815,105
Age Eligible for Retirement	Age 60	Age 53

Note: For first 30 years of employment.

Total Compensation Comparison Trend

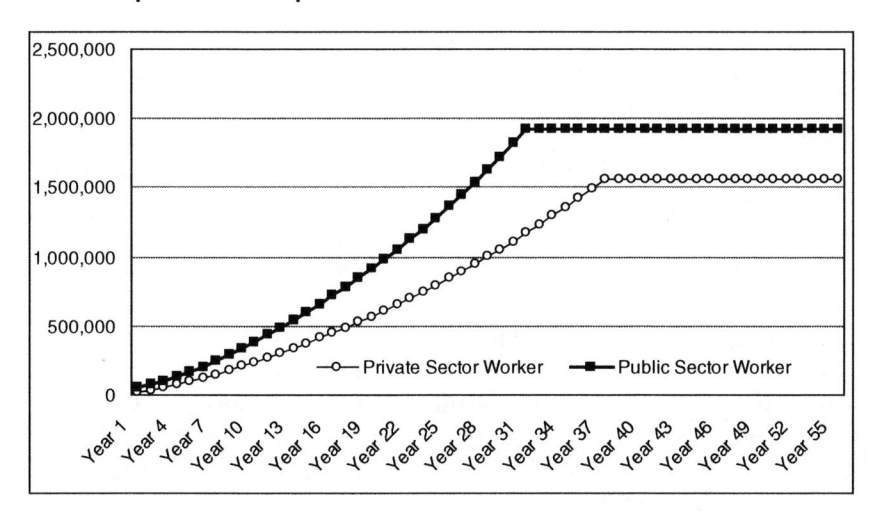

Next, it is assumed that the janitor in the private sector also contributes to a 401(k), or individual retirement account. Again, the public sector janitor does not participate in a 401(k) or similar private retirement account. Nevertheless, the private sector janitor contributes 5.4 percent of his/her salary with an additional employee match of 2.1 percent. Based on IRS guidelines, the maximum contribution cannot exceed $16,500 annually, which is automatically adjusted for in the model. It is anticipated that earnings on invested dollars will continue until age 60, with return rates declining every ten years. An annual rate of return is assumed to be 7.0 percent for years 1 through 10, dropping 1.0 percent every decade thereafter until retirement. Once the janitor is retired, the rate of return is less aggressive, staying at 3.5 percent in retirement.

Figure 5.1 demonstrates wage and salary compensation during both the public and private sector janitors' careers, in which the private sector janitor begins with a lower annual salary that will never become closer to his or her counterpart in the public sector. Notice the slow growth in wage and salary compensation for the private sector janitor when compared to the public sector equal. It is important to note that the private-sector janitors' final year of salary is significantly less than that of the public sector employee, who retired seven years prior.

Figure 5.2 illustrates the total compensation gained during both the public and private sector janitors' careers, and broken down by compensation instrument. Note the comparison between the private sector retirement contributions and those provided and largely funded by the public sector janitor's public employee retirement system. (Refer to Appendix 1 for the assumptions that were used in this model.)

While the public sector janitor does not participate in Social Security or a 401(k) program, he/she does participate in a public employee retirement system (PERS). The employee contributes 4.6 percent of wages to the system while the employer contributes 9.0 percent. The average rate of return is assumed to be 6.5 percent, but it is important to note that if the internal rate of return does not meet expectations for promised benefits, PERS can simply raise contribution rates on the employee/employer or lower benefits for new employees. There is no such option in the private sector.

The model also assumes that public and private sector employees can retire at different ages without penalty. The private sector employee must work until the age of 60 before retiring, while the public sector janitor can retire seven years earlier, at age 53. Additionally, while each jurisdiction and bargaining agreement is different, it is assumed that private sector employees will retire with 56 percent of their final three years' average salaries. Payments will come from Social Security and 401(k) returns. Public sector janitors will collect 71 percent of their final three years' average salaries.

Lastly, public sector janitors receive health care as a subsidy during retirement. Janitors receive approximately $7,980 per year, or $665 a month, in a health-care subsidy when beginning retirement, with an annual inflation adjustment of 3.0 percent. The private sector janitor receives no subsidy and likely receives health care through the federal Medicare program.

As we move the levers up and down, and turn different compensation tools off and on, we begin to see the real differences between public and private sector employee compensation over a lifetime. Comparing strictly wage and salary compensation, public sector janitors will tend to earn $82,866 in their last year of employment (year 30). Although private sector janitors will continue to work for seven more years, their salary in the last year of work will only reach $62,011. For the first 30 years of employment, public sector janitors will have been compensated more than $1.8 million, while janitors working their entire lives in the private sector will have earned approximately $753,800 less.

Assuming both public and private sector janitors live until the age of 78, the gap in retirement compensation continues. Public sector janitors tend to enjoy 24 years of retirement, with pension payments and post-retirement health-care benefits totaling more than $2.6 million dollars. Seven years after the public sector janitor retires, the private one can finally put up his or her mop and enjoy the sunset years. However, compensation that the private sector retiree receives from Social Security payments and 401(k) distributions will total $638,100 less than those of their counterpart from the public sector.

Aggregating salaries, paid retirement benefits, less employee contributions, and adjusting for the percentage of retirement benefits attributable to employees' direct contributions, private (58.3 percent) and public sectors (33.8 percent) respectively, an average annual compensation can be computed over the entire employees' adult lifetime of 55 years. With the variables where they stand, private sector janitors throughout their life would receive an average annual compensation of $40,002. On the other hand, public sector janitors would receive an annual compensation package averaging $61,931. While the input variables are standard assumptions based on historical averages and national figures, the compensation differences between employees in the two sectors, who most likely perform the same job, are striking. Remember that private sector janitors tend to start out at a pay level 25.0 percent less than their public sector equivalents.

The White-Collar Model

Using the same methodology and model, but replacing the blue-collar janitor with a white-collar civil engineer (Figures 5.3 and 5.4), it is easy to see how

Figure 5.3 **Comparative Analysis of Wage and Salary Levels: Hypothetical National Engineer**

Wage and Salary Compensation-Public Sector Employee

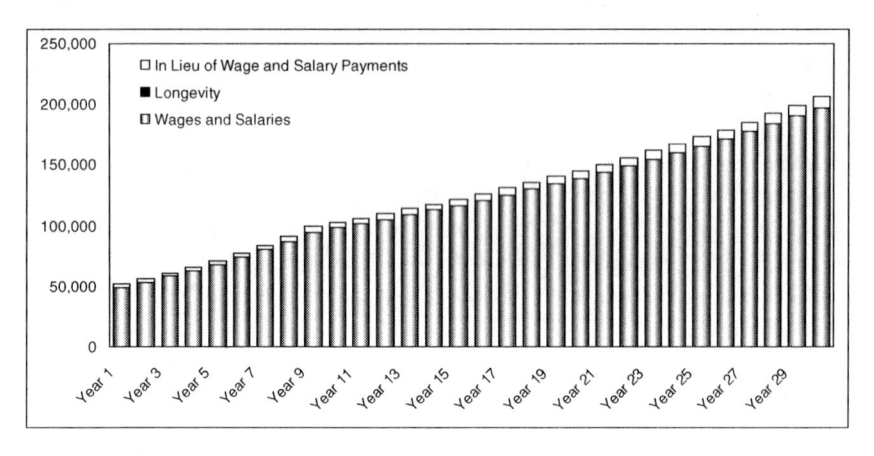

Note: Assumes public employee retires after 30 years of service.

Wage and Salary Compensation-Private Sector Employee

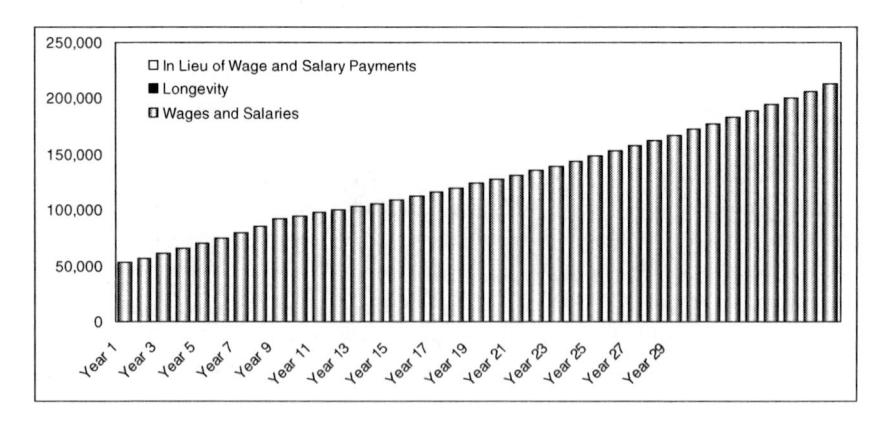

Wage and Salary Comparison

	Private Sector Employee	Public Sector Employee
Wages and Salaries		
General Wages and Salaries	$3,363,094	$3,820,421
Longevity Pay	$—	$—
In Lieu of Wage and Salary Payments	$—	$175,739
Total Wages and Salaries Paid	$3,363,094	$3,996,160
Average Annual Salary	$112,103	$126,082
Average Annual Increase	4.12%	4.89%
Age Eligible for Retirement	Age 60	Age 53

Note: For first 30 years of employment.

Wage and Salary Compensation Comparison Trend

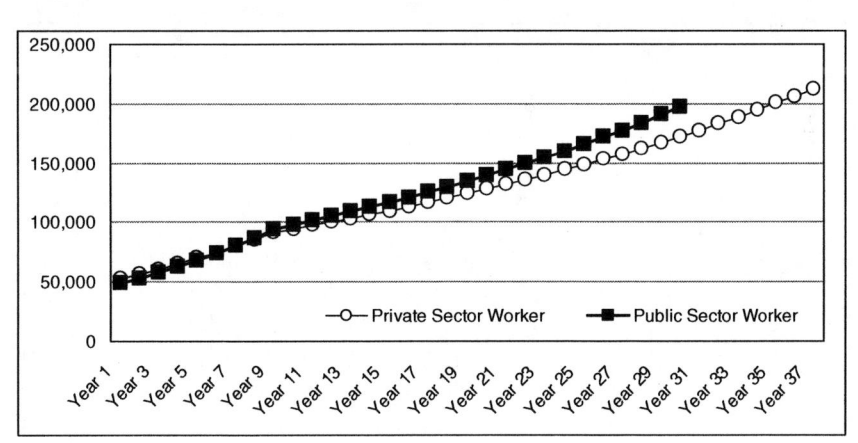

Figure 5.4 **Comparative Analysis of Combined Compensation: Hypothetical National Engineer**

Combined Compensation: Public Sector

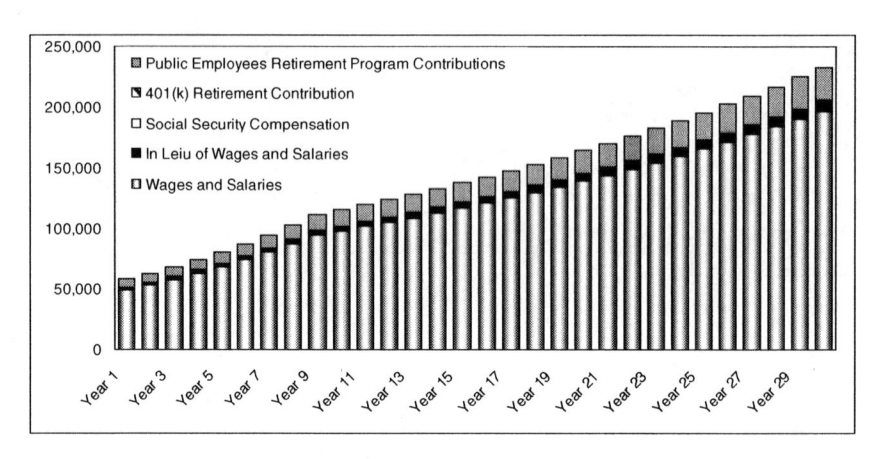

Note: Assumes public employee retirees after 30 years of service.

Combined Compensation: Private Sector

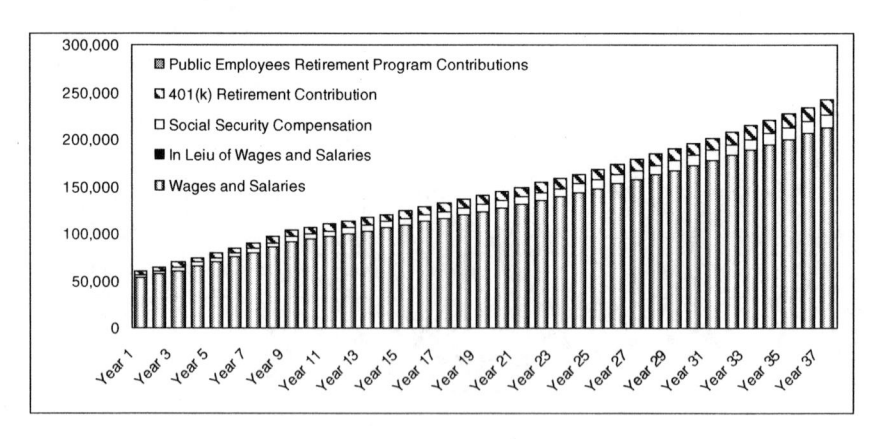

Note: Assumes public employee retires at age 60.

Total Compensation Comparison

	Private Sector Employee	Public Sector Employee
Wages and Salaries		
General Wages and Salaries	$3,363,094	$3,820,421
Longevity Pay	$—	$—
In Lieu of Wage and Salary Payments	$—	$175,739
Total Wages and Salaries Paid	$3,363,094	$3,996,160
Average Annual Salary	$112,103	$126,082
Average Annual Salary Increase	4.12%	4.89%
Retirement Benefits		
Employer-Paid Social Security	$208,512	$—
Employer Contributions to 401(k) Program	$70,625	$—
Employer PERS Contributions	$—	$325,450
Total Employer-Paid Retirement Benefits	$279,137	$325,450
Combined Compensation Levels	$3,642,231	$4,321,610
Age Eligible for Retirement	Age 60	Age 53

Note: For first 30 years of employment.

Total Compensation Comparison Trend

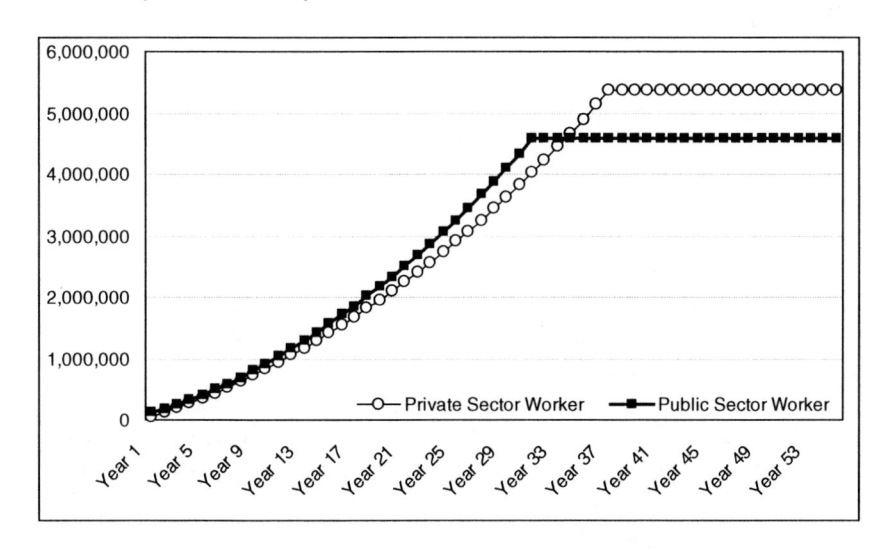

the compensation gap between the public and private sector swells. Figure 5.3 shows that the private sector engineer earns a higher salary than the matching public sector engineer at the career start. However, it is clear that the public sector engineer earns a higher salary when she/he retires after 30 years of employment. While the private sector engineer earns more salary at the end of his or her career, this engineer must work an additional seven years before retiring. Figure 5.4 illustrates the total compensation trends for both the public and private sector engineers, again clarifying the compensation sourced to retirement tools provided to each engineer during his or her career. Notice that the public sector engineer has been retired for three years before the private sector engineer, who is still employed, overcomes the public-private compensation gap. Appendix 2 includes the assumptions used in this model.

The BLS (2009c, 2011c) estimates that the median starting salary for a civil engineer is $53,151, while the same occupation in the public sector has a median starting salary of $49,154, or approximately 7.5 percent less. With all other variables remaining equal to the janitor example, the public sector engineer will be receive an annual compensation package (salaries, benefits, less employee contributions) averaging $136,040 per year over his/her lifetime. Comparing that to the average annual compensation of $109,499 for a private sector engineer indicates that working in the private sector means earning nearly $1.5 million dollars less than someone in the same job in the public sector over the same lifetime. Adding insult to injury, the public sector engineer will also retire seven years before the private sector employee.

Summary

It is important to stress that each occupation in both the public and private sectors is unique. That being said, one must demonstrate caution before assuming that all public sector employees earn more in compensation than do their private sector counterparts. This model was built to display the difference in the various compensation tools used by employers in both sectors of an economy. One cannot use the model and its inputs to assume that the outputs are concrete on a national or even regional level. Nevertheless, the model can be used as an effective tool to more clearly understand total compensation levels at the local level, where the inputs can be defined more precisely. The model can also be used to more fully understand and disclose the positive or negative impact on employee compensation, especially when tweaking variables. This model does not end the debate on comparative compensation analysis. It is a tool that helps illustrate the impact of lifetime compensation and how a defined benefit pension, retiree health care, and early retirement can increase the divide between the two sectors.

6
Pensions Gone Wild!

All public sector employees working full time for the federal, state, or local government, and the vast majority of private sector employees working for either medium or large employers, receive some type of employer-sponsored pension benefits. These benefits can generally be divided into two types of plans: *defined benefit* and *defined contribution.* In a defined benefit plan (DB), the employer guarantees a certain level of retirement benefits to the employee based on several factors, such as the employee's age, years of employment (or a combination of years and age), and final average salary. When the requirement for retirement is based on age, the employee must reach a certain age before he or she can retire without a penalty. The age requirement is usually accompanied by an obligation for a minimum number of years in service (five-year vesting is most common). Under the years of service requirement, an employee can retire at any age and collect benefits, as long as he or she has worked for a certain number of years. Under a combination of age and years of service, an employee can retire with benefits as long as the age and years of service add up to the required number. For example, the "Rule of 80" is a term often used when an employee's age and years of service must equal 80. This type of plan provides flexibility for the employee in meeting the requirements. The final average salary is based on a certain number of years employed (usually the average salary for the last few years of employment or the highest several years), and there is a vesting period. Typically, employees are required to contribute to the plan. The amount they need to contribute is the subject of much debate (Peng 2009).

In a defined contribution (DC) plan, the employee sets aside a certain percentage of his/her salary in a tax-deferred individual account that allows investments. DC plans essentially transfer the responsibility and risk of managing retirement plans to employees. Typically, the employer will match a part or the full amount of the employee contribution; 401k plans in the private sector and 403b plans in the public and nonprofit sectors are the most common types of DC plans available (Peng 2009).

A DB plan differs from a DC plan in that it provides employees, upon retirement, with annual pension payments equal to a previously agreed-upon percentage of their wage, as opposed to a DC plan in which employees receive the sum of the contributions, with interest, that they have paid into their pension fund throughout their career. In a DB plan, the benefits are earned during the employees' working years; however, they are not paid until after retirement, which has created problems in funding these deferred benefits. DB plans are most common in the public sector, where approximately 90 percent of public employees are covered. In the private sector, the DC plan is most common. Approximately 21 percent of private workers still have a DB plan (Bureau of Labor Statistics [BLS] 2007, 2008). There is one exception. Individuals working in higher education institutions traditionally participate in DC plans.

The advantage of the DB plan is clearly for the participant and includes the guarantee of a certain level of pension benefits after retirement based upon the plan's formula. Public DB plans are almost always indexed for inflation, and longevity of the retiree is not an issue because the pension is guaranteed for as long as the individual retiree lives. The most significant disadvantage is for the plan's sponsor and is associated with the funding risk, characterized as "both short-term volatility in pension contribution and the long-term uncertainty in required funding to meet future pension obligations" (Peng 2009, 183). The disadvantage for the employee is the plan's lack of portability. If a worker leaves before being vested, s/he will receive no retirement benefit. The employee can move his/her contribution but loses any ability to participate in the pension plan. Even if a worker becomes vested with the organization, they are penalized if they leave before the required retirement age. The penalty depends on the defined benefit plans provision and benefit formula. Thus, "job-changers who are in defined benefit plans will have lower lifetime pension wealth than single-career workers" (Clark and McDermed 1990, 26). This lack of portability reduces mobility among workers in defined benefit plans and can result in employees remaining in a job or with an organization for the sole purpose of retaining their pension even if they are burned out or job productivity is below par. It can also impact upward mobility. It is becoming much more common among younger generation of workers to move from job to job, city to city, or state to state for career advancement.

The advantage of the DC plan for the employer is that it reduces financial risks because the employer does not guarantee benefits. The pension and funding risks rest solely with the employee, and are subject to economic conditions and the investment strategies of the individual account. The cost of the plan is immediate and transparent. Given the increase in life expectancy, risk is compounded by the fact that it is difficult to gauge the level of financial resources a retiree will need to fund retirement: essentially, the employee covered by a DC plan runs the risk of outliving her pension assets (Peng 2009).

Private DB plans have been steadily declining since the 1980s due to employer cost and funding risks. The cost-saving mechanism inherent in DC plans for private companies has led to the rise of DC plans from 7 percent of all private sector workers in the late 1970s to 27 percent in the late 1990s. There was also a reduction of DB plans for the same workers from 28 percent to 7 percent during the same period of time. The number of DB and DC plans essentially reversed during this time period (Yi 2010).

In addition to the benefit plans mentioned above, public sector workers also are eligible for additional benefits often referred to as other postemployment benefits (OPEB). The most significant OPEB is a postemployment health-care subsidy, but other benefits include vision, dental, life, disability, and long-term care insurance. While the level of health-care benefits offered to public sector retirees varies significantly among local and state entities, retiree health-care subsidies are available in all 50 states for public sector retirees because they can usually retire earlier than the minimum age of coverage offered by Medicare (which covers people over the age of 65).

Public Pension Plans in the United States

Pensions in the public sector existed in the United States prior to the Constitution. Private and public sector pensions for civilian employees came about around the turn of the twentieth century, though those serving military duty have enjoyed pensions for a much longer time. The history of public pension plans can best be explained as a general expansion of coverage among different groups of public employees. According to Peng (2009), there were two unique features of public pension plans: different pension plans for employees based on the type of work performed, and some members of public pension plans being covered by the federal Social Security program.

General pensions were first provided in the United States as early as the colonial period for American colonists who became disabled in battle. Pension coverage was expanded to military members during the Revolutionary War. Native Americans were also individually provided pensions in the various colonies. The Colonial Congress also independently created pensions for Native Americans and the army. Pensions continued to be offered by Congress through the nineteenth century to "provide replacement income for soldiers injured in battle, offer performance incentives, to arrange for orderly retirements, and to respond to political pressure" (Clark, Craig, and Wilson 2003, 3).

The nineteenth-century pension system for the navy is of particular interest because it was funded with the profits derived from selling captured prizes. This created an unpredictable funding system, dependent largely on whether the country was in a period of war or peace. The Navy Pension Plan was then formally created by Congress to better manage these funds. The trustees of this fund were given the freedom to invest it in diverse ways, including private equities. This gave Congress its first experience facing issues that arise when public money is used to buy private assets, aptly reflected by the current debate over whether or not to invest Social Security funds in the private market. Managing the naval pension fund in this way through the nineteenth century created a great loss of assets due to poor private equities. This resulted in Congress bailing out the fund. Political pressure also played a big role in the sabotaging of the fund, resulting in widely increased benefits that were unsustainable. In stark contrast, the army's pension system has always been financed via a pay-as-you-go mechanism based on revenues from the government's general fund. Historically, the Army Pension Plan has been seen as operating in a much smoother fashion due to this funding structure.

Pension plans began to be offered to public employees in states and municipalities in the late nineteenth century until World War I. These plans came about as an extension of military retirement plans. Before 1900, very few cities in the United States provided pensions to municipal workers. "In contrast, municipal workers in Austria-Hungary, Belgium, France, Germany, the Netherlands, Spain, Sweden, and the United Kingdom were covered by retirement plans by 1910" (Squier 1912, as cited in Craig 2010). In large part, these plans were meant to cover disability rather than retirement. Those that were retirement plans were typically funded with large contributions from employees.

The first-ever municipal public pension plan was established in New York City in 1857 for police officers. Soon after, police officers along with fire fighters began receiving disability/pension plans in other large cities. The second major group of public employees receiving pension plans were teachers. General state and local government employees were the last major group of civil servants to be granted pension benefits. Two minor types of employment, judges and elected officials, also began receiving pension benefits at the state and local level after general state and local servants began receiving them (Peng 2009).

In 1911, Massachusetts became the first state to offer a pension plan to general state employees. The Massachusetts plan operated similarly to contemporary cash-balance plans. Workers paid up to 5 percent of their salaries into a trust fund, received benefits directly upon retirement, and were required to retire between 60 and 70 years of age. When the employee retired, the state bought an annuity equal to twice the worker's contribution plus interest. The market sometimes determined the interest rate, at other times it was determined by the portfolio of assets, and at other times it was determined by the state legislature. This plan provided an early model for public sector pension plans before being replaced by a defined benefit pension system.

Federal pensions were not created in abundance until the passage of the Federal Employees Retirement Act in 1920. Before 1920, federal employees were granted pensions on a case-by-case basis. This act created a system in which U.S. civil service workers earned pensions after 15 years of service and, depending on the job, reaching 62, 65, or a maximum of 70 years of age. Worker contribution was set at 2.5 percent and pension earnings ranged from 30 percent to 60 percent of average salary in the final ten years of employment. "After 1920, pension coverage in the public sector was relatively widespread, with all federal workers being covered by a pension and an increasing share of state and local employees included in pension plans" (Clark, Craig, and Wilson 2003, 5).

Until the latter part of the nineteenth century, pensions in the private sector were nonexistent. In 1875, American Express Corporation adopted the first formal employer-provided pension plan. This did not begin a trend in the private sector as there were only twelve private pension plans in 1900, mostly provided to employees of railroads, public utilities, and financial institutions. There was no guarantee that employees were going to receive these plans since employers could terminate employees at any point. Further, the early private sector pension plans were less than generous. General Electric Company had a fairly middle-of-the-road plan at the time, offering employees with tenure longer than 20 years a 1.5 percent earning of average pay over the last ten years of work.

Unlike the public sector, which always offered disability coverage as part of its pensions, the private sector did not have such coverage before workers' compensation was created in 1910. Before this time, private sector workers carried the burden of having to prove to a judge or jury that the employer failed to provide "due care" in the workplace in the event of an injury. Further, widows of employees who died as a result of a work-related injury were given a one-time payment of about a half-year's pay (Clark, Craig, and Wilson 2003). The rise of pensions in the private sector was slow, with about 15 percent of the private workforce covered by 1940. According to Clark and McDermed (1990), soon after pension coverage began to quickly expand due to higher individual tax rates, changes in collective bargaining regulations concerning pensions, and national economic policies including wage and price controls that excluded pension payments.

By 1941, all states except Idaho had some kind of pension plan and 46 percent of all state and local employees were covered. There was, however, a good deal of variation in these plans concerning coverage and the types of employees covered. By 1952, three-fourths of public employees were covered, and by 1972, 90 percent of public servants had pension coverage (Peng 2009). The rapid coverage of civil servants can be attributed in large part to the passage of the Social Security Act in 1935. The Social Security program provides retirement, disability, and survivor benefits to all workers covered by the program. While workers in both the federal public system and the private sector were required to join the program, state and local governments were initially prohibited. At the time, Congress was concerned whether it had the constitutional authority to tax state and local governments to fund the program. State and local governments were eventually given the option to join the program in the 1950s. Not all states chose to do so. Public employees in Alaska, Colorado, Louisiana, Massachusetts, and Nevada do not participate in the Social Security program, and in several other states, such as California, Illinois, and Texas, over half of the public employees are not covered by Social Security (most of them being teachers) (Munnell 2005; Peng 2009).

The Pension Benefit Guaranty Corporation

In 1963, over 4,000 Indiana autoworkers lost all or most of their pensions when the car manufacturer Studebaker ended its pension system, which had promised robust retiree benefits. Though tragic, this incident was legal as there was no protection for workers should their employer change policies. Without protection, workers all around the country were forced to put their hopes in the gamble that companies would deliver on the retiree benefits as promised. This soon changed, thanks to New York senator Jacob Javitz. In 1967, Senator Javitz introduced reform legislation to Congress to protect benefits for millions of private sector workers (Pension Benefits Guaranty Corporation 2011). His work was initially opposed by big business, though with continued work, and public support for reform gaining momentum through avenues such as NBC's 1972 documentary *Pensions: The Broken Promise*, the Employment Retirement Income Security Act (ERISA) was finally passed in 1974 (*Time* 1974).

ERISA laid the groundwork for a pension insurance program, effectively protecting pension benefits for workers in the private sector. The law does not require any private employer to establish a retirement plan. It only requires that those who do so meet certain minimum standards, including the protection of the plans, vesting, funding, fiduciary duties, disclosure, and reporting. The Pension Benefit Guaranty Corporation (PBGC), a federal corporation, was created by Congress in the 1974 ERISA to provide pension insurance for participants in private defined benefit plans. It is important to note that public sector pension plans are exempt from ERISA. However, despite the lack of federal legislation, state and local governments have established a series of laws and resolutions that provide similar protections for employees (Peng 2009).

PBGC's first premium collection regulation was published in September of 1974. Peter J. Brennan was the labor secretary and chairman of PBGC's board of directors at the time and he named Steve Schanes the first executive director. PBGC also consisted of a seven-member presidentially appointed advisory committee, which, along with the board of directors, developed PBGC's early regulations.

The first action by the PBGC was the issuance of a check for $104.75 to a member of the International City Bank of New Orleans Employment Retiree Plan in February of 1975. PBGC's work protecting and insuring benefits for insured pension plans has been ongoing to date, with PBGC currently paying pensions for 1.3 million people, many of whose former employers are no longer in business. Over 44 million workers in the private sector currently have pensions covered under PBGC's protection in more than 29,000 defined benefit pension plans. While PBGC covers these workers in the private sector, no such legislation has been created to serve a similar mechanism in the public sector.

In more recent years, the Securities and Exchange Commission (SEC) has also begun to look more closely at the pensions of big companies. In October of 2004, the SEC began investigating how GM, Ford, Delphi, Navistar, and Boeing account for their retiree benefits (*The Economist* 2004). This was in response to the growing pension deficits of these companies and the volatility of company profits due to dependence on the value of these liabilities. Lastly, the SEC was interested in monitoring companies for "the potential for mischief," given that companies have a great deal of flexibility in how they measure pension obligations and assets based on factors such as how long employees will work, how much health care they will need, and when employees will die. Further, the SEC is monitoring the discount rates companies use to value pension liabilities as an area of concern (*The Economist* 2004).

PBGC Gets in over Its Head

Companies typically calculate their present pension obligations by computing a discount rate to what they will owe in the future, since pension liabilities are future liabilities. Using this mechanism creates a situation in which companies should put more money aside when interest rates drop in order to adjust for slower growth. What remains elusive is establishing a proper rate for pension accounting (Lowenstein 2005).

Some have suggested that corporations have been gaming the system by using the highest rate allowable, which shrinks their reported liabilities and thus their funding obligations (Lowenstein 2005). PBGC uses the current market rate to determine what a plan's true liability is. The disparity between PBGC calculations and those of companies for the same pensions is often large. For instance, in 2005, General Motors would claim their pension fund to be totally funded. PBGC found that this fund to be $31 billion underfunded at the time (Lowenstein 2005).

As interest rates began to fall in the early 2000s, pension liabilities grew. The skyrocketing pension liability was a result of falling stock prices, plunging interest rates, and a recession in the early 2000s. PBGC began to assume responsibility for pensions for a number of large companies that could no longer remain viable with the pensions they carried. Bethlehem Steel, United Airlines, Kemper Insurance, and Kaiser Aluminum are among the many companies who were in dire enough straights to hand over the burden of their liabilities to PBGC in order to remain in existence. PBGC made the error of charging premiums below what was needed to be sustainable. This cheap insurance incentive allowed many companies to provide pensions that they could not afford. This, coupled with relaxed rules, created a situation in which pension sponsors continued to provide inadequate funding.

Under ERISA, United Airlines failed to provide contributions to its pension plans from 2000 to 2002 when it was headed into Chapter 11 bankruptcy. Even worse, United increased pension benefits by 40 percent for 23,000 ground employees while simultaneously asking Congress for emergency relief. Bethlehem Steel failed to contribute to their pension liabilities for the three years prior to turning these liabilities over to the government, while also increasing benefit enhancements. This was all directly prior to filing for Chapter 11 in 2001, and again, was all legally permitted under ERISA. Bradley Belt, then director of PBGC, had this to say in a Senate Committee on Finance hearing in June, 2005 regarding ERISA at the time: "United, US Airways, Bethlehem Steel, LTV and National Steel would not have presented claims in excess of $1 billion each—and with funded ratios of less than 50 percent—if the rules worked" (Lowenstein 2005, "The Surprisingly Pliable System of Pension Accounting" section, para. 8).

Public Sector Unions

Public sector unions, which give employees the political and bargaining power to increase benefits, have also been found to be related to public pension underfunding in several studies (Marks, Raman, and Wilson 1988). Mitchell and Smith (1994) found that the unionized public sector employees had lower levels of actual contributions made into pension funds. Likewise, Johnson (1997) noted that public sector benefits are more generous than those in the private sector because government has the ability to underfund the pension plans. He also found a positive correlation between public sector unions and pension benefit increases.

However, not all studies have shown this correlation. Analysts such as Joshua Rauh now focus mostly on the process of determining the cost of pensions. Rauh states, "The amount they have to be contributing could potentially be two to three times as much as they're contributing now. . . . If you don't want to count on the stock market to pay for all this, this is what you're going to have to contribute" (quoted in Walsh 2011). Steve Kreisberg, research director for the American Federation of State, County and Municipal Employees, fears that politics are painting an unfavorable picture of the situation. "We think there's an agenda . . . these numbers have become intensely politicized, and they're being distorted in a way that does real harm to real people" (Walsh 2011).

Sylvester J. Schieber recently completed a study comparing public pensions among all fifty states. His study differed from others in that it looked at how much of a worker's paycheck would be replaced by a pension when that worker retires, rather than simply on the dollar figure that a worker's pension would provide. This method effectively eliminates disparities between regions. Schieber was surprised at his results. He found no correlation between collective bargaining rights for public workers and the amount of workers' paychecks that would be replaced by pensions. Neither were the most generous states necessarily the states with the highest rates of collective bargaining in the public sector. Schieber states, "I had expected that the unions would be a significant force . . . I was surprised at the results" (Walsh 2011).

Wisconsin, with its average $26,500 a year in pension payment per retiree, turned out to have the eighth-richest pensions of any state. Wisconsin replaces 57 percent, on average, of workers' pay upon retirement. Colorado is by far the most generous of states, replacing an average of 90 percent of final salary with pensions. Further, annual compounding is calculated in Colorado so that the current rate of inflation is included. Another key piece of the equation relevant to the Colorado system is that public workers there are not permitted to participate in Social Security.

Certainly shocking to many, Schieber's study found that Georgia's public pensions are three times as generous as Vermont's. In Vermont, half of the public workers have the right to collective bargaining; in Georgia this right doesn't exist. Furthermore, though Vermont has an astounding rate of collective bargaining rights among public workers, their pensions only provide, on average, 20 percent of workers' pay. Schieber had expected, "rich pensions to go hand in hand with collective bargaining" (Walsh 2011). Schieber's research further explored reasons why seemingly inexpensive pensions such as Wisconsin's are so costly. Schieber concluded that low interest rates, generous retiree health benefits, and workers' ability to retire early as long as they have worked for thirty years are greatly responsible for the lack of sustainability of the current pension system. The few remaining companies in the private sector that offer pensions to employees without requiring them to be age 65 to retire are seldom taken up on their offer due to employees' fear of losing health insurance benefits before qualifying for Medicare. Schieber states, "By the time the typical private-sector worker has retired, the teachers, the highway patrolmen and these folks have already gotten $200,000, $300,000, $400,000 in pensions" (Walsh 2011). The pension deficit is astounding, and even with public sector employees' willingness to contribute a greater share of the cost in Wisconsin, it isn't enough.

The Price of Public Pensions and How We Got Here

As mentioned earlier, most public sector workers have defined benefit plans and these benefits are earned during the employees' working years, but are not paid until after retirement. The promises made to public sector employees for pension, health care, and other retirement benefits have escalated to the point of a fiscal crisis. Pension and retiree health-care plans across the United States are seriously underfunded, the result of overly generous promises, unrealistic expectations of stock market returns, a failure to plan prudently, and risky political behaviors.

Several factors have contributed to this financial mess. First, many state and local governments have effectively borrowed against the value of pensions by deferring contributions into the future. The result has been to transfer current fiscal deficits into future debt, with interest. Second, state and local governments have expanded benefits and offered cost-of-living increases without paying attention to the long-term price tag or figuring out how to pay for them. High-risk investment assumptions were attractive to elected officials and fund managers prior to the Great Recession. Strong market returns made it easier to justify benefit enhancements. Third, state and local governments have offered retiree health-care benefits without adequately paying for them (The Pew Center on the States 2010). Finally, recent investment losses during the Great Recession have severely undermined the fiscal health of many state and local governments.

In 1994, rules issued by the Governmental Accounting Standards Board

(GASB) required states to report on pension benefits that are actuarially determined, and required reporting and funding in a way that the costs would be recognized and funded in a period when the pension was earned by the employee rather than when it is paid to the employee during retirement. However, no such information was required for other postemployment benefits until 2004. States are now required to complete their calculations of the long-term cost of both pension and nonpension retiree benefits.

Estimates of the unfunded pension and health-care liabilities are shocking. As these liabilities have come to light, so has a financial crisis, exacerbated by the Great Recession, that is producing higher taxes and less money for education, health care, and other essential services, as well as an inequitable financial burden for future generations (Coggburn and Kearney 2010; Neumann 2010). In its study on underfunded state retirement systems, titled "The Trillion Dollar Gap," the Pew Center on the States (2010) finds that "states and participating local governments face a collective liability of more than $3.35 trillion for the pensions, health care and other retirement benefits promised to their public sector employees. They have put away $2.35 trillion in assets to pay for those promises—leaving a shortfall of more than $1 trillion that states and local governments will have to pay in the next 30 years" (15). The study notes that this finding is actually an underestimate. The first reason is because it totals assets in states' retirement benefit systems in June, at end of fiscal year 2008, which doesn't account for the rest of 2008. The second half of 2008 was when the financial market collapsed. Also, the funding gap will likely increase over the next several years due to the effects of the market's collapse because most state retirement systems operate in such a way that gains and losses are spread out over time.

A study by Novy-Marx and Rauh (2011) suggests that the numbers are actually higher when looking at the unfunded liability for major pensions in the fifty states. Their study indicates that the collective liability totals $4.43 trillion, with unfunded liabilities approaching $3.20 trillion using U.S. Treasury discount rates. Novy-Marx and Rauh contend that government accounting rules currently used by state and local governments obscure the real magnitude of public pension liabilities. Specifically, Government Accounting Standards Board (GASB) ruling 25 stipulates that public pension liabilities are to be discounted at the expected rate of return on pension assets. The authors argue that this procedure creates a significant bias in the measurement of these public liabilities and that discounting these liabilities at the expected rate of return on assets runs counter to the entire logic of financial economics. The authors suggest that liabilities are even larger than their projections under broader concepts that account for projected salary growth and future services.

Little Hoover Commission Report

A report by the Little Hoover Commission (2011) in Sacramento comes to a more disturbing conclusion: many state and local government employees have been promised pensions that the public could not have afforded even had there been no market crash. This contradicts numerous union officials, who contend the financial problems of many state and local pension programs have been overblown. A study of public pensions in California assembled to better understand the scale of the problem and to develop recommendations to control growing pension costs in state and local government, concluded that the state's pension plans are overextended in their promises to their current workers and retirees, and that pension costs to the state will crush government, severely reducing services and requiring the layoff of employees.

The Little Hoover Commission report suggests that while investment losses in 2008–2009 significantly impacted the system, other factors contributed to the unsustainable pension environment, including the offering of more generous benefits to employees. These included provisions that provide extra credits to retire early, more favorable methods for calculating pension benefits based on single highest year of compensation, and lowered retirement ages. The report also noted that the system banked on high fund returns and an aggressive investment strategy and that it lacked oversight, accountability, and transparency. The Little Hoover Commission recommended that the legislature give state and local governments explicit authority to aggressively deal with the crisis, including the ability to alter the future, unaccrued retirement benefits for current employees, and to mandate hybrid models for new hires that would retain the defined benefit formulas but at lower levels, combined with an employee-matched 401(k)-style defined contribution plan. The commission also recommended that more transparency and accountability measures be required, including submitting pension increases to voters.

Unfunded Pensions and State Debt

State debt is continuing to rise, largely due to unfunded pension liabilities. In some especially hard hit, such as Illinois, the state is borrowing more money to cover pensions, and thereby going further into debt. In 2003, Illinois borrowed $10 billion and deposited the money into its pension funds to make up for years of failing to contribute required annual payments. The return on this investment did not meet its target and Illinois was strapped with even more debt. In 2010, Illinois made another attempt to meet its obligations by selling $3.5 billion in pension bonds. Actions like this are being labeled as "fiscal sleight of hand" by major news outlets (Cooper and Walsh 2010).

An article in *The Economist* (2010) identifies similar issues with the way that state pension liabilities are calculated. As it stands now, individual states discount their pension liabilities by an assumed rate of return on assets of about 8 percent. Unfortunately, pensions have not gained returns this high in the last decade and with the current state of the stock market, are not expected to do so in the near future. David Crane, an economic adviser to former California governor Arnold Schwarzenegger, goes so far as to call setting the expected return rate of 8 percent "Alice-in-Wonderland accounting" (quoted in *The Economist* 2010, 18). Nevertheless, the burden still falls on the state to fund the pensions whether it hits its target return or not. On the basis of discounting the states' pensions by yield on U.S. Treasury bonds, the total pension liability for the states is $5.3 trillion. This is much higher than the $1.9 trillion liability states have on the books. The total shortfall is $3.4 trillion (*The Economist* 2010).

Other mechanisms to hide the true liability of local governments come in the form of changing credit ratings. Credit-rating agencies have raised credit ratings in local governments in the last year because of the unlikelihood of municipal defaults in comparison to corporate defaults. The new, higher credit ratings are not based on the actual financial state of municipalities. Rauh and Novy-Marx's (2011) findings were echoed in the *New York Times* article by Cooper and Walsh (2010), who explained that states and municipalities use accounting methods that would not be allowed in the private sector so as to lower their pension liabilities on the books. Increased underfunding for pensions in the private sector is also occurring, due in part to discount rates for valuing pensions. Pension liabilities in the private sector have increased due to declining discount rates, the ongoing effects of the depressed financial market since 2000, and the ageing workforce.

As highlighted by Orin S. Kramer of the *New York Times*, "The S.E.C. is now making inquiries about the underfunding of other public pensions, and its assertiveness is welcome. But this effort cannot ultimately fix the problem, because all the S.E.C. can do is force states to follow the budgeting rules that are set by the Governmental Accounting Standards Board. These rules offer, at best, only the illusion of transparency, because they allow governments to base their budgets on economic fictions" (Kramer 2010, A17). Contrary to the private sector's mechanism of valuing assets, government accounting standards allow pension systems to measure their assets based on average value from years past. This creates an unrealistic asset value that is much higher than actual worth. In addition, public pension funds are also given the freedom to make predictions about future returns that would be considered overly optimistic by most investors. These unrealistic assumptions about future returns are factored in to measure the fund's current status, creating the semblance of a well-funded pension system. These poor accounting rules have significantly contributed to the underfunding of state public pensions (Kramer 2010).

Looking at unfunded state pension liabilities in comparison to the payroll covered by plans shows that in 2008, the unfunded liability exceeded covered payroll in 22 states. In 7 of these 22 states, the unfunded liability was more than double the covered payroll. As recently as the year 2000, state-run pension plans had excess coverage of $56 billion. Between 2000 and 2008, assets could not keep up with growing pension liabilities. By 2006, only six states had fully funded pensions, down from over 50 percent of states having fully funded pensions in 2000. Just before the financial market collapsed in 2008, the number of states with fully funded pensions had dipped to four: Florida, New York, Washington, and Wisconsin.

Retiree Health Care and OPEB

Underfunded pensions are only half of the financial deficit borne by states. The other half come in the form of retiree health care and other postemployment benefits (OPEB). Similar to pension benefits, these OPEBs are earned during the employee's work tenure and are paid out after retirement. In 2004, the Government Accounting Standards Board (GASB) began to require governments to report their liabilities for retiree health care and nonpension benefits. They did so with the creation of Statements 43 and 45. Prior to this, there was no requirement to calculate and/or report long-term liabilities. For these benefits, the Pew Center on the States (2010) found that only two states (Alaska and Arizona) have more than 50 percent of the assets to fund long-term liabilities and that there was nearly $381 billion in unfunded OPEBs in 2007. As of fiscal year 2008, this translates into states collectively carrying $587 billion in long-term liability with only 5.44 percent of it covered. Total OPEB liabilities are essentially equal to unfunded OPEB liabilities. This is due to several factors, including states failing to prefund OPEB liabilities, making poor investment choices, applying faulty actuarial assumptions, deferring employer contributions, and diverting or borrowing pension fund assets (Coggburn and Kearney 2010). Another striking reality is the continuous "graying" of the workforce. This, combined with the escalating rate of inflation in health-care and prescription drug costs, adds immensely to the cost and unfunded health-care liability for employees, retirees, and dependents.

Even in states that have minimal retiree health-care liabilities, the cost is high. Iowa, Kansas, North Dakota, South Dakota, and Wyoming are examples, as they assist retirees with paying premiums. Instead, they allow retirees to stay on the plan that active employees have. This drives up the cost of the plan, since retirees are generally older and thus more susceptible to health problems. Connecticut has one of the largest health-care liabilities ($26 billion). As of 2008, it had no funding set aside to pay for this liability. Hawaii is another example of zero funding being set aside to pay for a $10 billion liability (The Pew Center on the States 2010).

Most states fund retiree health-care and nonpension benefits on a pay-as-you-go basis, arguing that this, along with the lack of legal barriers to changing benefits, makes the high cost more feasible to fund than the cost of pensions. This is less comforting when we consider that the substantially growing number of retirees and rising cost of medical treatment each year far outweigh the average expenditure increases. Paying more now will keep costs from getting out of hand in the future. Continuing to ignore the underfunded state retirement benefit systems will only exacerbate extensive annual costs that come with unfunded liabilities, lower bond ratings, less money for services, and higher taxes (The Pew Center on the States 2010).

The Pew Center on the States' 2010 report reviews several factors that have contributed to the largely underfunded state retirement systems, including: the volatility of pension plan investments; states falling behind in their payments; ill-considered benefit increases; and other structural issues. These factors, culminating with the Great Recession of 2007–2009, created a *perfect storm* for severe retiree benefit system deficits.

The volatility of pension plan investments was the first contributing factor. "In calendar year 2008, the median investment loss for public pension funds was 25.3 percent," according to the Pew Center on the States (2010, 23). In the past several decades, restrictions on making investments in equity, real estate, and private equity have loosened greatly. In 1990, 38 percent of pension plan assets were invested in equities. By 2007, the percentage of assets invested in equities had jumped to 70 percent of all state pension plan assets. This is a far cry from the 1970s, when state pension systems made conservative investments with slow but steady returns. As returns continued to be strong, pension assets shot up dramatically during the 1990s, leading to overfunding. Then contribution rates were lowered, creating a system that was even more vulnerable to the changes in the market of the early 2000s and the last few years.

The second factor identified in the Pew report (2010) as contributing to state retiree system deficits is states' falling behind in payments. This was largely seen in states that relied on a pay-as-you-go plan, which paid out retiree benefits from current state revenues. As the number of retirees began to grow faster than the number of new employees, states began to fall farther and farther behind. Rhode Island's Employee Retirement System is an example, as they adopted a pay-as-you-go method from 1936 to the late 1970s.

Since then, the system has made 100 percent of its actuarial contributions and is only 57 percent funded. Consistently low contributions have created a situation in which "21 states failed to make pension payments that averaged out to 90 percent of their actuarially required contributions," in the last five years (The Pew Center on the States 2010, 24).

As already mentioned, many states began to seriously reduce contribution rates to retirement plans in the late 1990s and early 2000s as a result of the strong market of the 1990s. By doing so, intergenerational equity was violated. The concept of intergenerational equity states that a generation that benefits from particular public service should also be the generation that pays for it. By reducing contribution rates to pension plans, states created a funding shortage and passed the bill on to the next generation. Not only was the financial obligation shifted to the next generation, but it was done at an increasing cost (Peng 2004). States justified shifting funds away from pensions by pointing to the fact that retirement systems were 100 percent funded, therefore financial support could be moved elsewhere to fix fiscal problems and balance budgets. The release of the GASB's new standard for reporting in 2004 was the first time most state governments actually calculated the long-term impact of retiree health care and nonpension benefits and began setting aside funding for them (The Pew Center on the States 2010).

The Departure from Fully Funded Pensions

Former New Jersey governor Christine Todd Whitman's actions in the mid-1990s exemplified this kind of shifting funding away from fully funded pensions to other areas. In the *New York Times*, columnist Bob Herbert (1995) decried "Mrs. Whitman's decision to withhold billions of dollars that should be going into the public employee pension funds over the next few years, and using the bulk of that money to balance the state budget." In doing so, the governor pushed off the funding of pension and effectively implemented a buy-now, pay-later economic policy. Not only was Governor Whitman diverting funding away from the pension system, she was doing so with drastic measures.

The New Jersey Education Association found that employer contributions to the pension system in 1995 were reduced by amounts up to 96 percent of contributions made in the early 1990s. "By all accounts, the employer contributions have been reduced by nearly $1 billion a year" (Herbert 1995). Even in 1995, at a time when New Jersey's pension system was fully funded, there was concern over this kind of practice. Richard C. Leone, former New Jersey state treasurer, explained, "there is no question but that this is creating future debt . . . this is just another way of getting around the balanced-budget requirement, a kind of deficit spending. It is the sort of thing that comes back to haunt you" (quoted in Herbert 1995). Given the data presented in Pew's research, Leone's words could not have been more prescient.

Two years later, in 1997, Governor Whitman continued this pattern by proposing to borrow $2.75 billion to help close a deficit in the state pension fund. This plan included borrowing proceeds and investment gains from the pension system to reduce the state's $4.2 billion pension deficit. This proposal brought significant attention to the widespread changes Whitman had been making to the pension system since 1994. These changes were vital in paying for her significant tax cuts, the basis of her platform for reelection. From 1994 to 1997, New Jersey had cut its scheduled contributions to pension funds by over $3 billion. This fueled the Democrats' criticism of Whitman, who accused her of paying for her tax cuts by mortgaging the state's future (Preston 1997).

Even before Whitman, Democratic governor James Florio pushed the Pension Revaluation Act through the legislature in 1992. The effects of the act's adjustments included the state gaining the power to cut pension contributions by more than $1.5 billion in 1992 and 1993, before Whitman even took office in 1994. Douglas Forrester, former assistant state treasurer under Governor Thomas Kean, referenced Florio and Whitman's accounting changes as "the one-two punch from which the retirement system has never recovered" (Benner 2009). In an attempt to make up some of the pension system's losses, New Jersey put its hopes in the leveraging of the stock market by selling $2.75 billion of bonds paying 7.6 percent interest, with proceeds going to the pension funds. Whitman described this as the Pension Security Plan and assured everyone that it would save taxpayers about $45 billion. This turned out not to be the case as the fund has earned less than 6 percent annually since the plan's creation. U.S. representative Leonard Lance, a Republican legislator in New Jersey from 1991 to 2008, identified this as a questionable strategy even in the private sector and called it unacceptable as a matter of public policy (Benner 2009).

Unfunded benefit increases is the third factor reported on in the Pew Center's "Trillion Dollar Gap" report. In the 1990s and the early part of the 2000s, states began to significantly increase employee benefits. Many states, such as New Mexico, did so in lieu of raising salaries but failed to add funding mechanisms to adjust for the long-term cost. Several states increased benefits to cover cost-of-living increases and changed retirement formulas, resulting in retroactive benefit increases for current employees. Mississippi is another example of a state that increased benefits drastically without budgeting for the cost. In 1998, Mississippi had an 85 percent funded Public Employee Retirement System, with full funding projected for another 10 years. By

2008, the same system was funded 73 percent, with full funding projected to be 30 years away.

The Pew Center report cites several other structural issues that have additionally contributed to underfunded retirement benefit systems. Early retirement is the first, and is a common tactic of governments attempting to reduce the present size of the workforce. When the retirement age is lowered, positions vacated by those who take advantage of early retirement are often filled by new workers. Any savings through the cutting of short-term costs is far overshadowed by the cost of covering a greater number of retirees for additional years. Additionally, early retirement disrupts actuarial assumptions by adding more years of coverage than are accounted for to retirement benefits. Connecticut, Maine, and Vermont all experienced a large number of early retirees being replaced by new, younger workers in 2009.

Cost-of-living adjustments (COLA) offered on an ad hoc basis, as in Georgia in 2008, create an even greater strain than those incorporated by some states annually because they had not been previously accounted for. Georgia's 2 percent COLA increases added to its pension liability by $188 million. In an attempt to increase long-term fiscal responsibility, Georgia's legislature passed a law in 2010 that eliminated COLAs for new hires when they retire.

Sharing excess returns has also contributed to retirement system underfunding. In Oregon, a money-match system was put in place that allowed employees to receive any additional return on the state's matched investment if there is a return greater than the state had predicted. This worked well in good years. However, when the investment return was lower than the state's estimate, Oregon was responsible for making up the difference. If the additional returns were put into a reserve account rather than credited to members, it would likely have balanced out the good and bad years. In the 1990s, many Oregonians retired with pensions that exceeded their final salaries as a result of being credited the increased amount of the state's investment. In the economic downturn of 2001–2003, Oregon's pension system went from 100 percent to 65 percent funded. The state froze the money-match program and stopped crediting amounts to members that returned more than their investment. Oregon also took out a pension bond to help cover pension liability.

An issue that contributes to the cost of pension systems, and has yet to be significantly dealt with by states, is known as double dipping. Double dipping is the practice of employees retiring, receiving pensions, and then returning to work for a new salary. In Utah, the number of state employees who were double dipping rose from 125 in 1995 to 2,166 in 2008. This has recently gained a great deal of media attention.

Deferred retirement option plans (DROPs) have been adopted by many states in an attempt to offset double dipping while simultaneously retaining valuable workers. DROPs attempt to maintain retiring employees on salary for several years in order to train other employees. The incentive is that these employees get to continue receiving their salary while the pension benefits that they would have been collecting had they retired are kept for them in special accounts. First created in Baton Rouge, Louisiana, in the 1980s as an incentive to retain police and fire protection workers, DROPs gradually became available to other state and local government workers (Peng 2009). While the retention of skilled workers can be a significant benefit of the program, there has also been much controversy about these plans. One of the selling features of the program was that it would be cost-neutral; however, there is little evidence that that has been the case. According to Peng (2009), to really determine the full cost of the program, the employer must compare the age of the employees who enter into a DROP program to the age of those who retire with a DROP program. In Arizona, in the mid-2000s, a DROP plan was passed by the legislature and later repealed before it ever went into effect, after a study indicated that it would cost $45 million annually in employer contributions (The Pew Center on the States 2010).

A final issue, referred to in the Pew Center's "Trillion Dollar Gap" report as the additional structural factor that contributes to the increased deficit in retirement benefit system funding, is the spiking of final salaries. Workers know that their pensions will be calculated based on their final salaries and they have learned how to boost them before retiring. They do this by working additional overtime, as those with the longest tenure have the seniority to do so. Commonly, workers save sick leave and ask for temporary promotions or last-minute raises as other ways of boosting their final salary. Newspapers in Delaware detailed in 2008 how correctional officers were working extra overtime to raise pensions. The Pew Center on the States (2010) reports that "Georgia recently cracked down on agencies that were giving large raises to employees at the end of employment as a way of increasing pension benefits" (29).

"Enron by the Sea": San Diego (A Case Study)

San Diego's pension problems began in 1996, when, to help pay for renovations at the convention center, site up the upcoming Republican National Convention, money was diverted from the city's pension fund rather than raising taxes or issuing bonds to cover the expense. This was the beginning of a pattern in San Diego of using the pension's pot of money to fund other services. Due to this underfunding, the city of San Diego now needs to divert an increasing amount of its budget, up to one-half of its general fund by 2025, to stabilize its retirement system for city employees (San Diego Grand Jury

2010). As Former San Diego City Attorney Michael Aguirre observed regarding the practice: "The key, Nobel Prize–winning breakthrough in economics was the discovery that the unfunded pension liability was a big hole where you could hide your debt" (*CQ Researcher* 2006, 150).

Not only was this kind of chipping-from-the-pension-fund behavior occurring, but to make matters worse, in 2002, the city offered 25 percent pension increases to city employees in lieu of raises while simultaneously lowering the city's annual contributions to the pension fund. The *San Diego Union-Tribune* called this a "corrupt scheme," stating, "the City Council agreed to increase pension benefits significantly if the retirement board, controlled by labor unions and other city employees, approved a plan allowing the city to underfund the pension system" (*CQ Researcher* 2006, 150). This deal allowed union officials to increase pensions while violating tax rules.

Denial of the severity of financial difficulty for the city of San Diego came from Mayor Dick Murphy in 2004, despite the pension deficit's rising to nearly $1 billion. In 2005, the city began spending in an attempt to make up losses to the pension fund, doubling its annual contributions from approximately $80 million to $160 million. At this time, Councilman Scott Peters announced the city's plan to continue raising contributions to over $200 million, despite the city's budget totaling only $2.5 billion. The city was also spending heavily on legal bills, estimated at $10 million by Michael Aguirre. On January 6, 2006, five former trustees, the former pension system's director, and a staff attorney were indicted for conspiracy and fraud (*CQ Researcher* 2006).

In the November 2010 election, Proposition D was presented to San Diego citizens to increase funding for the pension deficit. It failed to be voted in and in response, San Diego mayor Jerry Sanders along with three council members garnered enough signatures to place the Comprehensive Pension Reform initiative on the city ballot in June 2012. The initiative would eliminate guaranteed pensions for all new city hires except police officers and offer them 401(k) accounts instead (Gustafson 2012). The annual pension payment, paid mostly from the city's operating budget of $1.1 billion, is continuing to grow in attempt to pay off the $2.1 billion debt from benefit boosts in 1996 and 2002. It is expected that the annual payment will rise from $229 million this year to $318 million in 2015 and $512 million by 2025. Opposition to Sanders's proposal has come from labor unions, suggesting that ending pensions for new hires will do nothing but create poverty for future city employees and will not solve the city's budget crisis. Some of these arguments rest on the fact that city employees opted out of Social Security in 1982 and therefore have no safety net, with a pension entirely dependent on the stock market. Sanders has addressed this concern and shared the possibility that some workers might be allowed back into the Social Security system; however, their ability to rejoin the federal Social Security system is still in question.

Where Do We Go from Here?

While reform of public sector pensions is inherently difficult, a mix of cost-cutting and revenue-enhancing changes are needed to avoid a complete financial meltdown along with a potential federal taxpayer bailout. The most significant problem consists of the promises made to existing employees. Legal protections and court decisions have been pretty clear that these promises cannot be withdrawn. While private sector employers can restructure their pension plans, it is much more challenging for public sector organizations to do so. The best that can be done is to change the plans for new employees (*The Economist* 2011b). This will need to be done by establishing two-tier pension and OPEB programs. Doing so will allow reduced retirement and health benefits to be available for employees hired after a specific date and at the same time, maintain agreed-upon benefits for existing workers.

First and foremost, people need to work longer and the retirement age should be raised. Along with this, retirement before the official pension age must be curbed. Public sector employees should not be retiring earlier than private sector ones (*The Economist* 2011b). In preparation for the rising rate of retirees, governments are already beginning to raise the age of retirement in order to offset pension costs. Not only is the United States facing a serious pension debt, but life expectancy is continuing to rise. Since 1971, life expectancy has increased by four or five years in the developed world and is projected to increase an additional three years by 2050. Thus, people are living longer and retiring earlier. The average age of retirement is 63, which is almost an entire year younger than in 1970. Public sector employees can retire on full pension an average of five years earlier than their private sector counterparts (Clowes 2004). The advantage of raising the retirement age includes giving the employee more years of wages, governments gaining more in taxes and paying out less in benefits, as well as the fact that by having more people working, the economy grows at an increased rate (*The Economist* 2011b).

The fiscal crisis gripping Europe has pushed a number of countries such as Greece, Spain, Portugal, and Britain to adopt touch austerity measures including reduced pension benefits and increased legal retirement age in order to address the debt being created by the inability to finance their programs. Even Germany, France, and Sweden have raised the age of retirement. As Europe ages and its working population dwindles, the continent can no longer afford its growing number of retirees. However, this is not so easy in the United States, as there are extensive laws that protect pensions. "Municipalities in this country cannot easily follow suit even as financial problems mount, though, because reducing benefits for their existing employees is considered impossible under the current laws of most states" (Walsh and Schoenfeld 2010, A21).

Other two-tiered programs should include longer vesting requirements and scaled-backed benefits for retirement. Formulas that include years of service and age can also be adjusted so that components such as the final salary include a career average versus a formula based on a limited number of best or final years. Some states and cities are already adopting more modest retirement plans for future workers, though these changes create little savings initially and take a long time to significantly alter financial statements. Other states have reduced cost-of-living increases for retirees, causing a legal backlash. In Colorado, for example, cost-of-living adjustments are being reduced for current retirees. In response, retirees and those who are soon to retire have jointly filed lawsuits against the state and the courts are still deciding whether or not the move was legal. Another strategy being adopted is to tie cost-of-living increases to actual inflation rates. This would still protect retirees from rising living expenses (Weiss et al. 2008). Bolder strategies being considered by some states and local jurisdictions include having new employees operate under a defined contribution program instead of a defined benefit program. This would bring the public sector more in line with the private sector and allow for a more flexible workforce as well as boosting prospects for older workers (*The Economist* 2011b).

States, counties, and cities are also experimenting with hybrid plans that mix defined benefits and defined contribution plans (The Pew Center on the States 2007). Several of the plans emerging are designed to limit risk and market volatility in order to provide retirement security for employees. These approaches give employees the upside of a 401(k)-style plan such as portability and the ability to roll over retirement savings when the worker changes jobs without the downside of potential significant investment loses. In 2003, Nebraska instituted a new version of a state pension called the cash-balance plan. It required all new public workers to contribute 4.8 percent of their salary while the state contributed 6.8 percent of a salary match. While similar to a defined contribution plan, where the employee receives a payout upon retirement based on how much is in the plan, Nebraska guarantees a 5 percent annual investment return, dramatically reducing the risk for the employee (The Pew Center on the States 2010).

In 2010, Orange County, California, gave newly hired employees the option of choosing a lower fixed pension with a government-matched 401(k)-type component. The part that appeals to employees is a 7 percent increase in their take-home pay due to smaller deductions for their share of retirement contributions (Little Hoover Commission 2011). New employees in Atlanta will now be enrolled in a hybrid plan consisting of a traditional defined benefit pension and a defined contribution plan similar to a 401(k). Eight percent of their salaries will go toward the former, and at least 3.75 percent must go to the latter (the city will match employees' contributions up to 8 percent). Retirement ages will also rise, from 55 to 57 for police and firefighters and from 60 to 62 for other workers (*The Economist* 2011c).

Reform for current employees will require increased employee contributions for both retirement and OEMP benefits to better match rising costs. There needs to be a curtailing of abuses such as salary spiking and pension benefit increases as well as the narrowing of eligibility for public safety benefits to select groups (Weiss et al. 2008). In Newport Beach and other California beach communities, lifeguards were able to significantly increase their pension and OEMP benefits, as well as eligibility for early retirement, by falling under the public safety criteria.

Another major reform that appears to be needed is for state and local governments to fully fund their obligations—both pension and OPEBs—and to institute a moratorium on any new increases in benefits until this occurs. The Pew Center on the States (2007) has recommended the use of state or local trusts requiring that all the money going into them be used in a predetermined way—such as to pay for retirement benefits in years to come. The center cites two states that have successfully addressed management of their retirement system. Florida has fully funded its actuarially required contribution and follows conservative accounting principles in managing its obligations. Likewise, Georgia has had state laws for twenty years that require an actuarial study to determine the long-term financial impact on the system for any reduction or increase. This allows for informed and transparent decision making. Even in progressive and more liberal jurisdictions, such as the City of San Francisco, city law now requires a vote of the people for any pension increase. Voters must be fully informed of the current and future costs, and justification for the need to increase benefits.

Finally, the crisis has a good deal to do with the inherent conflict of interest that elected officials encounter when they have the option of awarding pensions to special-interest constituencies, including themselves, without citizens fully understanding what is going on and without the bills coming due until after they are long gone from office. As previously discussed, in order to either balance their budgets and/or to increase services, many politicians refuse to make the necessary contributions to pension funds, and/or they borrowed from the funds at the same time, creating deeper and deeper future shortfalls.

The lack of transparency and the secrecy that has often accompanied the awarding of pensions, OPEBs, and salary increases is deplorable and contrary to the public interest. Closed circles of elected officials, public managers, and union and employee groups have often deliberately hidden from public scrutiny the facts on what benefits have been awarded and what the real costs are associated with them as well as with deferred benefits. Public sector unions and employee groups have supported increasing benefits over wages because the costs are less transparent to the community and can be spread out over time. This is one reason that fringe benefits have grown substantially in the public sector: they are used as political payments for elected officials, and the public rarely is aware of what is being awarded to employee groups. The most effective measure public managers can employ to better manage these issues is to insist upon increased transparency in all aspects when dealing with public sector wages and benefits. This includes having more public discussions and deliberations on employee benefit packages as well as on long-term financial commitments that may affect future generations of public officials and taxpayers. State laws should be adopted that require an independent accounting of collective bargaining agreements and pension and other retirement benefits so as to clearly outline the current costs as well as the costs to future generations. Consideration should also be given to either establishing separate citizens groups to negotiate contracts on behalf of state and local governments, or for taking increases in pensions and retirement benefits to a vote of the people.

7
Rethinking Public Sector Employment

The years 2006 to 2011 have been marked by unyielding economic despair for many state and local governments. Nationwide, the decline in local governmental revenue has accelerated from 2007 to 2011, draining billions of dollars from essential services like public safety and critical safety-net programs for the poor and elderly. Sales taxes, property taxes, and other forms of local government revenues have been severely curtailed. Additionally, local governments have shed nearly half a million jobs and it is widely believed among financial experts that their recovery will lag years behind the private sector's rebound. Large budget shortfalls are jeopardizing the ability of cities and counties to perform core functions. Unlike the federal government, local governments cannot run deficits. To balance their budgets, they must cut spending, raise taxes, or both. Yet local jurisdictions attempting tax increases face tremendous obstacles as many localities have passed referendums prohibiting elected officials from raising taxes. Others have imposed restrictions that require super majorities or a popular vote. With so many families struggling, additional taxes are a hard sell politically. While cutting services may be more common, there are limits to what citizens will allow (Boyd 2009; Ginsberg and Horwitz 2009; Horwitz 2009; Shubik, Horwitz, and Ginsberg 2009).

States as well continue to struggle to balance their budgets at a time when revenues are down and demand for services is high. Attempts to reel in spending and identify new revenue sources dominate the agendas of state officials. More so than some local governments, states are also grappling with huge unfunded liability costs centered on public sector pensions and the cost of other postretirement benefits (OPEBs). The collective liability for state pension obligations exceeds $4 trillion, with unfunded liability approaching $3 trillion by some estimates. Since the unfunded actuarial liability of OPEB is much greater than the unfunded liabilities for pensions, the funding of OPEBs is expected to increase substantially in the future and will be placed in direct competition with the funding for pensions—since they all come out of the same operating budget (Peng 2009).

Difficulty raising or generating taxes to cover these unfunded liabilities has already surfaced. In states and local jurisdictions, payments to cover these liabilities are crowding out revenues for parks, road repair, schools, universities, and safety net programs for the poor and elderly. Stimulus funds from the 2009 American Recovery and Reinvestment Act have dried up and are no longer available to fill in gaps in revenue. These funds were essential in helping states fill the gaping holes in their budgets. With the drying up of these funds and the recession still lingering, more pain will surely follow. The debate occurring across each of the states and in regions and municipalities has been based on common questions: What are the tradeoffs? Should we save or invest? Borrow or pay as we go? When resources are scarce, which essentials become less so? In their book, *The Price of Government*, David Osborne and Peter Hutchinson (2004) offer a different approach to budgeting in the public sector, one that focuses more on buying results for citizens than cutting or adding to last year's spending program. They ask a fundamental question: What should governments do and what should they stop doing? The framework they offer is a rational one that realistically acknowledges the partisan divide that often accompanies these political processes. However, when significant portions of a state or local governments' general budget is consumed by simply making a required payment to a pension fund for current and former employees, the discussions become that more challenging.

The financial crisis, and associated media attention have placed public sector employment and, more specifically, the compensation for public sector workers under the microscope. Concerns about escalating employee wages/benefits and retirement/pension programs are expressed publicly on a daily basis. Headlines across the nation, including those of major publications such as *The Economist*, *Los Angeles Times*, *New York Times*, *USA Today*, and the *Wall Street Journal*, have underscored the widespread nature of the problem and have weighed in on the value and amount of benefit levels granted to public sector employees. In some cases, the media has gone to great lengths to pit private citizens against the public sector worker. Wage comparisons between the two are often mischaracterized and have failed to account for many differences in education and job type. The evidence suggests that the divide between the two is pretty close, with blue-collar workers making more in the public sector and white-collar workers making more in the private sector. However, in other cases, the media has simply chronicled the differences in benefits between the two sectors.

Compensation increases for state and local government employees have been trending upward for the last several years and have been substantially higher than those for workers in the private sector from (Brinner et al. 2008; Bureau of Labor Statistics 2009b). This is in sharp contrast to many private sector workers who have seen their wages and benefits reduced during the recession. Such has been particularly true with retirement plans, where employer contributions have been reduced and the stock market has decreased the value of individual pension plans. In reality, a guaranteed public pension, indexed for inflation for life coupled with lifetime retiree health benefits, is unheard of to most Americans. It is not sustainable. Most private sector workers lack a guaranteed pension and instead rely on a defined contribution program that they manage and that is subject to fluctuations in the stock market.

The media's focus on the differences in retirement and health-care benefits for public versus private employees created a clear sense of "pension envy" for many citizens. Fewer and fewer private workers today have the luxury of a traditional pension, and if they do, there is no guarantee that their employer won't freeze or cut benefits before or after they retire. Public pensions, on the other hand, appear to be sacrosanct. Taxpayers are jealous and many are asking why the public sector has richer benefits than the majority of working citizens paying the taxes. In other cases, news stories have brought to light obscene abuses in government pay.

In the working-class city of Bell, California, county executives, public safety officials, and elected city councilmen were receiving exorbitant compensation while going great lengths to hide it from the public. The *Los Angeles Times* reported that Chief Administrative Officer Robert Rizzo was earning $787,637—with annual 12 percent raises—and that Bell paid its police chief $457,000, more than Los Angeles police chief makes in a city of 3.8 million people. Additionally, some City Council members in the California community were pulling in $96,000 a year for part-time elected positions, amounting to 20 times the national average for similar positions. The council members allegedly increased their salaries by accruing stipends for serving on city commissions. Some of the commissions would reportedly hold meetings for just a few minutes a month, or in tandem with other meetings. More astounding was the news that Rizzo could draw $884,692 in his first year of retirement and at age 62, when he could also begin receiving Social Security payments, and that his annual pension would rise to $976,771, topping $1 million two years later. If he lives to age 83, his annual payout will rise to $1.48 million and draw lifetime pension payments exceeding $30 million (Sallant and Gottlieb 2010).

In Newport Beach, California, the media recently pointed out that its thirteen-member full-time lifeguard crew was receiving some very generous salaries, benefits, and overtime pay. With overtime only added in, more than half of the 13 cleared $100,000 and the rest made between $59,500 and $98,500. Adding in pension contributions, medical benefits, life insurance, and other pay, two battalion chiefs earned more than $200,000 in 2010, while the lowest-paid officer made more than $98,000. In addition, all lifeguards received $400 sunglass allowances and two cleared $28,000 apiece in overtime and night duty pay. The revelation that these lifeguards make as much as some CEOs has spurred rage among citizens (Flaccus 2011).

Public sector unions have often been singled out for criticism, and some governors, elected officials, and interest groups have exploited the financial crisis to further a political agenda for the total dismantling of collective bargaining rights for public sector workers. While public sector unions contribute to the problem by supporting the often unsustainable ways in which public employees are compensated, they are hardly the only culprit. Public sector unions are some of the most powerful interest groups in the United States, and their political machines have been used to drive up spending and to both elect and unseat the same people who determine their compensation.

However, the Great Recession was triggered by Wall Street and fueled by declining taxes on corporations and the rich. Elected officials deserve a good deal of the blame. They have chosen to award pensions and other deferred compensation to public employees without transparency and without the bills coming due until they have long left office. In order to balance their budgets, many have refused to adequately fund pension programs or have borrowed from them, creating huge shortfalls. While not engaged in the blatant political payoffs to special interest constituencies, such as public sector unions and employee groups, public managers have nonetheless been complicit in the problem. They often have failed to insist upon transparency in these practices and have often awarded many of these unsustainable benefits via a tight circle of insiders made up of elected official and union and employee groups. These practices to provide deferred compensation have been carried out in ways that often hide a full accounting of the total costs from the public and push a significant amount of the costs onto future generations of taxpayers, elected officials, and public managers. The result has been to transfer current fiscal deficits into future debt, with interest.

On top of this, civil service rules governing the personnel practices in the public sector are antiquated and have prevented the effective delivery of services. Rules and regulations have created a system that is overly bureaucratic and attracts individuals who crave security, at the expense of attracting the best and the biggest, who are needed to confront the many messy and intractable problems facing communities.

What is increasingly clear is that the current ways in which public workers are compensated via deferred benefits is not sustainable. The unrelenting financial crisis, coupled with the media attention it has received, has created the perfect storm in some respects. Like many crises, it has created an opportunity to rethink the larger issue of public sector employment. How should we manage, motivate, and compensate public sector employees? How do we ensure that citizens receive effective, efficient, and responsive services? The focus of this process of rethinking must be on the public interest, which implies a focus on such integrity in the delivery of services. The public interest is what needs to drive our rethinking.

The following is a series of proposed solutions, many of them covered in previous chapters, that can begin to rectify many of the problems associated with public sector employment. In numerous cases, best practices are already in place. In other cases, states and local governments need to simply be given the tools to create environments in which quality and responsiveness dominate the culture of public organizations and where the facilitation and/or delivery of services has public interest in the forefront of everyone's thinking. While not all of these recommendations can be implemented in all jurisdictions, it is clear that the time to act is now.

Increased Transparency

Government must be operated in an open and transparent manner. State laws should be enacted requiring full disclosure of all costs associated with wage/benefit increases or reductions for public employees. An independent analysis should be mandated similar to the ones enacted in Georgia, North Carolina, and Oklahoma that requires an actuarial study to determine the long-term financial impact on retiree benefits of spending decisions. These laws force legislators to consider how any change or adoption of new benefits could affect future generations of taxpayers, legislators, and public managers (The Pew Center on the States 2010).

Public notices and public hearings should be mandated and should occur prior to any adoption of new benefits or new collective bargaining agreements. All too often, jurisdictions circumvent open meeting laws by listing the wage or benefit increase, or ratification of a collective bargaining agreement, as an item in the consent agenda, requiring someone to request in person for it to be heard. If no one asks for the items to be heard separately, the entire consent agenda is approved with one motion and without any discussion. At other times, if the item is on the agenda for discussion, often the details and costly components of the agreement are not detailed in public or this is done in a manner that is not understandable to citizens. Not only should there be an independent analysis but there should be a public discussion of the current cost of any benefit or wage increase as well as a discussion of all future costs and how the state or local government will pay for them. States and local governments should also consider mandating that labor negotiations with unions and/or employee groups adhere to open meeting laws. The public interest is not well served when these discussions are held behind closed doors and in secret. Opening these negotiations to the public and the media will increase scrutiny and transparency.

Conflicts in Awarding Compensation Should Be Avoided

The conflict for many elected officials in awarding benefits to special interest groups, including themselves, is very clear and creates serious ethical problems. Elected officials often view bargaining with public sector unions as advantageous. By supporting public sector unions, elected officials create a political partnership of enormous magnitude. The political partner, the union, provides financial and in-kind contributions during elections that are ultimately funded and supplied by member dues and fees. Politically, the union becomes a potent source of political and financial support (Troy 2003). Where significant campaign funds can be funneled to candidates at the local level, often dwarfing what candidates can raise themselves, public sector unions have the ability to elect whom they want and punish those who do not support them. Keep in mind that these beneficiaries of union support are the same individuals who ultimately decide on the compensation for public employees. As a result, negotiations with unions in the public sector have an inherent bias toward higher salaries, more generous benefits, and more inflexible work rules. The Little Hoover Commission (2011) put it this way: "The ability or willingness of elected officials to hold the line on their own is in serious doubt" (iv).

Additionally, public managers often benefit from the very contracts that they negotiate. At the very least, they do not have as much to lose by not engaging in tough negotiations. Unlike their counterparts in the private sector, government unions are largely free from market discipline. There is no profit incentive to keep costs down, so most labor relations managers learn quickly that the conflict and discourse that often accompany negotiations can be avoided by not fighting or being tough. Without that profit incentive, there is, in the public sector, a tendency for managers to give greater concessions. Those concessions are primarily in nonpay areas (work rules and benefits) in which the public and the press are not nearly as likely to notice and create an uproar. Additionally, elected officials are prone to pressure negotiators to make peace with unions and grant favorable contracts.

In order to address the inherent conflict, either a separate citizen-appointed board should negotiate collective bargaining agreements on behalf of the public employer (subject to the elected official's ratifications and adoption), or citizens should be made part of the team of negotiators. Another clear way to avoid conflicts and unsustainable pensions and retiree health-care benefits that have been awarded is to require that any altering of benefits must be approved by voters. This system has actually been in place in the city of San Francisco for the past 100 years.

Pensions and Other Postemployment Benefits

Governmental estimates place the total state liability for pensions at more than $3 trillion with an unfunded liability of over $1 trillion. Other estimates suggest that the collective liability totals $4.43 trillion with unfunded liabilities approaching $3 trillion (Novy-Marx and Rauh 2011). It appears that many state and local government employees have been promised pensions that the public could not have afforded even had there been no Great Recession (Little Hoover Commission 2011), and that these unfunded liabilities could be the next "bubble" requiring a federal bailout. There is no question that many of the promises made to public employees are not sustainable. In the cities of Central Falls, Rhode Island, and Prichard, Alabama, the bubble did in fact burst. In Prichard, the city stopped paying retirees in 2009 after its pension fund ran out of money. The city of Central Falls is broke and headed for bankruptcy and they are asking retirees to agree to cutting existing pensions by 50 percent.

Legal protections and court decisions have been pretty clear that these promises cannot be withdrawn and that the best that can be done is to make changes for new employees. Serious consideration should be given by states to converting new employees currently on defined benefit (DB) plans to defined contribution plans or a hybrid model that would retain the defined benefit formula but at a lower rate, combined with an employer-matched 401(k)-style defined contribution plan. In order to minimize risks to the employee, hybrid plans much like the successful federal employee pension plans that retain a defined benefit plan at a lower level, while adding a defined contribution plan, as well as recently enacted plans in the state of Nebraska, Orange County, California, and the city of Atlanta, should be given serious consideration. These plans are similar to a defined contribution plan in that employees receive a payout upon retirement based on the actual money in their account; however, employees are guaranteed a certain level of annual investment return. Employees gain the benefit of a guaranteed return that is associated with the defined pensions model and the portability of moving the funds to another employer in the event that they change jobs.

In addition to the obvious benefits, moving employees to defined contribution or hybrid plans will significantly relieve the public employer of new, unsustainable debt in the future and will also be more in line with the reality of the new workforce. A huge problem with the defined benefit plan is its lack of portability and the fact that it contributes to employees staying with one employer no matter how unhappy or unproductive they are, or how much they desire to move. The characteristics of DB plans that result in a loss of pension wealth with job changes decreases mobility among workers. Increasingly, younger employees tend to move around from job to job, city to city, and state to state in search of new opportunities, promotions, and experiences. Defined contribution and hybrid plans allow for portability of their pension plans and would significantly change the culture of public institutions. They would allow for a more flexible workforce, infuse new ideas and talent into the work setting, boost prospects for older workers, and reduce the incentive to stay at one job for an entire career.

For those state and local governments deciding to keep defined benefit plans, there should be statewide moratoria on any new benefits until these are fully funded and/or mandating that all changes be fully funded upon inception. For current employees under existing DB plans, increased employee contributions for both retirement and OPEB will be needed to curtail risings costs. Curtailing abuses that allow spiking, narrowing the eligibility for public safety benefits to select groups, use of overtime for retiree calculations, and prohibiting any surpluses from going to the retiree area are just a few of the more immediate actions that can be implemented. Creating a two-tiered system for all new hires under DB plans should first and foremost focus on increasing the age for retirement and place penalties on those retiring before the official pension age. Longer vesting periods, scaled-back benefits, and use of actual inflation rates instead of automatic cost-of-living increases for pensions should be part of these new plans. "Golden handshake" agreements that provide extra service credit to retire early should be banned. Despite statements to the contrary by public agencies, these agreements seldom achieve any cost savings.

There also needs to be legislation requiring states to fully fund their obligations, both for pensions and OPEB. As previously documented, states and local governments have often failed to make their required payments and, thus, have exacerbated the problem and increased the debt. While most states have done a better job at funding their pension obligations (about 85 percent of the total bill), little has been set aside for retiree health care and other postemployment benefits. Ideally, state and local governments should fund retiree health-care benefits as they are earned. This would reduce the amount owed and increase intergenerational equity by not passing the costs on to further generations. However, since most states have not properly funded retiree health care, there is a good deal of catching up that will be required. On average, the annual contribution to pay for these costs is about three times what states currently pay each year for current retirees (The Pew Center on the States 2007).

As previously mentioned, fully funding these obligations will compete with contributions for pension obligations that are already consuming large parts of available funding and place greater demands for higher taxes, making less money available for education, health care, public safety, and other essential services. Statewide legislation should also be considered mandating that any increases be fully funded. Further, retirement boards and commissions overseeing state and local pension plans need to be restructured so that these boards have a majority, or at least a healthy minority, of independent members to ensure more objectivity and accountability.

State and local governments need more options. There seems to be a good deal of confusion about the legislature's role over pension policy, and the assumption that any changes must be negotiated through collective bargaining. In many instances, state laws can be amended to change how pensions are designed. In some cases, elected officials have chosen to skirt their responsibilities to make tough decisions on pensions for fear of retribution from powerful public sector unions. This lack of action confuses the lawmaking process with the bargaining process. State and local governments need to have the authority to restructure their pension and retiree health-care programs for their employees. In order for this to occur, the legislature needs to pass laws giving them explicit authority. Parameters must be set for some of the practices that are not in the public interest and that deal with the most expensive public sector employee benefits, specifically health insurance and pensions. Although it is important to maintain quality plans that will attract and retain quality employees, it is fiscally necessary to eliminate unsustainable excesses unheard of in the private sector. Because many states and local governments are in such financial straits with their pensions and retiree health-care benefits, it may be necessary for legislative bodies to allow for referenda to be presented to the public for a vote to approve increases to retiree benefits. As stated earlier, urgent action is needed to avoid a financial meltdown and to keep these obligations from consuming larger and larger portions of state and local government revenues.

Civil Service Reform

It has been widely acknowledged that the civil service system was established to combat abuses associated with the spoils system; however, it has now become the problem instead of the solution. The system places too much emphasis on security and longevity and not enough on performance. It has difficulty rewarding competence, quality, and entrepreneurial thinking. A system that grants salary increases according to seniority rather than performance or merit, and that makes raises and promotions appear automatic, also breeds mediocrity, complacency, and inefficiency. Legislation is needed to empower state and local governments to radically alter their civil service system.

Serious consideration should be given to converting state and local governmental employees to at-will employment. Several states have done this and the fears of returning to the spoils system have not materialized. While the return to at-will employment in some jurisdictions has clearly not been the panacea for all the ills associated with public employment, it has opened the door for more flexibility and responsiveness to citizens. Strong whistleblower protections, coupled with the protection of employees against partisan political coercion, can be codified in state law. Statewide reforms need to be mandated at the state level to empower state and local governments to position themselves in ways that will increase accountability, promote effective and efficient delivery of services, and encourage innovative and entrepreneurial thinking. Prohibiting seniority and bumping rights would also go a long way toward accomplishing this. Mandating performance-based pay and bonuses would change the organizational culture of many public agencies. Additionally, partnering with the nonprofit and private sectors to create new institutional arrangements for cross-boundary/cross-jurisdictional work would be of enormous benefit.

Collective Bargaining

Public sector unions are different than their private sector counterparts. Suggesting that they be treated differently does not constitute an attack of anti-unionism. Collective bargaining is often needed in the public sector to equalize power, but it is important not to ignore the fact that public employees already have much of this equality because of built-in civil service protections. This does not necessarily mean we should overreact, as Wisconsin has, by effectively wiping out public sector bargaining. However, as with many special interest groups, the focus of public sector unions is not always in the best interest of the public. While most states already prohibit strikes by public sector employees, the public interest demands that public employees not under strike any circumstances, in either essential or nonessential services.

Further, compulsory public sector bargaining laws give powers and privileges to unions at the expense of the rights of individual public employees. Forcing workers to enroll in a union and pay dues, and using these funds for political means, is contrary to individual rights and to the public interest. The notion that we should gloss over conflicts of interest or practices that do not serve the public interest because we need public sector unions as a counteroffensive to big corporations is the wrong kind of debate. The public interest is not served by spending large sums of money to influence elections and alter public policy. Further, the fight against the influence of big business, other special interests, and wealthy individuals, should not be carried out at the expense of public employment and the ability of public employees to deliver governmental services to citizens.

Appendix 1
Comparative Analysis of Compensation Levels

Hypothetical Public and Private Sector Employees: Janitors and Cleaners (Baseline Assumptions)

	Private Sector Employee	Regular Public Sector Employee	Notes
Employee's starting salary in 2008	$15,487	$20,645	See the U.S. Bureau of Labor Statistics, Occupational Employment and Wages, May 2009 (Private vs. State Employment), http://www.bls.gov/oes/2009/may/oes372011.htm. Note: starting salary is unknown. Using national average, and adjusted for bottom 10 percentile.
Annual rate of inflation (CPI—all urban)	3.05%	3.05%	See the U.S. Bureau of Labor, Consumer Price Index for All Urban Consumers (Table H).
Average collectively bargained COLA	0.00%	0.50%	Based on historical COLA.
Step increases			
Step 1	4.00%	5.00%	Hypothetical increases, 5% over 8 years generally assumed. Nine years for public safety.
Step 2	4.00%	5.00%	
Step 3	4.00%	5.00%	
Step 4	4.00%	5.00%	
Step 5	4.00%	5.00%	
Step 6	4.00%	5.00%	
Step 7	4.00%	5.00%	
Step 8	4.00%	5.00%	
Step 9	0.00%	0.00%	
Step 10	0.00%	0.00%	
Step 11	0.00%	0.00%	
Step 12	0.00%	0.00%	
Step 13	0.00%	0.00%	
Step 14	0.00%	0.00%	
Step 15	0.00%	0.00%	
Are step and inflation increases additive?	Y	Y	

Longevity

Is the employee eligible for longevity pay?		N	N
When does longevity pay begin?		Year 8	Year 8
What is the longevity base pay rate?		3.00%	2.00%

Note: Longevity has been eliminated in some jurisdictions. Other models differ materially.
Note: Only 7% of public sector employees have access to longevity pay; see http://www.bls.gov/ncs/ebs/benefits/2010/ownership/govt/table27a.pdf (table 41).
NV offers longevity pay or "nonproduction bonuses."

What is the longevity incremental pay rate?	0.50%	0.50%	
Longevity pay scale			
Year 1	$—	$—	http://dop.nv.gov/emphand.pdf
Year 2	$—	$—	http://dop.nv.gov/emphand.pdf
Year 3	$—	$—	http://dop.nv.gov/emphand.pdf
Year 4	$—	$—	http://dop.nv.gov/emphand.pdf
Year 5	$—	$—	http://dop.nv.gov/emphand.pdf
Year 6	$—	$—	http://dop.nv.gov/emphand.pdf
Year 7	$—	$—	http://dop.nv.gov/emphand.pdf
Year 8	$—	$—	http://dop.nv.gov/emphand.pdf
Year 9	$—	$—	http://dop.nv.gov/emphand.pdf
Year 10	$—	$—	http://dop.nv.gov/emphand.pdf
Year 11	$—	$—	http://dop.nv.gov/emphand.pdf
Year 12	$—	$—	http://dop.nv.gov/emphand.pdf
Year 13	$—	$—	http://dop.nv.gov/emphand.pdf
Year 14	$—	$—	http://dop.nv.gov/emphand.pdf
Year 15	$—	$—	http://dop.nv.gov/emphand.pdf
Year 16	$—	$—	http://dop.nv.gov/emphand.pdf
Year 17	$—	$—	http://dop.nv.gov/emphand.pdf
Year 18	$—	$—	http://dop.nv.gov/emphand.pdf
Year 19	$—	$—	http://dop.nv.gov/emphand.pdf
Year 20	$—	$—	http://dop.nv.gov/emphand.pdf
Year 21	$—	$—	http://dop.nv.gov/emphand.pdf
Year 22	$—	$—	http://dop.nv.gov/emphand.pdf
Year 23	$—	$—	http://dop.nv.gov/emphand.pdf
Year 24	$—	$—	http://dop.nv.gov/emphand.pdf
Year 25	$—	$—	http://dop.nv.gov/emphand.pdf
Year 26	$—	$—	http://dop.nv.gov/emphand.pdf

	Private Sector Employee	Regular Public Sector Employee	None
Year 27	$—	$—	http://dop.nv.gov/emphand.pdf
Year 28	$—	$—	http://dop.nv.gov/emphand.pdf
Year 29	$—	$—	http://dop.nv.gov/emphand.pdf
Year 30	$—	$—	http://dop.nv.gov/emphand.pdf
Year 31	$—	$—	http://dop.nv.gov/emphand.pdf
Year 32	$—	$—	http://dop.nv.gov/emphand.pdf
Year 33	$—	$—	http://dop.nv.gov/emphand.pdf
Year 34	$—	$—	http://dop.nv.gov/emphand.pdf
Year 35	$—	$—	http://dop.nv.gov/emphand.pdf
Year 36	$—	$—	http://dop.nv.gov/emphand.pdf
Year 37	$—	$—	http://dop.nv.gov/emphand.pdf
Year 38	$—	$—	http://dop.nv.gov/emphand.pdf
Year 39	$—	$—	http://dop.nv.gov/emphand.pdf
Year 40	$—	$—	http://dop.nv.gov/emphand.pdf

Social Security

	Y	N	
Does the worker participate in Social Security?			
What is the employer's Social Security contribution?	6.20%	6.20%	Social Security Administration, http://ssa-custhelp.ssa.gov/cgi-bin/ssa.cfg/php/enduser/std_adp.php?p_faqid=240&p_created=956850562.
What is the employee's Social Security contribution?	4.20%	4.20%	Social Security Administration, http://ssa-custhelp.ssa.gov/cgi-bin/ssa.cfg/php/enduser/std_adp.php?p_faqid=240&p_created=956850562.
What is the maximum earnings limit for Social Security?	$106,800	$106,800	Social Security Administration, http://ssa-custhelp.ssa.gov/cgi-bin/ssa.cfg/php/enduser/std_adp.php?p_faqid=240&p_created=956850562.
At what age can the employee begin to receive Social Security payments?	Age 66	Age 66	Social Security Administration, http://ssa-custhelp.ssa.gov/cgi-bin/ssa.cfg/php/enduser/std_adp.php?p_faqid=240&p_created=956850562.
What is the anticipated Social Security payment at retirement?	$9,077	$10,387	Use retirement benefits calculator to adjust each time, http://www.ssa.gov/retire2/AnypiaApplet.html.

139

Individual retirement account assumptions (401k)

Does the employer offer a 401(k) program?	Y	N	See http://www.401khelpcenter.com/benchmarking.html.
What share of the employee's income in contributed annually?	5.40%	5.40%	See http://www.401khelpcenter.com/benchmarking.html.
What is the amount of the employer match?	2.10%	2.10%	See Internal Revenue Service, http://www.irs.gov/faqs/faq-kw7.html.
What is the maximum 401(k) contribution amount?	$16,500	$16,500	See Internal Revenue Service, http://www.irs.gov/faqs/faq-kw7.html.
At what age can the employee draw against the account?	Age 60	Age 60	See Internal Revenue Service, http://www.irs.gov/faqs/faq-kw7.html. Actual age is 59 and 1/2 years of age.
What are the anticipated earnings on invested dollars?			
Years 1–10	7.0%	0.0%	General assumption.
Years 11–20	6.0%	0.0%	General assumption.
Years 21–30	5.0%	0.0%	General assumption.
Years 30+ (Pre-retirement)	4.0%	0.0%	General assumption.
Years 30+ (Post-retirement)	3.5%	0.0%	General assumption.

Public employees retirement program

Does the employee participate in a Public Employees' Retirement System (PERS)?	N	Y	
What is the employer's contribution amount?	0.00%	9.00%	PERS. Note: Contributions that are additional, deferred, or in lieu of wages are not included above or reflected as employee contributions here.
What is the employee's contribution amount?	0.00%	4.60%	PERS. Note: Contributions that are additional, deferred, or in lieu of wages are not included above or reflected as employee contributions here.
Assumed employee benefit share based on 401(k)-like investment analysis?	Y	N	Note: Nevada PERS contribution by employee is 0%, while that of employer is 20.5%
Assumed average rate of return for PERS investments	0.00%	6.50%	Based on average. However, if IRR does not meet expectations to meet promised benefits, PERS can simply raise contribution rate on employee/employer or lower benefit factors for new employees.

	Private Sector Employee	Regular Public Sector Employee	None
Retirement assumptions			
At what age can the employee retire without penalty?	Age 60	Age 53	PERS. Reflects 30 years for regular employees and 25 years for fire and police employees.
Employee will retire with what percentage of the employee's final three salaries?	56%	71%	PERS. Maximum allowable. Each jurisdiction and occupation may differ. NV is 75%. 56% for systems that include SS and 71% for systems that do not include SS coverage.
Post-retirement health-care subsidy			
Does the employer provide a health-care subsidy?	N	Y	PERS. Reflects 30 years for regular employees and 25 years for fire and police employees.
What is the base year subsidy amount?	0	$7,980.00	
What is the expected rate of annual adjustment?	0	3.0%	
Estimated annual subsidy			
Year 1	$—	$7,980	
Year 2	$—	$8,219	
Year 3	$—	$8,466	
Year 4	$—	$8,720	
Year 5	$—	$8,982	
Year 6	$—	$9,251	
Year 7	$—	$9,529	
Year 8	$—	$9,814	
Year 9	$—	$10,109	
Year 10	$—	$10,412	
Year 11	$—	$10,724	
Year 12	$—	$11,046	
Year 13	$—	$11,378	
Year 14	$—	$11,719	
Year 15	$—	$12,070	
Year 16	$—	$12,433	

Year 17	$12,806
Year 18	$13,190
Year 19	$13,585
Year 20	$13,993
Year 21	$14,413
Year 22	$14,845
Year 23	$15,291
Year 24	$15,749
Year 25	$16,222
Year 26	$16,708
Year 27	$17,210
Year 28	$17,726
Year 29	$18,258
Year 30	$18,805
Year 31	$19,370
Year 32	$19,951
Year 33	$20,549
Year 34	$21,166
Year 35	$21,801
Year 36	$22,455
Year 37	$23,128
Year 38	$23,822
Year 39	$24,537
Year 40	$25,273
Year 41	$26,031
Year 42	$26,812
Year 43	$27,616
Year 44	$28,445
Year 45	$29,298
Year 46	$30,177
Year 47	$31,082
Year 48	$32,015

http://www.ebri.org/pdf/briefspdf/EBRI_IB_01-2010_No338_RetHlth1.pdf.

	Private Sector Employee	Regular Public Sector Employee	None
Year 49	$—	$32,975	
Year 50	$—	$33,965	
Year 51	$—	$34,984	
Year 52	$—	$36,033	
Year 53	$—	$37,114	
Year 54	$—	$38,227	
Year 55	$—	$39,374	

CPI: The consumer price index (CPI) is a measurement of the average change in prices of goods and services from one period to the next within a defined economic region. Verbatim from the Bureau of Labor Statistics, the definition states: The CPIs are based on prices of food, clothing, shelter, and fuels, transportation fares, charges for doctors' and dentists' services, drugs, and other goods and services that people buy for day-to-day living. Prices are collected each month in 87 urban areas across the country from about 4,000 housing units and approximately 26,000 retail establishments—department stores, supermarkets, hospitals, filling stations, and other types of stores and service establishments.

COLA: The cost of living adjustment (COLA) is an annual adjustment in wages or entitlements used to offset a beneficiary's purchasing power caused by inflation.

IRR: The internal rate of return (IRR) is a measurement of the return on an investment over a defined period of time.

Appendix 2
Comparative Analysis of Compensation Levels

Hypothetical Public and Private Sector Employees:
Civil Engineer (Baseline Assumptions)

144

	Private Sector Employee	Regular Public Sector Employee	Notes
Employee's starting salary in 2008	$53,151	$49,154	See the U.S. Bureau of Labor Statistics, Occupational Employment and Wages, May 2009 (Private vs. State Employment), http://www.bls.gov/oes/2009/may/oes172051.htm. Note: starting salary is unknown. Using national average, and adjusted for bottom 10th percentile.
Annual rate of inflation (CPI—all urban)	3.05%	3.05%	See the U.S. Bureau of Labor, Consumer Price Index for All Urban Consumers (Tab H).
Average collectively bargained COLA	0.00%	0.50%	Based on historical COLA.
Step Increases			
Step 1	4.00%	5.00%	Hypothetical increases, 5% over 8 years generally assumed. Nine years for public safety.
Step 2	4.00%	5.00%	
Step 3	4.00%	5.00%	
Step 4	4.00%	5.00%	
Step 5	4.00%	5.00%	
Step 6	4.00%	5.00%	
Step 7	4.00%	5.00%	
Step 8	4.00%	5.00%	
Step 9	0.00%	0.00%	
Step 10	0.00%	0.00%	
Step 11	0.00%	0.00%	
Step 12	0.00%	0.00%	
Step 13	0.00%	0.00%	
Step 14	0.00%	0.00%	
Step 15	0.00%	0.00%	
Are step and inflation increases additive?	Y	Y	
Longevity			
Is the employee eligible for longevity pay?	N	N	Note: Longevity has been eliminated in some jurisdictions.

When does longevity pay begin?		Year 8	Year 8
What is the longevity base pay rate?		3.00%	2.00%	Other models differ materially. Note: Only 7% of public sector employees have access to longevity pay. http://www.bls.gov/ncs/ebs/benefits/2010/ownership/govt/table27a.pdf (table 41).
What is the longevity incremental pay rate?		0.50%	0.50%	NV offers longevity pay or "nonproduction bonuses."
Longevity pay scale				
Year 1		$—	$—	http://dop.nv.gov/emphand.pdf
Year 2		$—	$—	http://dop.nv.gov/emphand.pdf
Year 3		$—	$—	http://dop.nv.gov/emphand.pdf
Year 4		$—	$—	http://dop.nv.gov/emphand.pdf
Year 5		$—	$—	http://dop.nv.gov/emphand.pdf
Year 6		$—	$—	http://dop.nv.gov/emphand.pdf
Year 7		$—	$—	http://dop.nv.gov/emphand.pdf
Year 8		$—	$—	http://dop.nv.gov/emphand.pdf
Year 9		$—	$—	http://dop.nv.gov/emphand.pdf
Year 10		$—	$—	http://dop.nv.gov/emphand.pdf
Year 11		$—	$—	http://dop.nv.gov/emphand.pdf
Year 12		$—	$—	http://dop.nv.gov/emphand.pdf
Year 13		$—	$—	http://dop.nv.gov/emphand.pdf
Year 14		$—	$—	http://dop.nv.gov/emphand.pdf
Year 15		$—	$—	http://dop.nv.gov/emphand.pdf
Year 16		$—	$—	http://dop.nv.gov/emphand.pdf
Year 17		$—	$—	http://dop.nv.gov/emphand.pdf
Year 18		$—	$—	http://dop.nv.gov/emphand.pdf
Year 19		$—	$—	http://dop.nv.gov/emphand.pdf
Year 20		$—	$—	http://dop.nv.gov/emphand.pdf
Year 21		$—	$—	http://dop.nv.gov/emphand.pdf
Year 22		$—	$—	http://dop.nv.gov/emphand.pdf
Year 23		$—	$—	http://dop.nv.gov/emphand.pdf
Year 24		$—	$—	http://dop.nv.gov/emphand.pdf
Year 25		$—	$—	http://dop.nv.gov/emphand.pdf
Year 26		$—	$—	http://dop.nv.gov/emphand.pdf

	Private Sector Employee	Regular Public Sector Employee	None
Year 27	$—	$—	http://dop.nv.gov/emphand.pdf
Year 28	$—	$—	http://dop.nv.gov/emphand.pdf
Year 29	$—	$—	http://dop.nv.gov/emphand.pdf
Year 30	$—	$—	http://dop.nv.gov/emphand.pdf
Year 31	$—	$—	http://dop.nv.gov/emphand.pdf
Year 32	$—	$—	http://dop.nv.gov/emphand.pdf
Year 33	$—	$—	http://dop.nv.gov/emphand.pdf
Year 34	$—	$—	http://dop.nv.gov/emphand.pdf
Year 35	$—	$—	http://dop.nv.gov/emphand.pdf
Year 36	$—	$—	http://dop.nv.gov/emphand.pdf
Year 37	$—	$—	http://dop.nv.gov/emphand.pdf
Year 38	$—	$—	http://dop.nv.gov/emphand.pdf
Year 39	$—	$—	http://dop.nv.gov/emphand.pdf
Year 40	$—	$—	http://dop.nv.gov/emphand.pdf
Social Security			
Does the worker participate in Social Security?	Y	N	
What is the employer's Social Security contribution?	6.20%	6.20%	Social Security Administration, http://ssa-custhelp.ssa.gov/cgi-bin/ssa.cfg/php/enduser/std_adp.php?p_faqid=240&p_created=956850562.
What is the employee's Social Security contribution?	4.20%	4.20%	Social Security Administration, http://ssa-custhelp.ssa.gov/cgi-bin/ssa.cfg/php/enduser/std_adp.php?p_faqid=240&p_created=956850562.
What is the maximum earnings limit for Social Security?	$106,800	$106,800	Social Security Administration, http://ssa-custhelp.ssa.gov/cgi-bin/ssa.cfg/php/enduser/std_adp.php?p_faqid=240&p_created=956850562.
At what age can the employee begin to receive Social Security payments?	Age 66	Age 66	Social Security Administration, http://ssa-custhelp.ssa.gov/cgi-bin/ssa.cfg/php/enduser/std_adp.php?p_faqid=240&p_created=956850562.
What is the anticipated social security payment at retirement?	$11,622	$11,622	Use retirement benefits calculator to adjust each time, http://www.ssa.gov/retire2/AnypiaApplet.html.
Individual retirement account assumptions (401k)			
Does the employer offer a 401(k) program?	Y	N	

What share of the employee's income in contributed annually?	5.40%	5.40%	See http://www.401khelpcenter.com/benchmarking.html.
What is the amount of the employer match?	2.10%	2.10%	See http://www.401khelpcenter.com/benchmarking.html.
What is the maximum 401(k) contribution amount?	$16,500	$16,500	See Internal Revenue Service, http://www.irs.gov/faqs/faq-kw7.html.
At what age can the employee draw against the account?	Age 60	Age 60	See Internal Revenue Service, http://www.irs.gov/faqs/faq-kw7.html. Actual age is 59 and 1/2 years of age.
What are the anticipated earnings on invested dollars?			
Years 1–10	7.0%	0.0%	General assumption.
Years 11–20	6.0%	0.0%	General assumption.
Years 21–30	5.0%	0.0%	General assumption.
Years 30+ (Pre-retirement)	4.0%	0.0%	General assumption.
Years 30+ (Post-retirement)	3.5%	0.0%	General assumption.
Does the employee participate in a Public Employees' Retirement System (PERS)?	N	Y	
What is the employer's contribution amount?	0.00%	9.00%	PERS. Note: Contributions that are additional, deferred, or in lieu of wages are not included above or reflected as employee contributions here.
What is the employee's contribution amount?	0.00%	4.60%	PERS. Note: Contributions that are additional, deferred, or in lieu of wages are not included above or reflected as employee contributions here.
Assumed employee benefit share based on 401(k)-like investment analysis?	Y	N	Note: Nevada PERS contribution by employee is 0%, while employer is 20.5%.
Assumed average rate of return for PERS investments	0.00%	6.50%	Based on average. However, if IRR does not meet expectations to meet promised benefits, PERS can simply raise contribution rate on employee/employer or lower benefit factors for new employees.

	Private Sector Employee	Regular Public Sector Employee	None
Retirement Assumptions			
At what age can the employee retire without penalty?	Age 60	Age 53	PERS. Reflects 30 years for regular employees and 25 years for fire and police employees.
Employee will retire with what percentage of the employee's final three salaries?	56%	71%	PERS. Maximum allowable. Each jurisdiction and occupation may differ. NV is 75%.
Post-retirement health-care subsidy			56% for systems that include SS and 71% for systems that do not include SS coverage.
Does the employer provide a health-care subsidy?	N	Y	PERS. Reflects 30 years for regular employees and 25 years for fire and police employees.
What is the base year subsidy amount?	$7,980.00	$7,980.00	
What is the expected rate of annual adjustment?	3.0%	3.0%	
Estimated annual subsidy			
Year 1	$—	$7,980	
Year 2	$—	$8,219	
Year 3	$—	$8,466	
Year 4	$—	$8,720	
Year 5	$—	$8,982	
Year 6	$—	$9,251	
Year 7	$—	$9,529	
Year 8	$—	$9,814	
Year 9	$—	$10,109	
Year 10	$—	$10,412	
Year 11	$—	$10,724	
Year 12	$—	$11,046	
Year 13	$—	$11,378	
Year 14	$—	$11,719	
Year 15	$—	$12,070	
Year 16	$—	$12,433	
Year 17	$—	$12,806	
Year 18	$—	$13,190	
Year 19	$—	$13,585	
Year 20	$—	$13,993	

Year	Amount
Year 21	$14,413
Year 22	$14,845
Year 23	$15,291
Year 24	$15,749
Year 25	$16,222
Year 26	$16,708
Year 27	$17,210
Year 28	$17,726
Year 29	$18,258
Year 30	$18,805
Year 31	$19,370
Year 32	$19,951
Year 33	$20,549
Year 34	$21,166
Year 35	$21,801
Year 36	$22,455
Year 37	$23,128
Year 38	$23,822
Year 39	$24,537
Year 40	$25,273
Year 41	$26,031
Year 42	$26,812
Year 43	$27,616
Year 44	$28,445
Year 45	$29,298
Year 46	$30,177
Year 47	$31,082
Year 48	$32,015
Year 49	$32,975
Year 50	$33,965
Year 51	$34,984
Year 52	$36,033
Year 53	$37,114
Year 54	$38,227
Year 55	$39,374

References

Adler, J. (2006). The past as prologue? A brief history of the labor movement in the United States. *Public Personnel Management*, 35(4), 311–329..

Agranoff, R., and M. McGuire. (2001). American federalism and the search for models of management. *Public Administration Review*, 61(6), 671–681.

Associated Press. (2008). Prison guards threaten "dismal" Schwarzenegger with recall. Fox News. September 8. www.foxnews.com/story/0,2933,419143,00.html (accessed June 1, 2011).

Ballenstedt, B.R. (2008). Pentagon drops plans to convert union employees to NSPS. *Government Executive*, September 30.

Barbash, J. (1984). Trade unionism from Roosevelt to Reagan. *Annals of the American Academy of Political and Social Science*, 473, 11–22.

Barro, Josh. (2011). Tools for better budgets: Options for state and local government to manage employee costs. Manhattan Institute for Policy Research, Issue Brief 9 (March). www.manhattan-institute.org/html/ib_09.htm (accessed July 11, 2011).

Belman, D., and J. Heywood. (2004). The structure of compensation in the public sector. *Public Finance Review*, 32 (6), 568–587.

Belman, D., J.S. Heywood, and J. Lund. (1997). Public sector earnings and the extent of unionization. *Industrial and Labor Relations Review*, 50, 610–628.

Bender, K.A. (2003). Examining equality between public- and private-sector wage distribution. *Economic Inquiry*, 41(1), 62–79.

Bender, K., and J. Heywood. (2010). Out of balance? Comparing public and private sector compensation over 20 years. Report, Center for State and Local Government Excellence, April.

Benecki, S. (1978). Municipal expenditure levels and collective bargaining. *Industrial Relations*, 27, 216–230.

Benner, K. (2009). The public pension bomb. *Fortune*, May 12. http://money.cnn.com/2009/05/12/news/economy/benner_pension.fortune/index.htm (accessed May 25, 2011).

Berry, J.M. (1989). Subgovernments, issue networker, and political conflict. In *Remaking American Politics*, ed. Richard A. Harris and Sidney M. Milkis. Boulder, CO: Westview Press.

Berry, S. (2011). American taxpayers are the new "Norma Raes." *Big Government*, March 2. http://biggovernment.com/sberry/2011/03/02/american-taxpayers-are-the-new-norma-raes/ (accessed March 30, 2011).

Biggs, A., and J. Richwine. (2011). Public-sector compensation: Correcting the economic policy institute, again. *Backgrounder* no. 2539 (March 31). www.heritage.org/Research/Reports/2011/03/Public-Sector-Compensation-Correcting-the-Economic-Policy-Institute-Again.

Blanchflower, D.A., and A. Bryson. (2004). What effect do unions have on wages now and would Freeman and Medoff be surprised? *Journal of Labor Research*, 25(3), 383–415.

Bloom, M. (2004). The ethics of compensation systems. *Journal of Business Ethics*, 52, 149–152.

Borjas, G.J. (2002). The wage structure and the sorting of workers in the public sector. NBER Working Paper no. 9313, October. Cambridge, MA: National Bureau of Economic Research.

Boyd, D.J. (2009). State/local employment up slightly since start of recession, but cuts are now under way. Fiscal Studies Report, August 20. The Nelson A. Rockefeller Institute of Government.

Brady, S. (2007). GASB 45 and other post-employment benefit promises: The fog is clearing. Policy Brief 07–7, September. New England Public Policy Center, Federal Reserve Bank of Boston. www.bos.frb.org/economic/neppc/briefs/2007/briefs077.pdf (accessed July 11, 2011).

Branden, B., and Hyland, S.L. (1993). Cost of employee compensation in public and private sectors. *Monthly Labor Review*, 116(5), 14.

Brinner, R.E., J. Brinner, M. Eckhouse, and M. Leahey. (2008). Fiscal realities for the state and local governments. *Business Economics*, 43(2), 55–63.

Brogan, D. (2011). NJBIA's Weekly Newsletter, July 1. www.njbia.org/news_cma_110701.asp (accessed July 5, 2011).

Brown, M.M., and J.L. Brudney. (1998). A "smarter, better, faster, and cheaper" government: Contracting and geographic information systems. *Public Administration Review*, 58(4), 335–345.

Browne, W.P. (1995). *Cultivating Congress: Constituents, Issues, and Interests in Agricultural Policymaking.* Lawrence: University Press of Kansas.

Bryson, A. (2001). Employee voice, workplace closure and employment growth. Research Discussion Paper no. 6. London: Policy Studies Institute.

Bureau of Economic Analysis. (2009). Employees rate bureau of economic analysis among top federal agencies. News release, U.S. Department of Commerce. www.bea.gov/newsreleases/general/oasnewsrelease.htm (accessed September 7, 2011).

Bureau of Labor Statistics (BLS). (2007). National compensation survey: Employee benefits in private industry in the United States, March 2007. Summary 07–05, August. www.bls.gov/ncs/ebs/sp/ebsm0006.pdf (accessed June 22, 2010).

———. (2008). National compensation survey: Retirement benefits in state and local governments in the United States, 2007. Summary 08–03, May. www.bls.gov/ncs/ebs/sp/ebsm0008.pdf (accessed June 22, 2010).

———. (2009a). Employer costs for employee compensation. News release, December 9. www.bls.gov/news.release/ecec.nr0.htm (accessed June 22, 2010).

———. (2009b). Occupational employment statistics, May 2009: 37-2011, Janitors and cleaners, except maids and house cleaners. www.bls.gov/oes/2009/may/oes372011.htm (accessed April 3, 2011).

———. (2009c). Engineers. In *Occupational Outlook Handbook*, 2010–11 ed. Washington, DC: U.S. Department of Labor. www.bls.gov/oco/pdf/ocos027.pdf (accessed April 3, 2011).

———. (2011a). Employee benefits in the United States—March 2011. News release, July 26. At www.bls.gov/news.release/pdf/ebs2.pdf (accessed September 19, 2011).

———. (2011b). Employment Cost Index—June 2011. News release, July 29. www.bls.gov/news.release/eci.nr0.htm (accessed October 12, 2011).

———. (2011c). Occupational Employment Statistics Query System. February 8. Washington DC, District of Columbia, United States.

———. (2011d). Table 1: Work stoppages involving 1,000 or more workers, 1947–2010. News release, February 8. www.bls.gov/news.release/wkstp.t01.htm (accessed July 7, 2011).

———. (2011e). Union members—2010. News release, January 21. www.bls.gov/news.release/pdf/union2.pdf (accessed October 12, 2011).

Burton, J. (1978). Public sector strikes: Legal, ethical, and practical considerations. Reprint series no. 448. Ithaca, NY: Cornell University, New York State School of Industrial and Labor Relations.

Bush, W.C., and A.T. Denzau. (1977). The voting behavior of bureaucrats and public sector growth. In *Budgets and Bureaucrats: The Sources of Government Growth*, ed. T.E. Borcherding, 90–99. Durham, NC: Duke University Press.

Butcher, D.R. (2011). What Americans Think of Labor Unions. *Industrial Market Trends*, March 1. http://news.thomasnet.com/IMT/archives/2011/03/what-americans-think-of-labor-unions-survey-findings.html (accessed March 30, 2011).

Clark, R.L., L.A. Craig, and J.W. Wilson. (2003). *A History of Public Sector Pensions in the United States.* Philadelphia: University of Pennsylvania Press.

Clark, R.L., and A.A. McDermed. (1990). *The Choice of Pension Plans in a Changing Regulatory Environment.* Washington, DC: AEI Press.

Clowes, M. (2004). Can public DB plans survive? *Pensions and Investments*, 32(20), 14–20.

Coggburn, J.D. (2006). At-will employment in government: Insights from the state of Texas. *Review of Public Personnel Administration*, 26(2), 158–177.

Coggburn, J.D., and R.C. Kearney. (2010). Trouble keeping promises? An analysis of underfunding in state retirement benefits. *Public Administration Review*, 70(1), 97–108.

Condrey, S.E. (2002). Reinventing state civil service systems: The Georgia experiment. *Review of Public Personnel Administration*, 22(2), 114–124.

Cooper, M. (2009). Government jobs have grown since recession's start, study finds. *New York Times*, August 20, A15.

Cooper, M., and M.W. Walsh. (2010). Mounting debts by states stoke fears of crisis. *New York Times*, December 5, A1.

CQ Researcher. (2006). Pension crisis: Are traditional pensions becoming obsolete? *CQ Research*, 16(7), 145–168.

Craig, L.A. (2010). Public sector pensions in the United States. EH.net, February 1. http://eh.net/encyclopedia/article/craig.pensions.public.us (accessed March 12, 2011).

Crane, D.G. (2011). Should public employees have collective bargaining? SFGate.com, February 27. http://articles.sfgate.com/2011-02-27/opinion/28635623_1_public-sector-private-sector-unions (accessed March 30, 2011).

Denhardt, R.B., and J.V. Denhardt. (2006). *Public Administration: An Action Orientation* (5th ed.). Belmont, CA: Thompson Wadsworth.

Denholm, D.Y. (2001). The case against public sector unionism and collective bargaining. Public Service Research Foundation, Vienna, VA. http://www.psrf.org/gur/caps.jsp.

Dray, P. (2011). Putting Wisconsin's union battle in historical context. *Fresh Air*

(NPR), March 8. www.npr.org/2011/03/08/134337221/putting-wisconsins-union-battle-in-historical-context (accessed March 30, 2011).

Duhigg, C. (2011). Public unions take on boss to win big pensions. *New York Times*, June 22, A1.

The Economist. (2004). Murk in the gloom. *The Economist*, October 30, 77–78.

———. (2009). Welcome to the real world. *The Economist*, December 10. www.economist.com/node/15065693.

———. (2010). Three-trillion-dollar hole. *The Economist*, October 14. www.economist.com/node/17251840.

———. (2011a). (Government) workers of the world unite! *The Economist*, January 6. www.economist.com/node/17849199.

———. (2011b). 70 or bust. *The Economist*, April 9–15, 13.

———. (2011c). Blood on the table, money in the bank. *The Economist*, July 7. www.economist.com/node/18928863?story_id=18928863&fsrc=rss (accessed September 7, 2011).

Edwards, C. (2010). Public sector unions and the rising costs of employee compensation. *Cato Journal*, 30(1), 87–115.

Elling, R.C., and T.L. Thompson. (2006). Human resource problems and state management performance across two decades: The implications for civil service reform. *Review of Public Personnel Administration*, 26(4), 302–334.

Farber, H.S. (1987). The recent decline of unionization in the United States. *Science*, 238, 915–920.

———. 2005. Nonunion wages and threat of unionization. *Industrial and Labor Relations Rewiew* 58(3), 335–352.

Fender, J. (2008). Vote unionizes state labor. *Denver Post*, June 12. www.denverpost.com/commented/ci_9556821?source=commented-news (accessed March 5, 2010).

Ferris, F., and A.C. Hyde. (2004). Federal labor-management relations for the next century—or the last? The case of the Department of Homeland Security. *Review of Public Personnel Administration*, 24, 216–233.

Flaccus, G. (2011). Most full-time Newport Beach lifeguard earn well over $100,000 per year. *Daily News*: Los Angeles, May 20. http://www.dailynews.com/politics/ci_18104856 (accessed December 16, 2011).

Fleet, S.H. (2007). Words of wisdom: Don't just stand there—do something! *Employee Benefit Plan Review*, August, 18–20.

Foster, K. (2000). Regionalism on purpose. Report, September. Cambridge: Lincoln Institute for Land Policy.

Frahm, K., and L. Martin. (2009). From government to governance: Implications for social work administration. *Administration in Social Work*, 33(2), 407–422.

Frederickson, H.G., and K.B. Smith. (2003). *The Public Administration Theory Primer*. Boulder, CO: Westview Press.

Freeman, R. (1986). Unionism comes to the public sector. *Journal of Economic Literature*, 24, 410–431.

Freeman, R., and J. Medoff. (1984). *What Do Unions Do?* New York: Basic Books.

Froomkin, D. (2011). Supreme Court strikes down Arizona law but leaves public financing intact. *Huffington Post*, June 27. www.huffingtonpost.com/2011/06/27/supreme-court-mccomish-bennett-arizona-public-financing_n_885200.html (accessed June 29, 2011).

Ginsberg, T., and L. Horwitz. (2009). Quiet no more; Philadelphia confronts the cost

of employee benefits. Report, June. The Philadelphia Research Initiative at The Pew Charitable Trusts.
Goldsmith, S., and W.D. Eggers. (2004). *Governing by Network: The New Shape of the Public Sector.* Washington, DC: Brookings Institution Press.
Gramlich, E., and D.L. Rubinfeld. (1982). Micro-estimates of public spending demand functions and tests of the tie bout and median voter hypotheses. *Journal of Political Economy,* 90, 536–560.
Greenhouse, S. (2007). Child care workers in New York City vote to unionize. *New York Times,* October 24. www.nytimes.com/2007/10/24/nyregion/24childcare.html (accessed September 26, 2011).
Greenhouse, S. (2011). Ohio's Anti-Union Law Is Tougher Than Wisconsin's. *New York Times,* March 31. www.nytimes.com/2011/04/01/us/01ohio.html. (accessed December 15, 2011).
Greenhut, S. (2009). *Plunder! How Public Employee Unions Are Raiding Treasuries, Controlling Our Lives, and Bankrupting the Nation.* Santa Ana, CA: Forum Press.
Greenspan, A., and J. Kennedy. (2007). Sources and uses of equity extracted from homes. Finance and Economics Discussion Paper 2007-20. Division of Research and Statistics and Monetary Affairs, Federal Reserve Board. www.federalreserve.gov/pubs/feds/2007/200720/200720pap.pdf (accessed July 5, 2011).
Gupta, N. (1997). Rewarding skills in the public sector. In *New Strategies for Public Pay: Rethinking Government Compensation Programs,* ed. H. Risher and C. Fay, 207–230. San Francisco, CA: Jossey-Bass.
Gustafson, C. (2012). Pension election rhetoric to ramp up. UT San Diego, January 8. http://www.utsandiego.com/news12012/Jan108/pension-election-rhetoric-to-ramp-up/?print&page=all (accessed January 8, 2012).
Heclo, H. (1978). Issue networks and the executive establishment. In *The New American Political System,* ed. Anthony King, 87–124. Washington, DC: AEI Press.
Heinrich, C.J., C.J. Hill, and L.E. Lynn, Jr. (2004). Governance as an organizing theme for empirical research. In *The Art of Governance: Analyzing Management and Administration,* ed. P.W. Ingraham and L.E. Lynn Jr., 3–19. Washington, DC: Georgetown University Press.
Herbert, B. (1995). In America; Whitman steals the future. *New York Times,* February 22. www.nytimes.com/1995/02/22/opinion/in-america-whitman-steals-the-future.html (accessed May 25, 2011).
Hindman, H.D., and D.B. Patton. (1994). Unionism in state and local governments: Ohio and Illinois, 1982–87. *Industrial Relations,* 33(1), 106–120.
Hirsch, B., and D. Macpherson. (2011). Union membership and coverage database. http://unionstats.gsu.edu (accessed September 7, 2011).
Honeycutt, J. (2007). The influence of organized employees in North Carolina's twenty-five largest cities. *Popular Government* (Fall), 26–29.
Horwitz, L. (2009). Layoffs, furloughs, and union concessions: The prolonged and painful process of balancing city budgets. Report, September 22. The Philadelphia Research Initiative at The Pew Charitable Trusts.
Hunter, W.J., and C.H. Rankin. (1988). The composition of public sector compensation: The effects of unionization and bureaucratic size. *Journal of Labor Research,* 9 (Winter), 29–42.
Hurd, R., and S. Pinnock. (2004). Public sector unions: Will they thrive or struggle to survive? *Journal of Labor Research,* 25(2), 211–221.

Husch, B., L. Cummings, S. Mazer, and B. Sigritz (eds.). (2011). The fiscal survey of states. Report, Spring. National Governors' Association and the National Association of State Budget Officers. www.nga.org/files/live/sites/NGA/files/pdf/FSS1106.PDF (accessed July 11, 2011).

Ichniowski, C. (1988). Public sector union growth and bargaining laws: A proportional hazards approach with time-varying treatments. In *When Public Sectors Workers unionize*, ed. R.B. Freeman and C. Ichniowski, 19–40. Chicago: University of Chicago Press.

Ingraham, P.W. (1995). *The Foundation of Merit: Public Service in American Democracy.* Baltimore, MD: Johns Hopkins University Press.

Johnson, C.M. (1992). *The Dynamics of Conflict Between Bureaucrats and Legislators.* Armonk, NY: M.E. Sharpe.

Johnson, R. (1997). Pension underfunding and liberal retirement benefits among state and local government workers. *National Tax Journal*, 50(1), 113–142.

Johnston, A., and B. Hancke. (2009). Wage inflation and labour unions in EMU. *Journal of European Public Policy*, 16(4), 601–622.

Kearney, R. (2003). The determinants of state employee compensation. *Review of Public Personnel Administration*, 23, 305–322.

———. (2009). *Labor Relations in the Public Sector* (4th ed.). Boca Raton, FL: CRC Press.

Kearney, R., and D. Carnevale. (2001). *Labor Relations in the Public Sector.* New York: Marcel Dekker.

Keefe, J. H. 2010. Are Wisconsin Public Employees Over-Compensated? Economic Policy Institute Briefing Paper, September. Washington, DC: Economic Policy Institute.

Kellough, J.E., and L.G. Nigro. (2002). Pay for performance in Georgia state government: Employee perspectives on Georgia gain after 5 years. *Review of Public Personnel Administration*, 22(2), 146–166.

Kettl, D.F. (2000). The transformation of governance: Globalization, devolution, and the role of government. *Public Administration Review*, 60(6), 488–497.

Klinger, D.E. (2006). Societal values and civil service systems in the United States. In *Civil Service Reform in the States: Personnel Policy and Politics at the Subnational Level*, ed. J.E. Kellough and L.G. Nigro, 11–32. Albany: State University of New York Press.

Kramer, L. (1962). *Labor's Paradox: The American Federation of State, County and Municipal Employees, AFL-CIO.* New York: Wiley.

Kramer, O.S. (2010). How to cheat a retirement fund. *New York Times*, September 11, A19.

Kroncke, C.O., and J.E. Long. (1998). Pay comparability in state governments. *Journal of Labor Research*, 19(2), 321–385.

Krueger, A.B. (1988). The determinants of queues for federal jobs. *Industrial and Labor Relations Review*, 41(4), 567–581.

Laslo, D., and D. Judd. (2006). Building civic capacity through an elastic local state: The case of St. Louis. *Review of Policy Research*, 23(6), 1235–1255.

Lasseter, R.W. (2002). Georgia's merit system reform 1996–2001: An operating agency's perspective. *Review of Public Personnel Administration*, 22(2), 125–132.

Lawler III, E.E. (2000). Pay strategy: New thinking for the new millennium. *Compensation and Benefits Review*, 32, 7–12.

Lee, R.D. (1979). *Public Personnel Systems*. Sudbury, MA: Jones and Bartlett Learning.

Leonard, J. (1992). Unions and employment growth. *Industrial Relations*, 31 (Winter), 80–92.

Lewin, D., T.A. Kochan, J. Cutcher-Gershenfeld, T. Ghilarducci, H. Katz, J. Keefe, D.J.B. Mitchell, C.A. Olson, S.A. Rubinstein, and C.E. Weller. (2011). Getting it right: Empirical evidence and policy implications from research on public-sector unionism and collective bargaining. Social Science Research Network, March 16. http://ssrn.com/abstract=1792942 (accessed March 30, 2011).

Lewis, G.B., and C.S. Galloway. (2011). A national analysis of public/private wage differentials at the state and local levels by race and gender. Working paper, February 10–11. Andrew Young Scool of Public Studies Research Papers.

Lieb, D.A. (2007). MO: Bargain rights for public employees. *Forbes*, May 30, 1–4.

Lind, M. (2011). Liberalism and the post-union future. *Salon*, February 22. http://politics.salon.com/2011/02/22/lind_unions_wisconsin/ (accessed March 30, 2011).

Linneman, P.D., and M.L. Wachter. (1990). The economics of federal compensation. *Industrial Relations*, 29 (Winter), 58–74.

Little Hoover Commission. (2011). Public pensions for retirement security. Report no. 204, February. www.lhc.ca.gov/studies/204/report204.html (accessed July 11, 2011).

Llorens, J. (2008). Uncovering the determinants of competitive state government wages. *Review of Public Personnel Administration*, 28(4), 208–326.

Lowenstein, R. (2005). The end of pensions. *New York Times Sunday Magazine*, October 30. www.nytimes.com/2005/10/30/magazine/30pensions.html (accessed March 15, 2011).

Luger, M. (2007). The role of local government in contemporary economic development. Lincoln Institute of Land Policy Working Paper. www.lincolninst.edu/pubs/dl/1254_Luger%20Final.pdf (accessed September 7, 2011).

Luo, M., and M. Cooper. (2011). Who's paid more? Experts can disagree. *New York Times*, February 26, A12. www.nytimes.com/2011/02/26/us/26salariesbox.html?scp=1&sq=Who%92s%20paid%20more?%20Experts%20can%20disagree&st=cse (accessed March 30, 2011).

Lyons, D. (2011). Bill Gates and Randi Weingarten: Can the billionaire philanthropist and the president of the American Federation of Teachers find common ground—and fix our nation's education system? *Newsweek*, January 3, 52–55.

Malanga, S. (2010). The beholden state: How public-sector unions broke California. *City Journal*, Spring. www.city-journal.org/printable.php?id=6086 (accessed September 7, 2011).

Maranto, R., and D. Schultz. (1991). *A Short History of the United States Civil Service*. Lanham, MD: University Press of America.

Mareschal, P.M. (2006). Innovation and adaptation: Contrasting efforts to organize home care workers in four states. *Labor Studies Journal*, 31 (Spring), 25–49.

Marin, B., and R. Mayntz. (1991). Introduction: Studying policy networks. In *Policy Networks: Empirical Evidence and Theoretical Consideration*, ed. B. Marin and R. Mayntz, 191–124. Frankfurt am Main: Campus Verlag.

Marks, B.R., K.K. Raman, and E.R. Wilson. (1988). Toward understanding the determinants of pension underfunding in the public sector. *Journal of Accounting and Public Policy*, 7(3), 157–183.

Marlow, M.L., and W. Orzechowski. (1996). Public sector union and public spending. *Public Choice*, 89, 1–16.

McKethan, A., D. Gitterman, A. Freezor, and A. Enthoven. (2006). New directions for public health care purchasers? Responses to looming challenges. *Health Affairs*, 25(6), 1518–1528.

McNichol, E., P. Oliff, and N. Johnson. (2011). States continue to feel recession's impact. Report, June 17. Center on Budget and Policy Priorities. www.cbpp.org/files/9-8-08sfp.pdf (accessed July 5, 2011).

Miller, G. (2010). Out of balance, or out of proportion? A new look at whether public employees are overpaid. *Governing*, May 6. www.governing.com/columns/public-money/Out-of-Balance-or.html (accessed September 7, 2011).

Miller, M.A. (1996). The public-private debate: What do the data show? *Monthly Labor Review*, 119(5), 18–29.

Mintzberg, H. (2004). *Managers, not MBAs: A Hard Look at the Soft Practice of Managing and Management Development.* San Francisco, CA: Berrett-Koehler.

Mitchell, O.S., and R.S. Smith. (1994). Pension funding in the public sector. *Review of Economics and Statistics*, 76(2), 278–290.

Moore, W.J., and J. Raisin. (1991). Government wage differentials revisited. *Journal of Labor Research*, 12(1), 12–33.

Morriss, A.P. (2001). Returning justice to its private roots. *University of Chicago Law Review*, 68(2), 551–78.

Munnell, A. (2005). Mandatory Social Security coverage of state and local government workers: A perennial hot button. CRR Issue in Brief No. 32. Boston, MA: Center for Retirement Research and Boston College.

Munnell, A., J. Aubry, J. Hurwitz, and L. Quinby. (2011). Unions and public pension benefits. Issue brief, July. Washington, DC: Center for State and Local Excellence.

Nalbandian, J., and C. Nalbandian. (2003). Contemporary challenges in local government. *National Civic Review*, 92(1), 83–91.

National Association of State Budget Officers (NASBO). (2007). State Expenditure Reports. http://nasbo.org/Publications/StateExpenditureReport/StateExpenditureReportArc hives/tabid/107/Default.aspx (accessed July 11, 2011).

———. (2010). State Expenditure Report 2009. December. http://nasbo.org/Publications/StateExpenditureReport/tabid/79/Default.aspx (accessed July 5, 2011).

———. (2011). State Expenditure Report 2010. December. http://nasbo.org/Publications/FiscalSurvey/tabid/65/Default.aspx (accessed July 5, 2011).

National Conference of State Legislatures. (2011). State Budget Update: March 2011. Report, April 19. www.ncsl.org/documents/fiscal/marchSBU2011freeversion.pdf (accessed July 20, 2011).

Neumann, J. (2010). State workers, long resistant, accept cuts in pension benefits. *Wall Street Journal,* June 29. http://blogs.cfed.org/cfed_news_clips/2010/06/state-workers-long-resistant-a.html (accessed December 23, 2011).

Nigro, L.G., and J.E. Kellough. (2008). Personnel reform in the states: A look at progress fifteen years after the Winter Commission. *Public Administration Review*, 68(s1), s50–s57.

Norcross, E. (2010). Fiscal evasion in state budgeting. Mercatus Center Working Paper No. 10–39, July. George Mason University.

———. (2011). Public sector unionism: A review. Mercatus Center Working Paper No. 11–26, May. George Mason University.

Novy-Marx, R., and J. Rauh. (2011). Public pension promises: How big are they and what are they worth? *Journal of Finance*, 66(4), 1211–1249.

O'Brien, K. (1994). The impact of union political activities on public sector pay, employment, and budgets. *Industrial Relations*, 22(3), 322–345.

Olsen, K. (2011). Tennessee trumps Wisconsin: Kills teacher collective bargaining. Dead. Big Government. http://biggovernment.com/kolson/2011/06/05/tennessee-trumps-wisconsin-kills-teacher-collective-bargaining-dead/ (accessed March 30, 2011).

Osborne, D., and T. Gaebler. (1992). *Reinventing Government: How the Entrepreneurial Spirit Is Transforming the Public Sector.* Reading, MA: Addison-Wesley.

Osborne, D., and P. Hutchinson. (2004). *The Price of Government: Getting the Results in an Age of Permanent Fiscal Crisis.* New York: Basic Books.

Peng, J. (2004). Public pension funds and operating budgets: A tale of three states. *Public Budgeting and Finance*, 24(2), 59–73.

———. (2009). *State and Local Pension Fund Management.* Boca Raton, FL: CRC Press.

Pension Benefit Guaranty Corporation (PBGC). (2011). History of PBGC. www.pbgc.gov/about/who-we-are/pg/history-of-pbgc.html (accessed March, 12, 2011).

Perloff, J.M., and M.L. Wachter. (1984). Wage comparability in the U.S. Postal Service. *Industrial and Labor Relations Review*, 38, 26–35.

Perry, J.L., and N.D. Buckwalter. (2010). The public service of the future. *Public Administration Review*, 70(s1), s238–s245.

The Pew Center on the States. (2007). Promises with a price: Public sector retirement benefits. Report, December 17. Washington, DC: Pew Center on the States.

———. (2010). The trillion dollar gap: Underfunded state retirement systems and the roads to reform. Report, February. Washington, DC: Pew Center on the States.

Pew Research Center for the People and the Press. (2011). Labor unions seen as good for workers, not U.S. competitiveness. Survey Report, February 17. Washington, DC: Pew Research Center. http://people-press.org/2011/02/17/labor-unions-seen-as-good-for-workers-not-u-s-competitiveness/ (accessed March 30, 2011).

Picard, D. (2003). *Wage Watch: A Comparison of Public-Sector and Private-Sector Wages.* Report, May. Ontario, Canada: Canadian Federation of Independent Business.

Pollack, E. (2010). Local government job losses hurt entire economy. Economic Policy Institute Issue Brief No. 279, May 27. www.epi.org/page/-/pdf/issuebrief279.pdf (accessed July 21, 2011).

Preston, J. (1997). Not a bumper-sticker issue, but some folks are curious. *New York Times*, May 25. www.nytimes.com/1997/05/25/nyregion/not-a-bumper-sticker-issue-but-some- folks-are-curious.html (accessed May 25, 2011).

Reich, R. (2011). The Republicans' three-part strategy. *Business Insider*, February 17, 2011. www.businessinsider.com/the-republican-strategy-2011-2 (accessed March 30, 2011).

Rauh, J.D. (2010). Are state public pensions sustainable? Why the federal government should worry about state pension liabilities. Social Science Research Network, May 15. http://papers.ssrn.com/sol3/papers.cfm?abstract_id=1596679 (accessed September 7, 2011).

Reilly, T. (2007). Management in local governments. *Administration in Social Work*, 31(2), 49–66.

Reilly, T., S. Schoener, and A. Bolin. (2007). Public sector compensation in local governments: An analysis. *Review of Public Personnel Administration*, 27(1), 39–58.

Riccucci, N. (2007). The changing face of the public employee unionism. *Review of Public Personnel Administration*, 27(1), 71–78.

Richwine, J., and A. Biggs. (2011). Are California public employees overpaid? Heritage Foundation Center for Data Analysis, Report No. 11–01, March 17. www.heritage.org/Research/Reports/2011/03/Are-California-Public-Employees-Overpaid (accessed September 7, 2011).

Ripley, R.B., and G.A. Franklin. (1991). *Congress, the Bureaucracy and Public Policy* (5th ed.). Belmont, CA: Wadsworth.

Risher, H. (1997). The search for a new model for salary management: Is there support for private sector practices? *Public Personnel Management*, 26(4), 431–439.

Risher, H., and C.H. Fay. (1997). *New Strategies for Public Pay: Rethinking Government Compensation Programs*. San Francisco, CA: Jossey-Bass.

Risher, H., C.H. Fay, and J.L. Perry. (1997). Merit pay: Motivating and rewarding individual performance. In *New Strategies for Public Pay: Rethinking Government Compensation Programs*, ed. H. Risher and C. Fay, 207–230. San Francisco, CA: Jossey-Bass.

Rutten, T. (2011). A tipping point for labor in America. *Los Angeles Times*, February 19. http://articles.latimes.com/2011/feb/19/opinion/la-oe-0219-rutten-20110219 (accessed March 30, 2011).

Salamon, L.M. (2002). The new governance and the tools of public action: An introduction. In *The Tools of Government: A Guide to the New Governance*, ed. L.M. Salamon, 1–47. New York: Oxford University Press.

Sallant, C., and J. Gottlieb. (2010). If forced out, Bell city manager would be highest paid retiree in state's pension system. *Los Angeles Times*, July 21. http://latimesblogs.latimes.com/lanow/2010/07/if-forced-out-bell-city-manager-would-be-highestpaid-retiree-in-states-pension-system-.html (accessed September 7, 2011).

Sanders, J. (2008). Governor vetoes collective bargaining for child-care workers. *Sacramento Bee*, March 21. www.freerepublic.com/focus/f-news/1989439/posts (accessed December 23, 2011).

Schieber, S. (2003). Pensions in crisis. *Pensions*, 9(3), 212–226.

Schneider, M. (2005). The status of U.S. public pension plans. *Review of Public Personnel Administration*, 25(2), 107–137.

Selden, S.C. (2009). Personnel and human resource management in the states. In *Public Human Resource Management: Problems and Prospects* (5th ed.), ed. S.W. Hays, R.C. Kearney, and J.D. Coggburn, 46–63. New York: Pearson Longman.

Shafritz, J.M. (2004). *The Dictionary of Public Policy and Administration*. Boulder, CO: Westview Press.

Shafritz, J.M., E.W. Russell, and C.P. Borick. (2011). *Introducing Public Administration* (7th ed.). Boston, MA: Pearson Longman.

Shaw, L.C. (1972). The development of state and federal laws. In *Public Workers and Public Unions*, ed. S. Zagoria, 20–36. Englewood Cliffs, NJ: Prentice-Hall.

Shaw, L.C., and T. Clark Jr. (1972). Collective bargaining and politics in public employment. *UCLA Law Review*, 19 (August), 887–1051.

Sherk, J. (2010). The new face of the union movement: Government employees. *Backgrounder* 2458 (September 1). www.heritage.org/Research/Reports/2010/09/The-New-Face-of-the-Union-Movement-Government-Employees (accessed March 30, 2011).

———. (2011). Time to restore voter control: End the government-union monopoly. *Backgrounder* 2522 (February 25). www.heritage.org/Research/Reports/2011/02/Time-to-Restore-Voter-Control-End-the-Government-Union-Monopoly (accessed December 23, 2011).

Shlaes, A. (2010). How government unions became so powerful. *Wall Street Journal*, September 4. www.cfr.org/publication/22887/how_goverment_unions_became_so_powerful.html (accessed September 4, 2010).

Shubik, C., L. Horwitz, and T. Ginsberg. (2009). Tough decisions and limited options: How Philadelphia and other cities are balancing budgets in time of recession. Report, May 18. The Philadelphia Research Initiative at the Pew Charitable Trusts.

Slater, J.E. (2004). *Public Workers: Government Employee Unions, the Law, and the State, 1900–1962*. Ithaca, NY: Cornell University Press.

———. (1976). Pay differences between federal government and private sector workers. *Industrial and Labor Relations Review*, 29 (January), 14–15.

Smith, S.P. (1977). *Equal Pay in the Public Sector: Fact or Fantasy*. Princeton, NJ: Industrial Relations Section, Department of Economics, Princeton University.

Spero, S.D. (1948). *Government as Employer*. New York: Remsen Press.

Squier, L.W. (1912). *Old Age Dependency in the United States*. New York: Macmillan.

State of Connecticut. (2011). Summary of tax provisions contained in 2011 Conn. Pub. acts 6. Department of Revenue Services, June 10. www.ct.gov/drs/cwp/view.asp?A=1514&Q=480936 (accessed July 11, 2011).

Stoker, G. (1998). Governance as theory: Five propositions. *International Social Science Journal*, 50(1), 17–28.

Sullivan, J. (2011). Reasons why managers oppose public sector unions. March 7. www.ere.net/2011/03/07/reasons-why-managers-oppose-public-sector-unions/ (accessed September 7, 2011).

Sylvester, S., and P. Longman. (2011). The fallacy of union busting. *Washington Monthly*, May/June. www.washingtonmonthly.com/magazine/mayjune_2011 features/the-fallacy-of-union-busting029139.php (accessed June 21, 2011).

Thomas, P. (2007). The challenges of governance, leadership and accountability in public service. In *Managing Change in the Public Services*, ed. M. Wallace, M. Forting, and E. Shneller, 116–135. Malden, MA: Blackwell.

Thompson, D. (2006). Prison guards' union launches TV attack on Schwarzenegger reforms. *Contra Costa Times*, August 7. www.freerepublic.com/focus/f-news/1679657/posts (accessed June 1, 2011).

Thompson, F.J. (2007). The Winter Commission: Deregulation and public personnel administration. In *Public Personnel Administration and Labor Relations*, ed. N. Riccucci, 180–184. Armonk, NY: M.E. Sharpe.

Thompson, J., and J. Schmitt. (2010). The wage penalty for state and local government employees in New England. Working Paper No. 232, September. Center for Economic and Policy Research and Political Economy Research Institute, University of Massachusetts, Amherst.

Time. (1974). The press: Who decides fairness? *Time*, February 4. www.time.com/time/magazine/article/0,9171,908437-1,00.html (accessed May 20, 2011).

Tobias, R.M. (2004). The future of federal government labor relations and the mutual interest of Congress, the administration, and unions. *Journal of Labor Research*, 25, 19–41.

Troy, L. (1994). *The New Unionism in the New Society: Public Sector Unions in the Redistributive State*. Fairfax, VA: George Mason University Press.

———. (2003). Are municipal collective bargaining and municipal governance compatible? *University of Pennsylvania Journal of Labor and Employment Law*, 5(3), 453–485.
U.S. Census Bureau. (2011a). Housing vacancies and homeownership (CPS/HVS). www.census.gov/hhes/www/housing/hvs/historic/index.html (accessed July 5, 2011).
———. (2011b). Median and average sales prices of new homes sold in United States. www.census.gov/const/uspriceann.pdf (accessed July 5, 2011).
———. (2011c). Type of financing of new single-family houses completed. www.census.gov/const/C25Ann/sftotalfinance.pdf (accessed July 5, 2011).
U.S. Office of Personnel Management (OPM). (2003). Biography of an ideal: A history of the Federal Civil Service. Washington, DC: U.S. Government Printing Office.
Vallenta, R. (1989). The impact of unionism on municipal expenditures and revenues. *Industrial and Labor Relations Review*, 42, 430–442.
Van Dijk, J., and A. Winters-van Beek. (2009). The perspective of network government. In *ICTs, Citizens and Governance: After the Hype!* ed. A. Meijer, K. Boersma, and P. Wagenaar, 217–234. Amsterdam and Fairfax, VA: IOS Press.
Van Riper, P.P. (1958). *History of the United States Civil Service*. Evanston, IL: Row, Peterson.
Venti, S. (1987). Wages in the federal and private sectors. In *Public Sector Payrolls*, ed. D. Wise, 147–182. Chicago: University of Chicago Press.
Walsh, M.W. (2011). The burden of pensions on states. *New York Times*, March 10. www.nytimes.com/2011/03/11/business/11pension.html (accessed March 12, 2011).
Walsh, M.W., and A. Schoenfeld. (2010). Padded pensions add to New York fiscal woes. *New York Times*, May 21, A21.
Weiss, L., T. Phoenix, R. Davenport, and W. Eggers. (2008). Paying for tomorrow: Practical strategies for tackling the public pension crisis. Deloitte Research Study, December 13. www.deloitte.com/view/en_VE/ve/industries/ps/74680ef5c5efd110VgnVCM100000ba42f00aRCRD.htm (accessed September 7, 2011).
Wellington, H., and R.K. Winter. (1971). *The Unions and the Cities*. Washington, DC: Brookings Institution Press.
West, J.P. (2002). Georgia on the mind of radical civil service reformers. *Review of Public Personnel Administration*, 22(2), 79–93.
Whalen, C., and M.E. Guy. (2008). Broadbanding trends in the states. *Review of Public Personnel Administration*, 28(4), 349–366.
Wicks-Lim, J. (2009). Creating decent jobs in the United States: The role of labor unions and collective bargaining. Political Economy Research Institute, University of Massachusetts, Amherst (September). www.peri.umass.edu/fileadmin/pdf/published_study/PERI_Unions_DecentJobs_August09.pdf (accessed September 7, 2011).
Ye, L. (2009). Regional government and governance in China and the United States. *Public Administration Review*, 69(1), 116–121.
Yi, Song. (2010). Book review: *Pension Dumping*. *Monthly Labor Review*, 133(1), 78–79.
Zack, A.M. (1972). Impasses, strikes, and resolutions. In *Public Workers and Public Unions*, ed. S. Zagoria, s101–s121. Englewood Cliffs, NJ: Prentice-Hall.
Zax, J., and C. Ichniowski. (1988). The effects of public sector unionism on pay, employment, department budgets and municipal expenditures. In *When Public Sector Workers Unionize*, ed. R.B. Freeman and C. Ichniowski, 81–106. Chicago, IL: University of Chicago Press.

Index

Italic page references indicate charts and tables.

Across-the-board wage increases, 29–30
Adams, John, 19–20
Advisory Board of the Civil Service (later named Civil Service Commission), 21–23, 25
AFGE, 49
AFL, 146
AFL-CIO, 51, 66, 69
AFSCME, 49, 53, 56, 69
AFSCME, Local 201 v. City of Muskegon (1963), 49
AFT, 49, 56, 69
Agency capture, 81
Aguirre, Michael, 120
Alabama, 17, 53, 131
American Express Corporation, 105
American Federation of Government Employees (AFGE), 49
American Federation of Labor (AFL), 46
American Federation of Labor and Congress of Industry Organizations (AFL-CIO), 51, 66, 69
American Federation of State, City and Municipal Employees (AFSCME), 49, 53, 56, 69
American Federation of Teachers (AFT), 49, 56, 69
American Home Mortgage, 5
American Recovery and Reinvestment Act (ARRA) (2009), 5, 126
Ameriquest, 5
Arizona, 14–16, 28, 56, 119
ARRA (2009), 5, 126
Assembly Bill 572 (Nevada), 4
Atlanta (Georgia), 131

Bank run (2007), 5
Bankruptcy, 5, 13, 108
Barbash, Jack, 43–44
Barnes, E. Richard, 62
Barro, Josh, 76
Baton Rouge (Louisiana), 119
Bear Stearns, 5
Bell (California), 127
Belman, D., 76

Belt, Bradley, 108
Bender, K., 77
Benecki, S., 86
Benefits. *See also* Pension plans
  cost of deferred, 73, 77–79, *79*, 87
  cutting, 12–13
  defined contribution plans, 101
  defined plans, 101–102
Berry, Susan, 44
Beshear, Steve, 56
Big business, collective bargaining as counter to, 70–71, 74
Bigelow, John, 21
Biggs, A., 77
BLS data, 75–76, 78, 100
Blue-collar model (janitor), 89, *90–93*, 94–95, *136–142*
Bonus leave component of contract, 84
Boston police strike (1919), 46
Branstad, Terry, 15
Brennan, Peter J., 107
Broadbanding, 35–36, 41
Buckwalter, N.D., 38
Budget gaps
  local, 125
  state
    California, 16
    Connecticut, 16–17
    filling, 14–15, 17
    Great Recession and, 6–7, *6*, *7*, *8*, *9*, 14
    hardship caused by, 125–126
    New Jersey, 8–10, 12–13
    Wisconsin, 12–13
Budget Repair Bill (Wisconsin) (2011), 12
Buffet, Warren, 5
Bumping rights, 29–30
Bureau of Economic Analysis data, 75
Bureau of Labor Statistics (BLS) data, 75–76, 78, 100
Burton, J., 53
Bush, George H.W., 52
Bush, George W., 29, 52, 57–58
Bush, Jeb, 35
Bustamante, Cruz, 64

163

California. *See also specific city and county in*
  budget gap, 16
  collective bargaining in, 48, 56, 60–64
  fiscal deficit in, 63
  pension plans in, 11, 63–64
  Proposition 13 in, 52, 61
  Proposition 98 in, 61
  public pensions study, 112
  unions in, 60–64
California Correctional Peace Officers Association (CCPOA), 62
California Public Employees' Retirement System (CalPERS), 11, 63–64
California Teachers Association (CTA), 61, 64
CalPERS, 11
Carnevale, D., 80
Carter, Jimmy, 29
CCPOA, 62
Center for Responsive Politics, 69
Central Falls (Rhode Island), 131
Certainty equivalent theory, 78
Chapter 9 bankruptcy, 13
Chapter 11 bankruptcy, 5, 108
Chicago, 24
Chicago Board of Education, 50
Christie, Chris, 8–10, 15, 59
Citizens United decision, 70
Civil Rights Act (1871), 49
Civil Service Act (1883), 22–24
Civil Service Commission (formerly Advisory Board of the Civil Service), 21–23, 25
Civil Service Reform Act (1978), 23–24, 57, 67
Civil service system
  Adams (John) and, 19–20
  broadbanding and, 35–36, 41
  Civil Service Reform Act and, 23–24, 57, 67
  corruption associated with early, 19
  cross-jurisdictional problem solving and, 38
  hierarchical structure and, 37–38
  Intergovernmental Personnel Act and, 19, 25
  local merit systems and, 24–26
  merit and, 18–28
  overview, 39–41
  Pendleton Act and, 22–24
  performance-based pay and, 26–28, 32, 36, 41, 73
  protections, 67
  public sector employment and, 18–19, 30
  public wage management systems and, new, 31–36
  reform, 32–36, 133–134
    barriers to, 28–31, 39–41
  seniority and, 29–30, 41, 73
  shared service systems and, 36–39
  spoils system and, 20–22

Civil service system *(continued)*
  state merit systems and, 24–26
  for teachers, 18
  Tenure of Office Act, 20
  Washington (George) and, 19
Civil War period, 22
Clark County (Nevada), 27
Clark, R.L., 105
Classification Act (1939), 23
Cleveland, Grover, 24
Cleveland (Ohio), 48
Clinton, Bill, 28–29, 52, 57
Coggburn, J.D., 33
COLA, 83, 89, 118, 122
Collective bargaining
  big business and, countering, 70–71, 74
  in California, 48, 56, 60–64
  contemporary status of, 53, *54–55*, 56–58
  current view of, 64–65
  essence of, 48–49
  expiration of agreement, 85
  in Florida, 48, 56–57
  in Georgia, 53
  government backlash against, 52
  historical perspective of unions and, 42–47, *43*, *45*, 71
  Kennedy's (John F.) executive order guaranteeing, 43, 50–52
  legislative process and, 49–52
  market economy and, 67–68
  National Institute of Municipal Law Officers report and, 47
  need for public sector, 134
  in New Jersey, 59–60
  overview, 71–72
  political decision making and, 67–68
  as political machine, 68–70
  public sector versus private sector, 65–68, 71–72
  resistance to, 47–48
  rethinking, 134
  Rhyne's view of, 47–48
  seniority and, 29
  at state level, trend to strip or scale back, 58–60
  state sovereignty and, 66–67
Colorado, 15, 109, 122
Commission on Organization of the Executive Branch, 23
Commonwealth of Virginia v. The County Board of Arlington (1977), 57
Comparative analysis of public sector versus private sector compensation
  blue-collar model (janitor), 89, *90–93*, 94–95, *136–142*
  compensation model, 88–89
  Great Recession and, 88
  overview, 100
  white-collar model (civil engineer), 89, 95, *96–99*, 100, *144–149*

INDEX 165

Compensation. *See* Comparative analysis of public sector versus private sector compensation
Compensation model, 88–89
Condrey, S.E., 34
Conflicts in awarding compensation, avoiding, 130–131
Connecticut, 13, 16–17
Contra Costa County (California), 64
Contracting out, 37
Coolidge, Calvin, 46
Cooper, M., 113
Cost-of-living adjustment (COLA), 83, 89, 118, 122
Council-manager form of government, 40
Cox, Jacob D., 21
Crane, David, 113
Credit-rating agencies, 113
Cross-jurisdictional problem solving, 38
CTA, 61, 64
Cuomo, Andrew, 60
Current Population Survey (BLS), 76

Dade County Classroom Teachers Association v. Ryan (1968), 56–57
Davis, Gray, 62–64
DB plans, 101–102
DC plans, 101
Deferred retirement option plans (DROPs), 11, 118–119
Defined benefit (DB) plans, 101–102
Defined contribution (DC) plans, 101
Delaware, 119
Democratic Party, 22, 63, 70
Department of Defense (DOD), 57
Department of Homeland Security (DHS), 57
Derivatives, over-the-counter, 5
DHS, 57
DOD, 57
Dotcom bubble, 3
Double dipping, 118
Dow, 5
Dray, Philip, 43
DROPs, 11, 118–119

Economic Policy Institute, 14
Economist article on pension liabilities (2010), 113
Education funding, 16
Elling, R.C., 26
Employee Retirement System (Rhode Island), 115–116
Employer's duty to bargain, 85
Employment. *See* Public sector employment
Employment Retirement Income Security Act (ERISA) (1974), 106–108
European pension plans, 104, 121–122
Europe's fiscal crisis, 121–122

Evaluation. *See* Public sector evaluation
Evanston (Illinois), 24
Even, William, 59
Executive Order 10988 (1962), 43, 50–52
Executive Order 11491 (1969), 51
Executive Order 12933, 57

Farber, H.S., 53, 80
Fallejo (California), 13
Fay, C.H., 31
Federal Aviation Administration, 52
Federal Employees Retirement Act (1920), 105
Federal government pension plan, first, 105
Federal Labor Relations Council, 51
Federal Reserve, 5
Federal Services Impasse Panel, 51
Ferris, F., 57
Firefighter contract negotiation, example, 83–85
First Amendment, 46
Fletcher, Ernie, 56
Florida
 aid to local government and, reduction of, 16
 civil service system reform in, 33–36
 collective bargaining in, 48, 56–57
 pension plans in, 123
 stimulus package, 15
Florio, James, 117
Forrester, Douglas, 117
401(k) programs, 94, 101, 122
Freeman, R., 80

Gaebler, Ted, 28
Gallup poll on unions (2010), 65
Garfield, James, 22
GASB, 78, 110–111, 113–114, 116
Gates, Bill, 18
General Electric Company, 105
General Fund (Arizona), 16
General Motors, 63
Georgia
 actuarial study in, 129
 civil service system reform in, 33–36
 collective bargaining in, 53
 hybrid pension plans in Atlanta, consideration of, 131
 pension plans in, 118–119, 123
Georgia State Merit System of Personnel Administration, 33
GeorgiaGain, 33–36
Golden handshake agreements, 132
Goldsmith, Stephan, 28
Gore, Al, 28–29
Governmental Accounting Standards Board (GASB), 78, 110–111, 113–114, 116
Gramm-Leach-Bliley Act, 5
Grant, Ulysses, 21–22

166 INDEX

Great Depression (1930s), 22
Great Recession (2008)
   American Recovery and Reinvestment Act and, 5, 126
   bank run before, 5
   budget gaps and, state, 6–7, *6*, *7*, *8*, *9*, 14
   comparative analysis of public versus private compensation and, 88
   dotcom bubble before, 3
   factors triggering, 128
   housing bubble and, 3–5
   irrational exuberance and, 4
   New Jersey example and, 8–10
   pension plans and, 111
   prosperity before, 3–4, 128–129
   public sector employment and, 4–11, *6*, *7*, *8*, *9*, 126, 128–129
   San Diego example and, 10–11
   September 11 terrorist attacks before, 3
   severity of, 5–6
   subprime mortgage scandal and, 4–5
   Wall Street ripple effect and, 5
Greenhut, S., 61
Greenspan, Alan, 4

Haslam, Bill, 60
Hatch Act (1939), 23
Health care, 9, 114–116
Herbert, Bob, 116
Heywood, J., 76–77
Hindman, H.D., 53
Holiday component of contract, 83
Hoover Commission, 23
Housing bubble, 3–5
Hunter, W.J., 80
Hurd, R., 42
Hutchinson, Peter, 126
Hybrid pension plans, 131–132
Hyde, A.C., 57

Ichniowski, C., 53, 86
Illinois, 15, 24, 50
Illinois Appellate Court decision (1966), 50
Indiana, 28, 106
Indianapolis, 28
Indianapolis Education Association v. Lewallen (1969), 50
Inflation rates, 122
Ingraham, P.W., 29
Insurance component of contract, 83
Interest rates, 108
Intergovernmental Personnel Act (1970), 19, 25
International City Bank of New Orleans Employment Retiree Plan, 107
Iowa, 15
Iron Triangle, 81–87, *82*
Irrational exuberance, 4
Issue networks, 81–82

Jackson, Andrew, 21
Javitz, Jacob, 106
Jefferson, Thomas, 20
Job bumping, 29–30
Job classification systems, 35–36
Job security, 30–31
Johnson, R., 109
Joint Select Committee on Retrenchment, 21
Jones, Shannon, 58
JPMorgan, 5

Kagan, Elena, 71
Kasih, John, 58–59
Kean, Thomas, 117
Kearney, R., 30, 42–43, 53, 80
Keefe, J.H., 76–77, 80
Kellough, J.E., 34
Kennedy, Edward, 58
Kennedy, John F., 23, 43, 50–52
Kentucky, 56
Kettl, D.F., 39
Kramer, Orin S., 113
Kreisberg, Steve, 109

La Follette, Robert, 46
Labor strikes, 67, 72
Lance, Leonard, 117
Lawler III, E.E, 31
Lehman Brothers, 5
Leibensperger, William, 58
Leone, Richard C., 116
Lincoln, Abraham, 21
Little Hoover Commission, 64, 112, 130
Llorens, J., 76
Lloyd-La Follette Act (1912), 46, 50
Local government. *See also specific city or county*
   budget gap, 125
   council-manager form of, 40
   first public pension plan in, 104
   liabilities of pension plans in, 113
   merit system in, 24–26
   monopoly premise and, 80–81
   Social Security Act (1935) and, 106
   trickle-down effect and, 16
   unions' effect on, 86–87
Longevity pay component of contract, 83
Long-term disability component of contract, 84
Los Angeles, 24, 64
Lottery money, 16

Malanga, S., 60–61
Malloy, Dannel, 13
Marc, William L., 20
Mareschal, P.M., 53
Marlow, M.L., 86–87
Maryland, 48, 53
Massachusetts, 24, 46, 104–105

McComish v. Bennett, 71
McDermed, A.A., 105
McGrory, Jack, 11
Meany, George, 66
Media, 126–128
Medicaid, 16
Medicare, 110
Medoff, J., 80
Merit pay, 26–27
Merit systems, 19–20, 24–26
Merit Systems Protection Board, 23–24
Michigan, 16, 49
Michigan Supreme Court ruling (1963), 49
Military pension plans, 103–104
Miller, M.A., 76
Miller, Zell, 33
Minnesota, 17
Mississippi, 117–118
Missouri, 56–57
Mitchell, O.S., 109
Monopoly premise, 80–81
Murphy, Dick, 120

Napolitano, Janet, 56
National Commission on the State and Local Public Service, 25
National Federation of Federal Employees, 46
National Institute of Municipal Law Officers report, 47
National Labor Relations Act, 67, 85
National Labor Relations Board, 85
National Performance Review (NPR), 28–29
National Security Personnel System (NSPS), 57
Navy Pension Plan, 104
Nebraska, 16, 131
Nevada, 4, 53
New Jersey
  budget cuts in, 15–16
  budget gap in, 8–10, 12–13
  collective bargaining in, 59–60
  Great Recession and, example of, 8–10
  pension plans in, 116–117
  public sector employment in, 8–10
  stimulus package, 15
New Jersey Education Association, 116–117
New Mexico, 117
New York City, 104
New York State, 16, 24, 60
Newport Beach (California), 127–128
Nigro, L.G., 34
Nixon, Richard, 23, 25, 51
Norcross, Eileen, 66, 85–86
North Carolina, 15, 57, 129
Novy-Marx, R., 111, 113
NPR, 28–29
NSPS, 57

Obama administration, 58, 63
Office and Professional Employees International Union (OPEIU), 53
Office of Personnel Management (OPM), 23–24
Ohio, 16, 48, 58–59
Oklahoma, 53, 129
O'Malley, Martin, 60
OPEB, 103, 114–116, 121, 123, 129, 131–133
OPEIU, 53
OPM, 23–24
Orange County (California), 122–123, 131
Oregon, 118
Orzechowski, W., 86–87
Osborne, David, 28, 126
Other postemployment benefits (OPEB), 103, 114–116, 121, 123, 129, 131–133
Outsourcing, 37
Overtime in boosting pension plans, 119

PATCO, 52
Patronage, political, 20–22
Patton, D.B., 53
Pay differentials, 74–77, 75, 80
PBCG, 106–108
Pendleton Act (1883), 22–24
Peng, J., 74, 103, 119
Pennsylvania, 48–49
Pension Benefit Guaranty Corporation (PBGC), 106–108
Pension plans
  in Arizona, 119
  in California, 11, 63–64
  in Colorado, 109, 122
  cost-of-living adjustment and, 118, 122
  deferred retirement option plans, 118–119
  defined benefit, 101–102
  defined contribution, 101
  double dipping and, 118
  in Europe, 104, 121–122
  first, 104–105
  in Florida, 123
  fully funded, departure from, 116–119
  future directions of, 121–124
  in Georgia, 118–119, 123
  Governmental Accounting Standards Board and, 110–111
  graying of workforce and, 114
  Great Recession and, 111
  high-risk investment and, 110
  historical perspective of public, 103–106
  hybrid, 131–132
  increases in future, mandates for fully funding, 133
  interest rates and, 108
  investment volatility and, 110, 115
  liabilities of, 108, 113–114
  military, 103–104
  in Mississippi, 117–118

Pension plans *(continued)*
  in New Jersey, 116–117
  in Orange County (California), 122–123
  Oregon, 118
  overtime in boosting amount of, 119
  payments, 74, 87
  Pension Benefit Guaranty Corporation, 106–108
  price of public
    departure from fully funded plans, 116–119
    factors contributing to, 110–111
    Little Hoover Commission Report (2011) and, 112
    other postemployment benefits and, 103, 114–116, 121, 123
    retiree health care and, 114–116
    San Diego case study, 10–11, 83, 119–121
    state debt and, 112–114
  public sector versus private sector, 121
  rethinking, 131–133
  retirement age and, raising, 121–122
  rise of, 105
  Rule of 80 and, 101
  in San Francisco, 123
  scrutiny of, by Securities and Exchange Commission, 107
  sick leave in boosting amount of, 119
  Social Security Act (1935) and, 106
  state comparison of, 109–110
  transparency and, lack of, 123–124
  underfunded, 110, 112–114
  unions and public sector, 108–110
  U.S. Treasury bonds and state, 113
  in Utah, 118
  in Wisconsin, 109–110
Pension Revaluation Act of New Jersey (1992), 117
Pensions (NBC 1972 documentary), 106
Performance-based pay, 26–28, 32, 36, 41, 73
Perry, J.L., 38
PERS, 94
Personnel Reform Act of Washington State (2002), 53
Peters, Scott, 120
Pew Center on the States, 111, 114–115, 117–119, 123
Pew Research Center for the People and the Press poll, 64–65
Philadelphia (Pennsylvania), 49
Phoenix, 28
Pinnock, S., 42
PMA, 29
Postal Clerks v. Blount (1971), 50
Postal Reorganization Act (1970), 51
Power of Municipalities to Enter into Labor Contracts (National Institute of Municipal Law Officers 1941 report), 47

Premium pay component of contract, 84
President's Commission on the Status of Women, 23
President's Management Agenda (PMA), 29
Price of Government, The (Osborne and Hutchinson), 126
Prichard (Alabama), 17, 131
Private sector. *See also* Comparative analysis of public sector versus private sector compensation
  collective bargaining versus public sector collective bargaining, 65–68, 71–72
  compensation versus public sector compensation, 73–77, 75, 79, 87
  liabilities of pension plans in, 113
  as model for public sector, 28, 36
  pension plans, 105, 121
  union membership in, 42–44, *43*
  unions in, 68
Privatization in public sector employment, 28, 37
Professional Air Traffic Controllers (PATCO), 52
Pro-growth tax reforms, 15
Proposition 13 (California), 52, 61
Proposition 98 (California), 61
Proposition 100 (Arizona), 14
Proposition D (San Diego), 120
Public Choice Theory, 86–87
Public employee retirement system (PERS), 94
Public Employee System (Mississippi), 117–118
Public pensions, California study on, 112
Public Safety Employer-Employee Cooperation Act (2008), 58
Public sector compensation. *See also* Comparative analysis of public sector versus private sector compensation; Pension plans
  benefits, cost of deferred, 73, 77–79, *79*, 87
  broadbanding and, 35–36, 41
  conflicts in awarding, avoiding, 130–131
  cutting, 12–13
  defined benefit plans, 102–103
  firefighter contract negotiation, example, 83–85
  growth in (1997–2007), 4
  Iron Triangle and, 81–87, *82*
  media stories about, 127–128
  merit pay and, 26–27
  other postemployment benefits, (OPEB), 103
  overview, 87
  performance-based pay, 26–28, 32, 36, 41, 73
  principles for determining pay and, 73–74

Public sector compensation *(continued)*
  private sector compensation versus, 73–77, *75*, *79*, 87
  public wage management systems and, new, 31–36, 41
  rise in, trend toward, 126–127
  transparency and, lack of, 83
  unions and, impact of, 79–81
Public sector employment. *See also* Civil service system
  civil service system and, 18–19, 30
  collective bargaining versus private sector collective bargaining, 65–68, 71–72
  Great Recession and, 4–11, *6*, *7*, *8*, *9*, 126, 128–129
  job security and, 30–31
  media and, 126–127
  in New Jersey, 8–10
  privatization and, 28, 37
  public interest in, 18
  recovery of, 13–17
  rethinking, 125–129
  in San Diego, 10–11
  state approaches to unions and budget cuts and, 12–17
  teachers and, 18
  transparency and, need for increasing, 129–130
  union membership in, 42–44, *43*, 46
Public sector evaluation, 27
Public wage management systems, new, 31–36

Queens College (New York) census data, 76

Rankin, C.H., 80
Rauh, Joshua, 109, 111, 113
Reading (Pennsylvania), 48–49
Reagan, Ronald, 52
Reinventing Government (Osborne and Gaebler), 28
Republican Party, 21, 69–70
Retiree health care, 114–116
Retirement Act (1920), 23
Retirement age, raising, 121–122
Rhode Island, 115–116, 131
Rhyne, Charles S., 47–48
Richwine, J., 77
Right-to-work laws, 80
Risher, H., 31
Rizzo, Robert, 127
Roosevelt, Franklin, 46–47, 50
Roosevelt, Theodore, 46
Rule of 80, 101
Rutan v. Republican Party (1990), 21

S corporation tax reform, 15
San Diego, 10–11, 83, 119–121
San Francisco, 24, 123, 131
Sanders, Jerry, 120–121

Schanes, Steve, 107
Schieber, Sylvester J., 109–110
Schwarzenegger, Arnold, 56, 62–64, 113
SEC, 107, 113
Second Hatch Act, 25
Securities and Exchange Commission (SEC), 107, 113
SEIU, 53, 56, 63
Senate Bill 113 in Tennessee (2011), 60
Seniority, 29–30, 41, 73
September 11 terrorist attacks (2001), 3
Service Employees International Union (SEIU), 53, 56, 63
Service First legislation (Florida), 34–36
Services and programs, reduction in, 16–17
Shared service systems, 36–39
Sherk, J., 44
Shift differential pay component of contract, 84
Sick leave in boosting pension plans, 119
Side bar agreement, 27
Smith, R.S., 109
Social Security, 89, 94
Social Security Act (1935), 106
Social Security Act (1939), 25
Society of Tammany, 22
South Carolina, 35–36, 57
Spitzer, Eliot, 56
Spoils system, 20–22
State Auditor's Office (Texas), 32
State Classification Office (Texas), 32
State Employees Association (North Carolina), 57
State government. *See also* Budget gaps, state *specific state*
  Collective bargaining and, trend to strip or scale back, 58–60
  filling budget gaps and, 14–15, 17
  first public pension plan in, 104–105
  Great Recession and budget gaps, 6–7, *6*, *7*, *8*, *9*, 14
  Iron Triangle and, 83
  liabilities of pension plans in, 113
  merit systems in, 24–26
  monopoly premise and, 80–81
  public employee unions and budget cuts and, 12–17
  retiree health care and, 114–115
  Social Security Act (1935) and, 106
  sovereignty, 66–67
  stimulus packages, 15
  surpluses, excess, 4
  trickle-down effect and, 16
  union membership in, 53, *54–55*
  unions' effect on, 86–87
Steward, Luther, 46–47
Stimulus packages, state, 15
Strikes, labor, 67, 72
Subprime mortgage scandal, 4–5
Sullivan, J., 30

Suntrust Banks, Inc., 36
Suppliers of public services and Iron Triangle, 86

Taft-Harley Act, 67
Taft, William Howard, 46
Tammany Hall, 22
Tax reforms, 15
Teachers' personnel system, 18
Tennessee, 60
Tennessee Valley Authority (TVA), 47
Tenure of Office Act (1820), 20
Texas, 16, 32–33, 48
There Is Power in a Union (Dray), 43
Thompson, T.L., 26
Three Strikes and You're Out law, 70
Tobias, R.M., 57–58
Transparency
  lack of, 83, 123–124
  need for increased, 128–130
Trickle-down effect, 16
Trickle-up effect, 4
"Trillion Dollar Gap, The" (2010 Pew Center on the States study), 111, 117, 119
Tropicana Products, Inc., 36
Troy, L., 65
Truman, Harry S., 23
Tuition fee component of contract, 84
TVA, 247
Tweed, Boss William, 22

Uniform and linen allowance component of contract, 84
Union power thesis, 80
Unions. *See also* Collective bargaining; *specific name*
  in California, 60–64
  contemporary status of, 53, *54–55*, 56–58
  current view of, 64–65
  Gallup poll on, 65
  government backlash against, 52
  growth of, 49–52
  increase in public sector, 39
  local government and, effects on, 86–87
  membership
    changes in, 42–44, *43*, 46, 53, *54–55*
    compulsory, 69, 72
  overview, 71–72
  pension plans and, public sector, 108–110
  Pew study on, 64–65

Unions *(continued)*
  as political activism of, 68–70
  in private sector, 68
  public sector compensation and, impact on, 79–81
  public service system protections and, 67
  state approaches to budget cuts and public employee, 12–17
  state government and, effects on, 86–87
  state sovereignty and, 66–67
  strikes and, 67, 72
  in Wisconsin, 58–59
  work stoppage trends, 44, *45*
United Auto Workers, 63
United Federation of Teachers, 56
U.S. Court of Appeals for the Seventh Circuit decision (1968), 49–50
U.S. Supreme Court, 21, 70
U.S. Treasury bonds, 113
Utah, 118

Vallejo (California), 64
Vallenta, R., 86
Vermont, 109–110
Virginia, 36, 48, 57

Wagner Act (1935), 46
Walker, Scott, 12, 58, 70
Wall Street, 5, 128. *See also specific company*
Walsh, M.W., 113
Walters, Dan, 64
Washington, George, 19
Washington State, 48, 53, 56
Wellington, H., 80
What Do Unions Do (Freeman and Medoff), 80
White-collar model (civil engineer), 95, 96–99, 100, *144–149*
Whitman, Christine Todd, 10, 116–117
Wicks-Lim, Jeannette, 70
Wilson, Pete, 63
Winter, R.K., 80
Wisconsin
  budget gap in, 12–13
  collective bargaining in, 134
  merit system in, 24–25
  pension plans in, 109–110
  unions in, 58–59

Zax, J., 86

About the Author

Dr. Thom Reilly obtained his doctoral degree in public administration from the University of Southern California (USC) and his MSW from Arizona State University. He has held senior executive level positions in the public, private, and nonprofit sectors. Currently, he is professor and director of the School of Social Work at San Diego State University and serves as executive director for the Caesars Foundation, a private charity. Reilly is the former county manager/CEO for Clark County (the Las Vegas Valley) and vice-chancellor of the Health Sciences System for the Nevada System of Higher Education; he was also responsible for the statewide child welfare system in Nevada. Reilly served as the former vice president of social responsibility for Caesars Entertainment, Inc. (a Fortune 500 company). Reilly is a fellow of the National Academy of Public Administration (NAPA).